A PILOT'S PERSPECTIVE

1st Edition

Published in 2012 by
Woodfield Publishing Ltd
Bognor Regis PO21 5EL England
www.woodfieldpublishing.co.uk

ISBN 1-84683-130-X

Printed and bound in England

Cover design by Rowland Henry

v 1.1

A Pilot's Perspective

*A former airline captain's reflections
on a lifetime of flying ~ 1950-2012*

CEDRIC FLOOD

Woodfield

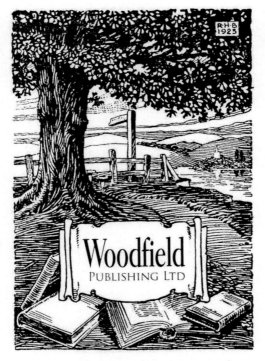

Woodfield Publishing Ltd

Bognor Regis ~ West Sussex ~ England ~ PO21 5EL
tel 01243 821234 ~ e/m info@woodfieldpublishing.co.uk

Interesting and informative books on a variety of subjects

For full details of all our published titles, visit our website at
www.woodfieldpublishing.co.uk

I dedicate this book to my wife, Theresa, who initially persuaded me to start writing and then put up with months of my absorption with the computer, and cups of tea going cold. Also my two sons, Peter and Brian, for their proof reading, and, at times, their unrequested advice!

~ CONTENTS ~

Preface

This is nothing special, just a collection of anecdotes and memories of fifty seven years (so far) flying aeroplanes.

Looking back I realise how lucky I have been. Lucky to have done just what I always dreamed of doing. Lucky to have enjoyed an easy going period in aviation which will probably never be repeated. Lucky to have survived many incidents which could have been disastrous and lucky at several points in my career when opportunities were presented to me just when I needed them, and probably not fully appreciated at the time.

I hope I can share some of the interest and enjoyment that flying has given me over the years.

Foreword

Very few people know precisely what they want to do in life from a very early age. And of this small group, even fewer actually see their aspirations fulfilled.

One such person is Cedric Flood, a good friend with whom I had the pleasure of sharing part of his life in aviation. As a very small boy he became interested in aeroplanes, and he achieved his ambition to become a pilot despite many obstacles along the way. It was a long and difficult road, but perseverance paid off, as you will see as you read this story of his life in aviation.

But Cedric became not just an ordinary pilot. During my own long airline career as a Training and Route Check Captain, I flew with many hundreds of pilots, but none were better than Cedric. Both as a pilot and as a captain, with the additional responsibilities that this carried, he was exceptional.

It was, therefore, both an honour and a privilege to accept Cedric's request to write a Foreword to his book, a book which, besides being an account of his own experiences, well illustrates a period which many regard as the Golden Age of Aviation.

Ken Wakefield MRAeS

Prologue

I was preparing my little aircraft, a Eurostar EV97A, for its first flight. I'd just spent six months to this point, assembling it from a kit in my garage. It was a very hot spell in July 2006 (hottest on record), when afternoon temperatures reached 35°C, so I'd arrived at the airfield early, at 0700, when the temperature would be reasonable. The airfield was Ince, just north of Liverpool, a microlight school and club base, with three grass runways, each about 400yds. As I worked on my aeroplane, a flex wing microlight flew overhead in the circuit at about 500ft. I looked up and, as I did, the pilot looked down and waved to me. I decided at that point that I had died and gone to Heaven!

An hour or so later, I opened the throttle, and my aircraft accelerated to about 45mph and lifted off for the first time. I climbed to 3,000 feet and did some stalls, one for each flap setting, and then back to Ince, to land and do a check over everything, as required in the test schedule. I flew twice more that day, doing nine landings in all, and was more than satisfied with my first attempt at building an aircraft.

I reflected on the flying I'd done to this point, fifty two years since my first solo, first milestone in a flying career, and fourteen years since I'd retired from the day job at British Airways. I thought it might be interesting to set down some of the experiences of those years. Now, after a further five enjoyable years flying my little aeroplane, I have decided that, before the memories begin to fade, I had better get on with it. If that memory lets me down and I get some facts slightly wrong, I apologise in advance. So, back to the beginning.

1. EARLY DAYS

In 1939, when I was two and a half years old, my parents and I moved to the new council estate at Speke, in south Liverpool. When the war started in September, work on the estate stopped for the duration, with only a relatively small number of houses completed, compared to the finished post war estate, so we lived in very rural environment, surrounded by fields and woods, altogether a very pleasant place for a growing youngster. Our house was close to Speke airfield, as it was then. The airfield was developed as part of the war effort, with an aircraft manufacturing company, Rootes, close by, building Blenheims and Halifaxes. Many lease lend aircraft came from the States to the docks in Liverpool to be assembled by Lockheed at Speke, creating a requirement for hard runways. The first Halifax flew from the grass airfield early in 1942 but by late 1942 three hard runways had been completed.

Our house was exactly half a mile from the start of the longest runway, 26, and just south of the centre line. This meant that landing aircraft flew past my bedroom window at about 150/200ft. Aircraft taking off on 08 also went past, but probably a little higher. All the aircraft built at Rootes, Hurricanes from the Polish squadron based at Speke, Spitfires, many other military types, all the American aircraft assembled by Lockheed at Speke, as well as the Rapides and DH86s of the Associated Airways Joint Committee, which operated scheduled services across the Irish Sea throughout the war; all these and more went past. I would often wander across the fields to the road at the threshold of 26 and watch the aircraft landing and taking off. I distinctly remember watching the elevator and rudder movements. By the time I was seven or eight I was a very critical (precocious) observer, deciding which was a good, or bad, landing.

I also remember, early in the war, standing at the front gate with my mother and a couple of neighbours and seeing the black crosses on a Ju88 which was being chased by two Hurricanes across Speke at about 1000ft. It was shot down and crash-landed near Bromborough on the Wirral. On one occasion, when I was about four or five, I awoke one morning to see a Spitfire (intact) in a field just opposite our house, with a solitary airman standing guard. It had landed short for some reason. I also remember when I was about three years old being carried by my father to a friend's house when we were 'bombed out' in the early hours by an unexploded bomb in a nearby back garden.

During the war, my grandmother brought me the 'Knockout' comic each week, which had a full-page cartoon of the 'Gremlins'. They were small creatures who were shown getting into every corner of an aircraft, causing problems for the pilot.

An interesting operation at Speke was the catapult, which was used to train Hurricane pilots who were going to be based on the CAM ships. These were merchant ships modified to carry a Hurricane and a fixed catapult, from which aircraft would be catapulted off if the convoy was attacked by bombers. After its mission, the Hurricane would fly to the nearest land, if it had enough fuel, or alternatively, it would ditch alongside the ship, or the pilot would bail out, and hopefully be rescued.

Just after the war, there was an emergency airlift of milk from Northern Ireland and Yorks, Lancastrians, Liberators and Haltons flew in at all hours, bringing milk for the mainland. In the immediate postwar years there were several foreign airlines – KLM, Sabena and Air France – operating from Speke, as they had done pre-war, as well as BEA, who had a large maintenance base. At this time Speke was equipped with GCA (ground controlled approach) radar but gradually the foreign airlines were poached by Manchester's Ringway and, shortly afterwards, the GCA followed them. This was a period when Speke was operated by the Ministry of Aviation on behalf of the city council. The Manchester council adopted a more aggressive approach to encourage airlines to start services, which, in due course, paid handsome dividends.

By the end of the war I was aircraft mad and my fate was sealed. I had several friends who were as keen on aircraft as I was. One in particular was Bernie Mackenzie. He was three years older than me but we spent a lot of time together 'spotting' aircraft and watching the flying at Speke. One summer we went to Luton Airport to stay with Bernie's father, who worked as an aircraft engineer for Percival Aircraft. We spent several happy days wandering around the local airfields, including Luton, Heathrow (when it just had a North

Terminal), Northolt, Denham, Elstree, Radlett and Blackbushe, spotting many aircraft types we hadn't seen before. At Hatfield we saw the prototype Comet and the new Heron and at Luton the Prince and P56 Provost.

When I was about eight or nine I was taken to Speke airport by my mother's younger brother. Uncle Bud, just demobbed post-war from the RAF, was employed by BEA as an engineer at their maintenance base at Speke. He took me on board a Dakota, sat me in a pilot's seat, and I particularly remember being shown how to open and close the cooling gills on the engine cowlings. Little did I realise then that a few years later I would be doing just that for real on the same aircraft.

In 1947, when I was ten, I passed the 'scholarship' exam, precursor of the eleven-plus, and gained a place at the Liverpool Institute, a grammar school in Liverpool city centre. During my last year, in the Upper Sixth, Paul McCartney was in the first year third form. Many years later he was involved in turning the old Victorian building into LIPA, the Liverpool Institute for Performing Arts. I visited it recently and was impressed with the modernisation of the old building, particularly the original semi-circular assembly hall. It had been transformed into a modern theatre, with an impressive control room.

Back in my schooldays, each morning one thousand boys filed into this huge hall with its upper gallery for morning assembly. The deputy head would stand on the stage maintaining discipline, trying to keep the boys quiet, and regularly telling miscreants to 'see me after assembly'. On the last day of my first term, I was intrigued when, as we were all finally seated, a low hissing started. I realised quickly that many boys were making this noise and, of course, it was impossible to tell which boys were doing it. As more boys joined in, including me, the noise rose to a crescendo. The deputy head was practically screaming for it to stop, but he had lost control. Finally, in a fury, he stormed off the stage. I almost felt sorry for him. An impressive demonstration of people power.

In 1949, I had my first flight. Every morning, from their maintenance base in Speke, British European Airways (BEA) positioned a Dakota, after servicing, to Manchester and another one back to Speke in the evening. BEA decided to fill the 32 seats in the Dakota by selling them cheaply to schools. My school arranged some flights and early on a miserable wet March 25th most of my fourth form from the Liverpool Institute flew to Ringway to spend the day at Belle Vue Zoo in pouring rain, then home to Speke in the evening. The two flights were mostly in cloud, so it wasn't an auspicious start to my airborne career.

When Bernie was sixteen in 1950, (and I was thirteen) he got a job as an apprenticed aircraft engineer at the flying club at Speke. Coincidentally, the licensed engineer, Basil Carlin, to whom Bernie was apprenticed, had just moved in to live opposite me in one of the new 'prefabs' which had recently been built to ease the postwar housing shortage. Very quickly I received permission to go down to the flying club and help Basil and Bernie in the hangar. I was issued with an old pair of white overalls and so started my aviation career.

I would come home from school, put on my overalls, jump on my bike and ride down to the club. It was a totally different world in those days, much more easygoing than the sterilised, rule-ridden society we have today. I would cycle to Speke Airport, ride in at the main entrance, past the big Number 1 hangar, then along the perimeter track, across the threshold of 17 runway, making sure no aircraft were landing, to the flying club. If I met an aircraft coming along the taxiway, such as a BEA Dakota, I would simply ride onto the grass alongside and wait for it to go by, waving to the pilots as they taxied past. Hard to believe now, I suppose, but that was the relaxed way of life then.

At the flying club, I quickly found my niche, cleaning cowlings, helping push aircraft in and out of the hangar, refuelling, checking oil between flights, and, of course, sweeping the hangar floor. I was in my element and happy. Every day I learned something new about aircraft. One particular job which I actually volunteered to do was to clean the aircraft after a passenger had been sick. This earned me half a crown, good money then for a thirteen year old, which the unfortunate pilot had to pay. Another job I remember, which would be frowned upon nowadays by 'elf and safety', was syphoning fuel. If money was tight, we would be asked to transfer fuel from several aircraft to one which was needed. This entailed sticking a short length of hose into a fuel tank, lowering the outside hose end to below the fuel level, and then sucking fuel up the hose. The trick was to remove your mouth from the hose just before the fuel arrived and stick the hose end in the fuel can. Of course, it frequently went wrong. Sometimes if you didn't suck hard enough the petrol didn't arrive and you had to repeat the process. The alternative was that you were slow removing your mouth and that meant a mouthful of petrol. I quickly learned to do it properly.

Another game was 'milking' the brass fire extinguishers of their CTC (carbon tetrachloride) content, which was a very useful cleaning agent for electrical components. Nowadays it is regarded as a carcinogen and quite dangerous. I wonder how we survived.

As an example of the easygoing style in those days, sometimes on a quiet summer evening we would wander out on to the airfield collecting mushrooms. If the area of grass opposite the club didn't produce the required crop, we would walk across runway 26/08, looking both ways first of course, to find more on the other side.

The club used Austers, a couple of Autocrats and a J4, all of which had the basic instrument panel, airspeed indicator (ASI), altimeter, turn and slip, and compass, plus engine revs (RPM) and oil pressure gauge, but no radio. The club was based at the northwest corner of the old Speke airfield, adjacent to the original airport buildings, Chapel House Farm. Prewar, this had been converted into the control tower and the farm buildings alongside made into a hangar (No. 50). We were in another big hangar (No. 34), which was built just before the war for the original Liverpool Flying Club. The club social side was accommodated in the building alongside, which was built in 1939 for the Civil Air Guard, a government sponsored organisation which subsidised flying for private pilots in return for an undertaking to join the air force in times of need.

Squadron Leader G.C. 'Wilbur' Wright, of Wright Aviation, was the boss and, as he lived across the river on the Wirral peninsular, sometimes he would be picked up from, or dropped off at, Hooton Park (the RAF airfield on the opposite bank of the River Mersey) in an Auster, flown by Johnnie Johnstone, the club manager. If it was an Autocrat, a three-seater, I would often be allowed to go along for the ride. Once when Wilbur was talking about flying he told us that he reckoned he could be put anywhere in the British Isles in his favourite aeroplane, a Mosquito, without a map, and he would soon know where he was. At the time I thought he was 'shooting a line', in the vernacular of the period, but many years later I remembered his words and agreed with him. A bit of height and good visibility helps a lot.

I also managed to fly with other people and quickly became part of the furniture. I flew with many of the club members and became a critical (still precocious) passenger, and would report my observations to the lads in the hangar. However, I learned a lot just sitting and watching.

Not long after we started there, the club won a contract to train ATC/CCF cadets to PPL (Private Pilot's Licence) standard on the RAF Flying Scholarship scheme. This required an aerobatic aircraft and soon we had some 'Maggies' – the Miles Magister in RAF form, the Miles Hawk Trainer 3 in its civil guise, G-ALOG, G-AIZL and G-AKRM.

I went flying in a Maggie one day with a club member who was usually quite good, but on landing he managed to get a bit slow and one wing dropped dramatically at about 50 feet. I clearly remember looking down the apparently almost vertical wing at the grass. He applied full power quickly and recovered to go around and try again.

The next stage of expansion for the club was getting the contract for Army Co-operation flying, which entailed flying various courses and heights, night and day, so that the army could practice their artillery, searchlight and radar procedures. This also required new aircraft, and Wilbur bought a Rapide, G-AHPT, and a Gemini, G-AKEM. I enjoyed going along on these exercises, there was usually a spare seat, particularly when the Rapide was on duty, and it often involved flying at night and sometimes in bad weather. These new aircraft had radio and blind flying instruments, which for me added a new dimension to flying. Wilbur also had the use of a Percival Proctor 5, G-AIAA, which belonged to a local solicitor, Mr T. Wayman-Hales.

Meanwhile, the engineering complement was increasing, of course, and a couple of the engineers, Cliff Watson and Gerry Smyth, had PPLs, and another, Nick Clements, was learning to fly. Cliff and Gerry were in the RAFVR (RAF Volunteer Reserve) at Woodvale, flying Chipmunks, and Cliff was doing his 'white' instrument rating. Cliff had learned to fly with the army and trained as a glider pilot at the end of the war. As the war ended before he was required, he had retrained as an aircraft engineer. I had been going on at the lads about spinning, and one evening Cliff said he'd take me and show me one.

We went off in one of the Autocrats and flew to the north of Liverpool, climbing to 3,000 feet. Cliff pulled the Auster up into a stall and, as it slowed, applied full rudder. The Auster rolled over into a spin but, as it did so, the propeller stopped. The engine's slow running speed was rather low and the slow speed and the entry into the spin were just enough to make it stop. After one quick turn of the spin, Cliff recovered and levelled off. We were now at about 2,500ft and, as the Auster didn't have a starter, Cliff wondered out loud if we had enough height for the only engine restart procedure we had available, which was diving to a speed which would rotate the prop. Deciding to give it a try, he pushed the stick forward. We accelerated and watched the stationary prop. As Cliff pushed the Auster more and more into what felt like a vertical dive, the speed built up, but our height rapidly reduced. I remember looking down at Aintree race-course and thinking that at least we would have somewhere decent to land, if all else failed. As the Auster accelerated and approached its VNE (never exceed speed) of 160mph, finally, at about 1,000ft, the prop kicked over and began windmilling. The engine restarted and we flew back to Speke, not wishing to risk another spin until the slow running was fixed.

My dream, of course, was to be a pilot. At that time the usual route was the RAF, and with this in mind I joined the RAF section of the CCF (Combined Cadet Force, previously the OTC, Officer Training Corps) at my school, the Liverpool Institute. My plan was to apply for a flying scholarship when I had the required qualifications, which were the proficiency badge and being 16 years old, and hopefully to do the training at my flying club. I worked my way through the CCF ranks and also learned a lot of theory, including navigation, princi-ples of flight, meteorology etc., which would be useful later. Ours was a fairly easy going CCF squadron and we were left largely to our own devices and had to find much of the information for ourselves. My school friend, Mike, was also keen on a career in the RAF, and together we gained the knowledge to pass both our proficiency and advanced proficiency badges. We ended up as sergeants, giving lectures on navigation etc. to the junior cadets.

Meanwhile, back at the club, I was getting as much flying as I could. Now and then, pilots would let me fly the aircraft, usually a bit of straight and level with an occasional turn or two. In the early days one of the instructors was a lady pilot called Vera Strodl, who had flown with the ATA (Air Transport Auxiliary) in the war. I did quite a bit of flying with Vera and she let me do mostly straight and level stuff and turns, on just one occasion attempting a landing. When the army co-op flying started, several commercial licensed pilots ap-peared, a couple full time, others just part time. I think the contract probably required a commercial pilot. One of these was Eric Minshaw, who became the club's Chief Flying Instructor. Eric who was ex Fleet Air Arm, had flown Corsairs in the Pacific and had been a prisoner of war of the Japanese for a couple of years. Eric was a taciturn, moody type who didn't talk a lot, but I got on with him, probably because I admired him. I flew with him when I could, particularly on army co-op flights. I think he recognised my enthusiasm. The Gemini only had one set of flying controls and on several occasions he swapped seats with me (with some difficulty) and let me fly this delightful little twin-engined aeroplane.

One of the best trips involved a couple of details of low-level exercises over Llanbedr airfield in Cardigan Bay, landing at Valley for a break at lunchtime. We were doing simulated strafing runs over gun emplacements and figure of eights over the airfield, at about 200/300ft. We swapped seats and Eric left me to it for half an hour or so, pretending to go asleep in the right hand seat. He wasn't asleep because a fist would come out to thump me if I strayed below 200ft, which he'd told me was the lower limit. I appreciated his trust in a fifteen-year-old and really enjoyed myself, but I go cold now to think of what would have happened if we'd had an engine failure!

'Dinger' Bell was the other full time commercial pilot. He had an instrument rating and was employed primarily to fly the Rapide and Gemini. 'Bunny' Bramson, of later fame, was one of the part time pilots who flew army co-ops, as was Len Mooney, an air traffic controller at Speke. One trip with Bunny I remember was an army co-op detail in northeast Lancashire. It was a triangular course over the hilly area between Blackburn and Bolton. I had been on the same course with another pilot a few days earlier. The aircraft was an Autocrat, as in the previous exercise. When we arrived in the area Bunny had difficulty deciding exactly where the course was. I remembered one turning point was a hill with a folly on top. We saw one and flew over to investigate but it turned out to be the wrong one. We wandered about for thirty minutes, trying to establish our whereabouts in relation to the hidden course, and then to the south we spotted an airfield. Bunny decided to fly to and identify it, which might help us to fix our position. As we approached, we could see a name in big letters on a hangar roof and when we were close enough to read it, realised it said 'Ringway'. At that point Bunny decided he'd had enough and we flew back to Speke.

One of my jobs during '52 when I was fifteen was pleasure flying. Dinger would taxi the Rapide up to the terminal building at Speke, with me in the back, holding a large wooden noticeboard, so big it had to stick out of the door. The notice board advertised pleasure flights (Speke to the Pierhead and back) at ten shillings per person, kids half price. I would take it up to the public balcony, retrieve our collapsible table from a cupboard inside, lean the board against it, and set up under the clock on the control tower to take bookings. When I had enough passengers for a flight, I'd tell Dinger, then make an announcement on the airport tannoy system that the Wright Aviation Pleasure Flight number 1 (or 2 or 3) was about to depart and dash down to the aircraft (with the cash box). I'd put the steps up to the Rapide and show the passengers on board, making sure they were strapped in, steps away, give Dinger the thumbs up, and the flight would depart. It was tricky getting an exact eight passengers each time, so we would often fly with six or seven on board, and sometimes I would stay on board for a trip.

It could be busy work at weekends or summer holidays as the balcony was often packed with people. Many years later, the public was excluded from the balcony as the railings were decreed to be too low to be safe. Before that happened there were many pictures of hundreds of girls on the balcony waving at the Beatles. I don't remember any falling over, but that's the ultra-safe sterilised world of health and safety we've inherited.

Another frequent job for me was helping Harry Robbins. Harry was an ex RAF flight engineer, whom Wilbur employed initially to make the advertising banners which he towed behind the Austers. We'd lay the banner out on the runway (in the reverse direction) alongside the aircraft, which peeled it off the ground as it took off. Wilbur would fly over the airfield when he finished his advertising display, release the banner and we would run to where it landed, roll it up and take it back to the hangar. Sometimes repairs were required if it had dragged on the ground during take-off. Harry was known as 'Harry the Banner', of course.

One of the club members arranged to hire an Autocrat, G-AIGP, to fly to France with his wife, and asked if the aircraft could be positioned to a disused airfield at Poulton near Chester to save him coming to Speke. Harry, who had a PPL, flew it there and I went with him for the ride. We landed at Poulton, where the man and his wife were waiting for us, and as Harry parked, I noticed that he switched the fuel off. This was unusual. The club pilots normally left the fuel on, mainly, as I understood, because frequent use of the valve caused the cork seals to leak. The engineers were the only people who checked that it worked correctly. The pilot loaded his luggage in the back, his wife in to the starboard seat and jumped in. Harry swung the prop, GP taxied the ten yards to the runway and the throttle was immediately opened for take-off.

Over the years I've noticed that I seem to have an almost psychic connection with mechanical things, and often get a 'feeling' when something is going wrong. It's been useful on occasions. As the Auster quickly accelerated down the runway, I had a feeling that something wasn't right. Sure enough, as the Auster lifted off, the engine stopped. The pilot, assuming Harry had left the aircraft ready to go, obviously hadn't done full pre take-off checks. Not a good idea. GP bounced back on to the ground, swung off the runway as there wasn't much of it left, and careered across the recently mown field, narrowly missing all the bales of hay. Harry went to swing the prop again. I didn't hear the pilot's comments and GP departed for France.

Another occasion when this 'feeling' occurred was when the Gemini had just finished its Certificate of Airworthiness overhaul. Eric was doing the test flight and, unusually, decided to fill all the seats. Cliff sat in front with Eric, and Gerry with me in the back. As we did the engine runs prior to take-off, with the parking brake on, the aircraft moved forward as power was increased. This wasn't unusual, so Eric then pushed the rudder over as each engine was tested. This applied differential brake and with parking brake on, increased the applied brake to each wheel in turn. However, when the second engine power was increased, there was a bang and the aircraft swung forward. The brake cable had broken.

"Never mind," said Eric, "We'll do the flight anyway".

We took off and did the full C of A air test, stalls, max speed etc., before returning to Speke. As we made our approach, I remembered the brake cable. I didn't say anything, assuming Eric would be aware of it, thinking it would be presumptuous of a schoolboy to speak at that point. We landed and sure enough Eric applied the brake. With only one brake operating, we swung abruptly off the runway on to the grass and continued swinging into the most vicious ground loop I'd ever experienced. The aircraft tightened more and more into the swing, and it felt like the undercarriage would go at any moment. Fortunately, it didn't, and we taxied carefully back to the club.

We often had a day out when the Rapide would position to an airfield to do pleasure flights at an air display. I joined the lads as a passenger and we enjoyed several days like this. One day out was when we all went to Blackbushe in the Rapide for the Farnborough Show in September 1952. It was the day when the DH110, with John Derry flying, broke up during its display, killing the crew, and its two engines crashed into the crowd, killing 28 people. The two engines, still howling, bits of piping hanging off, passed over our heads as the aircraft disintegrated and they landed on the hill behind us. We went home in a sombre mood.

Meanwhile, Mike and I applied for the flying scholarship with the CCF. During the summer holidays of 1953 we went to the Aircrew Selection Centre at RAF Hornchurch, for two days of aptitude and medical tests. It all seemed to go well, and at the end of the second day, I went before the President of the Medical Board for the results. He was sitting behind an impressive mahogany desk as I walked in, saluted, as was the form, and waited as he read through my documents.

"Well, I'm sorry, Flood," he said. "I'm afraid you've failed the medical on eyesight. You are hypermetropic, that means you are long sighted."

I nearly fell over. I had never considered the possibility of failure, particularly medical.

"Does that mean I won't be able to fly?" I gasped.

"Yes, I'm afraid so, but you can always be a navigator or radio operator," he replied.

Dreams and castles came tumbling down. This was not part of the plan and I wandered off in a daze. Mike also failed on eyesight and we travelled back home dismally reviewing our options.

That summer holiday was after I had taken GCE 'O' and 'A' levels, and I had obtained the two 'A' level passes that I would have required for Air Force entry. I had also considered staying on after the sixth form and trying for a scholarship to university, which would have helped the RAF route, but now...? My mother arranged a consultation for me with an ophthalmologist in Rodney Street, the centre of medical expertise in Liverpool. He provided me with an impressive report on my eyesight, which said that although I had a small degree of hypermetropia, it was well within the RAF limits, of which he was well aware, and overall I had no problems with vision. With the help of the Commanding Officer of my CCF squadron at school, I sent a copy of the report to RAF Home Command, but they completely ignored it and I heard no more. I didn't really appreciate at the time that about 200 cadets were competing for some 25 flying scholarships.

Soon after my Hornchurch visit, Wilbur entered the King's Cup Air Race at Coventry in one of the club Maggies, G-ALOG. We spent hours polishing it, and fitted ballast in the back cockpit so that Wilbur could fly it from the front. On the day, Dinger flew us all in the Rapide to Bagington, Coventry for the race. There was an air display, in which the most impressive item for me was Prince Cantacuzene flick rolling his Jungmeister just before touchdown, and then the race started. There were several circuits of the short course so the handicapped aircraft passed over the field several times. We were all staring at the horizon waiting to see them as they approached the field each time, and I was picking them out well before most of the lads could see them. After this happened on the first couple of circuits, Dinger turned to me and said,

"There's not much wrong with your bloody eyes!"

This pleased and encouraged me for the future. Wilbur was placed a creditable sixth in the race, unfortunately not able to compete with the dedicated racing men, and, disappointed, we flew back to Speke.

I went back to school for the 1953 autumn term wondering what to do next. On top of all this, Wilbur was in trouble with his flying club. To fund his fairly rapid expansion, he had borrowed money from one of the club members in the form of a debenture, which had been called in. Wilbur couldn't repay and the club was effectively insolvent. The lads who worked for him were obviously worried about their jobs. After my RAF rejection, I had been considering starting work at the club as an engineering apprentice, and then funding my flying training myself. However, Cliff, who was now the chief engineer at the club, advised me to wait to see what would happen, so I had gone back to school, ostensibly to try for a university scholarship.

What happened next at the club was a surprise. The debenture holder had negotiated with a company from Pwllheli, in North Wales, called Dragon Airways, and arranged for this company to take over the Wright Aviation assets, ie the club. Dragon Airways, a one man outfit, was operated by Maurice 'Guy' Guinane, previously a BOAC first officer on Argonauts. Dragon had one Rapide, and operated from Broom Hall airfield, Pwllheli, doing pleasure flights for the nearby Butlin's holiday camp.

Wilbur disappeared, and fairly quickly, in the autumn of 1953, Dragon Airways became the operator of what was previously Wright Aviation. The aircraft were repainted in Dragon colours, dark blue fuselage with a white top, and silver wings, replacing the club's cream and red colours. More staff were taken on and even more expansion was obviously intended.

Now another player entered the game. One of the club members, who had recently learned to fly and now had his PPL, was Reginald Gates, who had a wholesale fruit and vegetable importing business in Liverpool. He had planned an operation to fly mushrooms daily from Dublin to Speke. This was before refrigerated transport, and mushrooms had a very short life between being picked and then sold. Mr Gates had arranged with several mushroom growers in Eire for the mushrooms to be picked in the morning, driven to Dublin airport in the afternoon, then flown to Speke and put on trains from Liverpool that evening, so that they would be in the markets around northern England next morning, less than 24 hours after being picked. Mr Gates had discussed the operation with Wilbur, but, with the demise of Wright Aviation, he was now planning to set up his own operating company. Accordingly, he had approached several people at the club, with a view to employing them. 'Dinger' Bell, one of the commercial pilots, and Cliff had agreed to join this new company, as well as several other engineers. The company, called Federated Air Transport, would be a subsidiary of the fruit wholesale firm, Federated Fruit Co. Ltd, and would be operating with Anson and Rapide aircraft.

Once plans became firm, an Anson freighter was bought from Transair at Croydon, and a Rapide from Starways at Liverpool. Dinger was to be the only pilot, Cliff was chief engineer, but Nick, who had been interested, had backed out and decided to stay with Dragon. The other engineers were George Parkes, Stan Wright, and apprentice Malcolm Fraser. In December '53 Cliff offered me a job with Feds as an apprenticed engineer and I accepted.

That meant that I would be leaving school at the end of term, and I notified my headmaster, Mr Edwards. He wasn't impressed. He was an academic snob, and when I went to see him for my reference he made his views quite clear.

"You mean to say that you're going to wear overalls, Flood?" he bellowed at me.

"Yes Sir," I replied, and rendered him speechless.

He obviously thought that my career choice was beneath contempt, gave me my reference, and bid me farewell. The reference mentioned my academic achievements (doing both GCE 'O' and 'A' levels together when I was just sixteen), but he did say that my main interest was aeroplanes, so at least he got that right.

So this was it, I started with Feds (as everybody now called it) just before Christmas '53. We were based in hangar No.6, between the terminal building and the big No.1 hangar. Convenient, but it meant we had to taxi the aircraft from our hangar across an airport road to get to the apron. This required the airport managers to station men to remove a fence and stop any traffic whenever we moved the aircraft.

One consideration that was uppermost in my mind was that I wanted to learn to fly as soon as possible. I had mentioned this to Cliff, as I had thought I might be better off with Dragon, as they still operated the flying club. However Cliff reassured me that the boss, Mr Gates, intended to buy an Auster for his own use, and the engineers would be able to use it. Cliff and Stan had PPLs, and Malcolm was learning to fly, as I was intending to do.

Our first Anson G-AIPA was a MkI, and initially didn't have starter motors, although they were fitted later. The starting routine was for an engineer to put a long starting handle into the engine via the side cowling, and then wind furiously. Due to the gearing, a lot of turns of the handle produced a relatively slow engine turn over. When the pilot thought the engine was moving fast enough he would operate a booster coil by pressing a button and switch the magnetos on. With luck, the engine would fire as it went over compression, if not, the handle man would have a breather and start again. Of course, this routine meant that somebody had to accompany Dinger on every flight. I was more than happy to volunteer for this duty, and did quite a few hours in this role, mostly to Dublin, but also Manchester, Belfast etc. Stan also did some flights, as did Malcolm occasionally. As well as the daily mushroom flights, five days a week, we had a contract to carry the excess load of Sunday newspapers for Belfast from Manchester on a Saturday evening, when the BEA Dakota couldn't carry all of them because of a full load of passengers. All this was great for me, good experience, flying in all weathers day and night.

Dinger did all the flying, but I learned a lot just watching and listening. The Anson had the old RAF VHF radio equipment, TR1154/1155, large boxes with big yellow knobs, and they were mounted behind the pilot. Dinger insisted on changing channels on this himself, by reaching behind and doing it 'blind'. I would have been more than happy to do this for him, but Dinger was a bit of a 'one man band' and preferred to do it himself. Later we upgraded to Plessey VHF sets which had removable crystals for each frequency. One thing which was certainly my job was retracting and lowering the undercarriage. To do this, a handle protruded from the right side of the base of the pilot's seat, and it required 147 turns up, and 147 down, good exercise! Dinger was quite happy for the second man to do this. As well as the usual undercarriage red and green indicator lights the Anson had mechanical indicators. These were two little round knobs, by the throttle pedestal, which emerged and pushed a flap aside to show themselves when the undercarriage was locked down. As an unofficial modification they always had a smiling face painted on them. So as you finally finished the 147 turns of winding the undercarriage down, these two little happy faces appeared to make you feel a bit better. Dinger wasn't one to share the flying, and I only remember a single occasion, flying one night from Belfast to Dublin, when he let me do a bit of straight and level.

At Ringway and Nutts Corner, bad weather approaches were carried out using GCA (ground controlled approach), a radar talk down which was the best option if available. At Speke, it was SBA (standard beam approach), which was a pilot interpreted aural system of 'A's and 'N's either side of a constant note which was the approach centre line, with a couple of fan markers at inner and outer points (threshold and about 4 miles). En route navigation was by radio range, which also was 'A's and 'N's, the constant note aligned with the airway. Burtonwood was our local range and was aligned with airway Green Two to Dublin and Amber One to the north. Our Anson didn't have ILS or even ADF, but it did have a medium frequency (MF) beacon receiver to receive the radio range and NDBs (non-directional beacons), and this was connected to an indicator with 'twitcher needles'. These two needles pivoted at the bottom and each side of the indicator, and when they crossed in the centre that indicated that you were heading straight for the beacon, if they crossed either side of centre it indicated a turn that way was required. As the beacon was approached the needles rose up on the gauge the nearer the aircraft got to the beacon. 180° ambiguity was a problem, resolved by DR navigation, or by watching the twitchers, if they moved up the instrument you were getting nearer, if they dropped down then you were going away. ADF, automatic direction finding, followed soon after for us, with a relative bearing indicator giving a positive steady bearing indication to the beacon. RMIs (radio magnetic indicators) were far away in the future. One other option was QDMs and QTEs, magnetic bearings to, and true bearings from, an airfield homer station on VHF.

As we progressed into 1954, I was enjoying the engineering work and the flying, but one problem remained, which was to learn to fly. I began to have doubts when the boss, Mr Gates, started being checked out on the Rapide by 'Bunny' Bramson, one of the part time commercial pilots who used to fly army co-op flights for Wright Aviation. This indicated to me, correctly as it turned out, that he wasn't going to buy an Auster for his, or our, use.

The next event of note for me was when Dragon borrowed our Rapide for a week or so. During this time it had an ignition problem and Cliff and I went down to the club to do a magneto change. While we were working on the engine, Sid Lester, the new chief engineer at Dragon, came over to chat, and said to us that he could do with a couple of good engineers, and if we were interested to let him know. Cliff brushed it off, of course, as he had no intention of going back to where he had been, in a lesser position than before. However I considered Sid's offer seriously, as I now realised the only way I was going to learn to fly was at somewhere like Dragon and the flying club, as the possibility of doing this at Feds was becoming increasingly unlikely.

After we finished work at Feds, I would often go down to the club to chat to the lads and see how things were going, so on one of these occasions, I asked to see Sid, and told him I would like to accept his offer of a job.

"Oh, I didn't want just another apprentice," he said, to my dismay. "But leave it with me and I'll let you know," he smiled, and I left not knowing quite where I stood.

A week or so later he contacted me and offered me a job. I think he'd had a word with Nick to check whether I was worth the bother, and Nick had given me the OK.

So in April '54 I moved from Feds, back to the club where I had started, and settled in again working on the aeroplanes as before. Dragon had plans for expansion, had ordered three De Havilland Herons, two Mark 2s, and a Mk 1, and became the first English operator of the type. I think Jersey Airlines had actually been the first but they didn't qualify. We were still operating from Broom Hall, Pwllheli, doing pleasure flights for Butlin's, and also operating scheduled flights to Pwllheli from Liverpool and Stoke on Trent with the Rapides. Soon after I started with Dragon, I was posted, effectively, to Broom Hall to look after the aircraft there. There was another apprentice, Roy Roylance, with me, but as he had a driving licence, his main job was driving the 12 seater bus (previously used at Ronaldsway Airport, Isle of Man) between the airfield and the holiday camp bringing the passengers to fly. We had an old Chevrolet desert truck as a fire engine/rescue vehicle which we drove around the airfield each morning. As it had a cracked cylinder block and no cooling water, we had to be careful not to drive it for too long.

We were billeted at the Victoria Hotel in Pwllheli, but we had a bronze (staff) badge for Butlins which gave us free access to the camp, including the evening variety shows, and initially we also had our midday meal there. It wasn't very satisfactory, eating in a huge dining hall with all the happy campers, so we arranged for all our meals to be at the hotel, but kept our access to the camp, which filled in the odd evening. Several musicians and a very attractive girl singer from the camp also stayed in the hotel, and occasionally they would have an impromptu musical evening in the residents lounge, which we enjoyed.

I was at Broom Hall for about three or four months, looking after the Rapide based there for pleasure flying, and also the Rapides which operated scheduled flights from Liverpool and Stoke on Trent at weekends bringing holiday makers for Butlins. The grass airfield had two runways, one roughly north/south about 600yds the other east/west 400yds. The longer runway had quite a slope to the south, so the airfield created interesting problems for the pilots, weighing up wind and slope combinations. The scheduled aircraft with up to eight passengers and fuel for Liverpool or Stoke was often very tight for take-off, and at times it was interesting.

The pleasure flying Rapide usually kept the fuel on board down to about ten gallons a side (about one hour's flying) which helped. In fact the previous year when Captain Guinane was operating at Pwllheli he had been caught out on a pleasure flight when low stratus suddenly covered the field and, as he didn't have enough fuel to divert to Valley, 25 miles away, had to put the Rapide down in the best field he could find. He went through a couple of hedges and the aircraft was written off, but he and the passengers were unscathed.

One day when Eric was doing the pleasure flights, he was landing on the short, 400yd, runway with a strong westerly wind. There was a steep incline just before the runway which obviously caused some interesting wind effects. The Rapide dropped a wing just before the threshold and although Eric recovered with lots of power, he ended up in the cornfield alongside the runway. I spent the next couple of hours removing corn from the Rapide's cowlings.

By August 1954 I was back at Speke again and getting desperate about learning to fly. We (engineers) used to talk flying all the time, and in tea breaks when the instructors would often join us for a cup of tea, we'd have long theoretical discussions about all sorts, such as, did an aircraft actually stall in a stall turn, and so on. Being an opinionated seventeen year old I would argue with the instructors, with all the arrogance of youth.

I'd had no formal flying training at this point, so I asked Nick, who now had his PPL, if he would let me try some take offs and landings if I paid for an hour's flying. We, as staff, were allowed 50% discount on flying rates, which meant £1.10s.0d per hour (£1.50 in current money). Nick readily agreed and one evening we went off in G-AIPH, the flapless Auster J4, and did as many circuits as we could in the hour. I really enjoyed it, the first time I had been allowed to properly try take offs and landings, and I learned a lot. I now had my SPL (Student Pilot Licence) and desperately wanted to get on with training.

So, it was back to work in the hangar, until one Sunday evening in late September when Nick and I were on duty. The flying had finished and we were thinking about putting the aircraft in the hangar. Eric wandered over and said to Nick, (and I'll never forget his words),

"Come on, Nick, let's see what this bloke can do".

He told me to get in the left hand seat of G-AIBZ, an Autocrat, with flaps, Nick climbed in the third seat at the back, and Eric jumped into the right hand seat. I wasn't really sure what was going on, and thought we were just going to have a flight to see what Eric thought of my chances.

After we started up, I taxied out to runway 35, did the checks and engine run up, then lined up and took off. I flew round the circuit and made an approach and a reasonable landing, even though the flapped Auster was a bit different from 'PH without flaps. We cleared the runway on to the grass, and Eric told me to taxi back to the start of the runway by the runway control caravan and stop there. He then unfastened his seat belt and said,

"Get out, Nick, he doesn't need us", and they both climbed out.

This was it. I wasn't really sure it was happening, but I wasn't going to back out. With a green light from the caravan, I lined up on the runway again and opened the throttle. Airborne on my own, I concentrated hard, and carefully flew round the right hand circuit. As I turned on to base leg and started the glide approach I saw the caravan giving me a red light. I opened up again and flew along the runway at 1,000ft and started another circuit. Next time on base leg, another red light! I couldn't understand it but I knew Eric and Nick were in the caravan and thought Eric had decided to wind me up by making me go around a few times, as he had that sort of twisted sense of humour. Third time on base leg, another red light! I decided Eric was really pushing me to the limit, until I spotted a BEA Dakota downwind left hand and realised the tower controller had told the caravan to keep me airborne until it had landed to avoid the possibility of me making a mess on the runway and inconveniencing the scheduled flight. A real confidence booster! Next time around on base leg I got a green from the caravan and started my approach. There was a bit of a crosswind from port and as I rounded out and held off I started drifting to starboard. Just before I touched I decided there was too much drift, so full power and round again. Next time I had the aircraft rounded out and held off before the drift started so I landed and taxied back to the caravan. Eric and Nick climbed in and we taxied back to the club.

"Everythin' comes to them as waits," grinned Eric in his best Cheshire agricultural accent. I didn't care, I was walking on air. I'd done it, my first solo.

Next day, after work, I couldn't wait to fly again. Eric did one quick circuit with me, and then let me do a few more solo circuits. I was a pilot!

But what is it that pride comes before...? The third evening I logged out again for some circuits but this time we were using a grass strip between the runways, which was into-wind. This strip was about 300 yards long and had a concrete hut, the VHF Homer building, in the middle, but just off to one side. I took off with no problem but, as I came in to land, the short strip obviously affected my judgement and I touched down a bit fast and bounced. Full power and round again, no problem, but this happened on the next two landings as well. On my fourth approach and I could see the sun was just about to touch the western horizon. I had a feeling of panic. It would be dark in half an hour and what if I couldn't sort this out before then! However, my fourth attempt went well and I landed successfully. I couldn't quite understand what I was doing wrong and went home worrying about it, so much so that, soon after I went to bed, I woke up and was violently sick. It had clearly upset me, mentally and physically. The next day I went to my mentor, Nick, and told him about it.

"Yes, I was watching," he said. "You just weren't holding off long enough; you were trying to rush the landing because of the short strip."

Pretty obvious, really, when it was pointed out like that, but I had learned the lesson.

I carried on flying as much as I could. In our lunch hour several of the engineers would go off for a short flight and, if the tide in the river was out, three or four aeroplanes would tail chase along the channels in the Mersey mud banks, as low as we could go, occasionally hitting each other's slipstream as we tried to keep in line. It frightens me now to think about it. When we flew in the lunch hour, with no instructors around, we'd fly for twenty minutes and book ten, to keep the costs down.

The day after Boxing Day 1954, Bernie and I were the only two who had turned in, just in case anybody wanted to fly. We'd pushed the aircraft out but nobody came; even the instructors hadn't bothered to turn in. As the day wore on, I decided that I would fly myself. I had about seven hours solo logged by now and although, strictly speaking, I needed to be authorised by an instructor, I was quite happy to forego that requirement. I took off in BZ and decided I would do a short local flight. I had done quite a few stall turns as a passenger with several club pilots, even on one occasion sitting in the third seat when an instructor showed a pilot how to do them. The stall turn was the limit of the aerobatic capacity of the Auster, particularly as it only had lap straps fitted. Nevertheless, with all the confidence of youth, I decided I would try a stall turn. I had a good look around and my height at 1,500ft seemed plenty. I eased the stick forward and, as the aircraft accelerated, pulled gently back and applied full power. As BZ reached an almost vertical climb, I was watching the speed and as it fell quickly to 60mph I checked the climb and applied full left rudder.

If I had done no more it would probably have been a very reasonable stall turn. However, one instinctive habit I had been developing was a frequent scan of the instruments, particularly the airspeed indicator. I had already learned that this was 'good practice'. I had also learned during my few solo hours that falling airspeed should be countered by easing the stick forward, the rate of forward movement being more or less in proportion to the amount of loss of airspeed. So as the poor old Autocrat rotated from the vertical and the nose swung down past the horizon, I glanced at the airspeed. It was, quite correctly for a stall turn, decaying very rapidly past about 30 mph and heading very positively towards zero! The pitot head was on the port wing, which accentuated the effect. With the lightning reaction of a very inexperienced and startled seventeen-year-old pilot, I slammed the stick fully forward.

Still with full power on, the Autocrat did exactly as it was bid. The nose tucked sharply under and the aircraft was inverted! This was my first experience of negative G, at least as pilot-in-command, and I fell as far as the lap strap would allow, which meant my head hit the Perspex roof, hair tangling with the silly elevator trim situated on the X-shaped cross member above. With my right (throttle) hand I grabbed this cross member and pushed myself hard back into the seat. The other hand was still on the stick and (I will never forget the view I had of Hale lighthouse as I looked up, or rather down, through the Perspex roof) I pulled hard back...

The resultant manoeuvre, the second half of a loop, must have looked very impressive from the ground or water but I don't care to remember how few feet of height remained at the bottom of the recovery. I flew very slowly and carefully back home. We had a good look around the aircraft but it was fine; Austers are tough aircraft. I didn't try a stall turn again for some time and, when I did, it was above 3,000 feet! This was probably my first serious encounter with Lady Luck or my Guardian Angel – whoever she is – but we were destined to meet again on several occasions over the coming years.

One evening, when I was the last hangar representative, I thought I'd do a couple of circuits before putting the aircraft away and pre-pared BZ. On checking the fuel, about six gallons were showing on the little rotary indicator on top of the fuel tank, forward of the instrument panel. This was enough for more than one hour's flying but I knew the gauge read high with the tail on the ground, so I lifted the tail and from there I could see that there seemed to be plenty.

I taxied out, lined up and opened the throttle. As the Auster accel-erated and the tail came up, the gauge indicated lower, as expected, but, due to the acceleration and bouncing, the reading was swinging between about two and six gallons. I decided that discretion was the better part of valour, closed the throttle and taxied back to the club to put more fuel in, which is what I should have done before, of course. Unfortunately, the only other person in the hangar and office was Captain Guinane, the boss. Air traffic had phoned to say an Auster had aborted a take-off and he met me as I switched off. I explained what had happened but he wasn't convinced, obviously thinking that I had only noticed how much fuel I had when I started to take off. He then proceeded to give me a lengthy lecture and demonstrated to me how to pre-flight the aircraft properly. I bit my lip and accepted all this, by which time it was too late to fly anyway.

During all this time, of course, I was doing my main job, working on the aircraft. We would often work quite late, finishing jobs required for tomorrow. One evening we had an interesting experi-ence. Eric had been to the Isle of Man in the Rapide, to bring a casualty (a body, in fact) from the TT races. Nick, Bernie and I had put all the aircraft in the hangar and, just about midnight, were preparing to go home. All the hangar lights were out and Nick was putting the lights out in the crew room when suddenly the hangar was lit up as the landing light in the nose of the Rapide switched on.

There were tales around the airport about a 'ghost'. Various sightings had been reported, alleged to be the ghost of Tom Campbell Black, a famous racing pilot who had won the 1934 Great Air Race to Australia in a DH Comet. He was at Speke in 1936, in his Mew Gull 'Miss Liverpool', for its naming at an air display before competing in a race to Johannesburg. Tragically, a landing RAF Hawker Hart collided with the Mew Gull as it was taxiing and Campbell Black was killed.

We didn't believe these ghost tales, of course, but it was a few minutes before we plucked up the courage to go to the Rapide. The Rapide door was closed and when we went on board we found the landing light switch was on. It was a very positive switch, so there was no chance of it having been left in an intermediate position and moving to 'on' by itself. There was an odd sweet smell in the aircraft, probably a residue from the coffin that had been airlifted from the Island. We switched the landing light off and, very quickly, locked up and left. The next day, in daylight, it all seemed a bit like a dream.

Eric didn't bother me again until I'd done about ten hours solo, when he asked me for my logbook. I had 'rescued' my logbook from the drawer in the flight office, where there were always a couple left by people who had planned to start flying but then given up. I couldn't afford to buy one; I needed all my money for flying. So, with a white label stuck over the name page, I had a logbook. Eric saw how much flying I'd done and said, "This is no good. Get another logbook and change some of this flying to dual with me – and put some dual in before you went solo."

I did as I was told and awarded myself six and a half hours dual with him before going solo. Eric was happy and left me alone again. Subsequently, I put some of my solo flying as dual with Eric.

Without much (or, in fact, any) formal instruction, just being left to fly and work it out on my own, it could be interesting at times. Initially I had trouble with crosswind landings but one day I was landing with a fresh north-westerly on runway 26 and, as I held off and started to drift across the runway, I decided that, rather than go around, I would try something different. I put some power on, just enough to stop the speed decaying further, and flew the Auster back to the middle of the runway. I then eased the power off again, held off and, just before it touched, used rudder to bring it back in line with the runway. It was a moment of truth. I realised exactly what the controls were for, quite simply, to control the aeroplane, and if I used them correctly it would do exactly what I wanted it to do. All this early flying was based on my bible, the Air Publication (AP) 1979A *Elementary Flying Training*.

I carried on towards the forty-hour requirement for the PPL. During this time Eric left the club and we had a new CFI, Dickie Holmes. I decided I would like to fly the Maggies and Dickie checked me out and I flew them quite often. Dickie wasn't as easy going as Eric and actually had the nerve to ground me for a week. I was flying a Maggie and managed to run off the taxiway on to the grass in front of the control tower, due mainly to indifferent brakes (my excuse) and air traffic reported the incident to him. Apart from that incident, I completed my 40 hours without too much trouble. I did my cross country in the Maggie OG – Speke to Meir (Stoke on Trent) to Blackpool and back to Speke. After completing the written exams, I did my flying test with Dickie and finally I had my PPL.

It was several years before I realised the time to be logged in my logbook should include all the time taxying, from taxi out to taxi in. I see from my log at that time, and later, that many of the flights were of 10, 15 and 20 minutes duration (the airborne time). We (engineers) did have a habit of booking the minimum time on the sheet in the Flight Office, to keep the cost down, often logging 10 or 15 minutes when we'd probably flown 20 or 25, actually airborne. It was four or five years before I read the notes in my flying logbook and realised I'd probably got quite a few more hours than shown. At that stage I didn't realise how important flying time could be later, for licence qualification, etc.

By now, Dragon was operating its DH Herons, two Mark 2s and a Mark 1. The Heron was a four-engined, fourteen-seat mini airliner, developed from the twin-engined DH Dove, and they were being operated on scheduled services to and from Liverpool, Manchester, Glasgow and Newcastle-upon-Tyne. I had a few trips sitting in the co-pilot's seat of the Heron as they were operated by a single pilot. We also occasionally had the opportunity to fly an Auster, to position urgent spares or ourselves to do an equally urgent job on an aircraft. The generator quill drive on the Gipsy Queen 30 engine was a frequent snag when it sheared, but easy to fix. The Heron's Gipsy Queen 30-2 engines, a development of the Gipsy Queen 2 in the Proctor, had an innovative single lever throttle control with automatic pitch selection.

Being an apprentice, one of my duties was to do the messages, on my bike, for the engineers and the office girls. Three apprentices shared this, but it did seem to be my turn quite often! We would be sent for fish and chips at lunchtime, or cakes, cigarettes, etc, morning or afternoon. One of the office girls was very pretty and her frequent request was for SR toothpaste. As she had such perfect teeth, I have used SR toothpaste myself ever since. Her boyfriend was a Dakota first officer with Lancashire Aircraft Corporation at Blackpool. After a few months with Dragon, she left to start flying with them as an air hostess. Sadly, soon after, we heard that she had been killed when a Dakota, with just crew on board, crashed trying to land in fog in Germany. Over the years this sort of event became an unfortunately regular occurrence, when news arrived that another friend or acquaintance somewhere in the aviation world had been killed.

Our hangar workforce had expanded to cope with airline flying and several of the lads (engineers) who didn't fly were very good and shared the cost with me when I took them flying. I had my PPL in June 1955 and during that summer kept building my hours. I flew to Blackbushe in September, with two of the lads, to visit the Farnborough Show. I see from my logbook that one of the first trips after getting my PPL was in a Maggie with an ex RAF wartime pilot who wanted to fly but didn't have a valid licence. I was talked into going with him to make it legal and we spent an hour doing aerobatics. I enjoyed it, as I had already done some aerobatics when I went along on an air test in a Maggie for Certificate of Airworthiness renewal. I was talked into that one as well when none of the other lads would volunteer, not being too keen on the aerobatic bit.

Working for Dragon, a small but expanding airline, meant that I got to know the pilots who worked with us. They were an interesting and mixed bunch. One ex RAF pilot, of whom the boss, Captain Guinane, thought highly, became a training captain on the Heron. Len Levene used to leave his logbook in the flight office (which, of course, we read) with newspaper cuttings about his air display feats in the RAF. Another pilot was Mac, a Glaswegian. Mac told us an amusing tale about doing a check flight with Len at Renfrew when Len reprimanded him in the circuit for being 10° off the downwind heading for the runway. Mac told us he had been flying at Glasgow for years and said to Len, "Look, laddie, I fly down Sauchiehall Street until I come to the pub at the end, then I turn left and pass the next two pubs and then if I turn left I'm on finals for the runway."

Mac navigated by pubs in the air and on the ground but I don't think Len was impressed. They both went with Dragon to Newcastle, then to Hunting Clan. We heard that Mac had left under a cloud when he turned up to fly a Heron one morning slightly the worse for wear after a night in one of his pubs and the chairman of the company happened to be a passenger. Len went on from Dragon to Hunting, which was absorbed into British United, then British Caledonian, but unfortunately died when the Learjet he was flying in his spare time flew into a mountain in Switzerland.

During the summer of 1955, rumours began to circulate about where the company was heading. For a time, a move to Manchester seemed a possibility, as we used to go to Ringway most weekends to do Check 2s on the Herons, but eventually it was confirmed that Dragon Airways was merging with Hunting Clan (a much larger airline) and moving base to Newcastle-upon-Tyne. Captain Guinane offered me the position of flight clerk on the Herons at the new base, which would mean flying as a glorified steward but also doing loadsheets, passenger and baggage handling, etc. He obviously thought he was doing me a favour and it was a nice gesture but I declined, graciously, I hope, as it didn't really fit in with my plan for the future, whatever that was. Airline flying was not in my ambitious sights at the time (how wrong could I be?).

One of my last flights with Dragon was a trip in an Auster to Nottingham, Tollerton, with Nick.

Most of the lads in the hangar had elected to go with the company, Nick included, and I didn't know what to do. However, before Dragon moved, Nick told me that one of the club members, Jack Green, a PPL holder, was thinking of starting a new flying club and had approached Nick with a view to employing him. Nick wasn't interested, as he had decided to go to Newcastle, but he suggested to Jack that he might consider me. Jack wanted someone who could look after the aircraft and preferably also be a flying instructor. Nick was a licensed engineer but didn't really fancy flying instruction. Jack and I met and he told me his plans. I said the job was just what I wanted, looking after the aircraft wasn't a problem, as Cliff at Feds agreed to oversee me as an apprentice and cover our maintenance. On the flying side, I now had about 80 hours and only needed 100 to go for my assistant instructor rating. Jack and I visited Ken Harvey who had agreed to be the club CFI and would oversee my instructing until I had 400 hours and could get a full rating. Ken was the test pilot at Speke for Airwork, who were overhauling and modifying North American F86 Sabres and Lockheed T33s. He was very pleasant and agreed to do the ten hour course of training which I needed before I could apply for the assistant instructor rating to my PPL. A week or so later, we flew together for an hour or so and he said, "Oh, you'll be fine; just put ten hours with me in your logbook and when you've got your 100 hours, apply for the test".

This was just like Eric all over again. As well as Ken, Jack had organised a couple of part-time instructors to help out at weekends.

In October 1955 I started working for Jack Green at the Merseyside and North Wales Flying Club for £5 a week. I was his sole employee, except for the part time barman. I worked seven days a week from 0830 until dark, or about 1700 in the winter, but I was now in my element and my dreams were starting to come true. Initially, we were in hangar 39, which had been an RAF motor transport maintenance unit. This hangar, a dark, dismal one with no electrical power, was next to the Chapel House Farm building, the original airport terminal in the Thirties. The bar and social side were in the same building as before, and I spent my first couple of weeks repainting and decorating it while the aircraft were being organised. However, within weeks we had moved to the old pre-war Chapel House hangar, No.50, on the other side of the Chapel House Farm building.

This hangar, part of the original airport buildings of the thirties, was excellent for us, light and airy with power laid on, offices, with telephones, and workshops built on at the side from the original sandstone farm buildings, and lovely pre-war concertina-type hangar doors, which one man could operate easily.

The first aircraft Jack bought from Dragon was G-AHAK, a Taylorcraft Plus D two-seater with just a 10-gallon fuel tank. Shortly after starting operations, Jack arranged for the Autocrat G-AJAE to join us. This aircraft belonged to the Royal Artillery Flying Club and had been with Wilbur's club for some time previously, under an arrangement whereby the club maintained and operated it and the few Royal Artillery members who wanted to fly it did so whenever they required.

By January 1956 Jack had bought Auster J4 PH from Dragon, the flapless two-seater in which I'd done the circuits with Nick just before my first solo. Sometime later he bought G-AGVI from Dragon, an Autocrat with a long-range belly tank. Unfortunately BZ, my first solo aircraft, had disappeared and I never saw it again.

To get my hours up, I did as much flying as I could and organised the flying for the PPL members of the new club as they joined. Most of them had been members of the old club. I would also take people flying who came to try it, on a trial flight basis. I did stretch my qualifications to the limit, at Jack's insistence, by checking people out before they flew for the first time with us.

One of the first longer trips in my new job was taking AK to Thruxton in Wiltshire for an engine change. I arranged with Eric Roberts, one of the Dragon engineers who had stayed in Liverpool when Dragon left and who now worked for Lockheed Hydraulics in Speke, to fly AE down to bring me home.

The forecast on the day wasn't good, with an approaching warm front. We set off and soon met a southerly wind with broken low stratus. At first I thought we could stay on top and pressed on but, eventually, the broken stratus became almost solid and I realised that this plan wasn't going to work. I turned back, with Eric in AE following me (no radio) and flew back until we could descend through gaps in the cloud and continue at a lower level.

We managed to fly down valleys below cloud, avoiding the high ground in Shropshire and Worcestershire, until I realised that, with AK's 10-gallon tank and the backtracking, I was now becoming seriously low on fuel. I looked at the map for somewhere to land and saw an airfield at Pershore, apparently disused. We had planned to land for fuel anyway, at Staverton in Gloucestershire, and I was already planning how to get fuel from there to Pershore. On arriving overhead, the airfield appeared well maintained and the runway we chose to land on was in as good a condition as Speke. There were several buildings around the perimeter but we parked the two aircraft at the end of the runway to plan our next move.

Almost immediately, a Land Rover came hurtling around the taxiway towards us. When it arrived, two security men in uniform got out and demanded to know what we were doing. They told us that the airfield was a highly secret, supposedly secure, radar research establishment. I explained our predicament and, thankfully, they agreed we could fly to Staverton in AE to bring fuel for AK. They just wanted to be rid of us as soon as possible.

Eric and I flew to Staverton, borrowed a five gallon can, filled it with fuel and flew back to Pershore. We put the fuel in AK, then flew the two aircraft to Staverton, refuelled them both and continued to Thruxton. We left AK for its engine change and flew back to Speke in AE, another lesson learned. Not really; just until the next time!

By December 1955 I had the required 100 hours and applied for my assistant instructor rating flying test. I was given a date in January at Leicester East airfield, with none other than Bunny Bramson, the Guild of Air Pilots and Navigators (GAPAN) examiner. I had flown a lot with Bunny, a delightful character, at the old club when he used to do army co-op flying for Wilbur. I'd flown with him in Austers, Maggies, Proctor, Gemini and the Rapide and hoped this might give me an edge for the test. However, 'the best laid plans', etc...

On the appointed day the weather was dreadful, with rain and low cloud. I set off in PH and, approaching Stoke on Trent, I was down to about 400ft to keep clear of the cloud. Map reading was difficult in the Potteries, so I decided I would follow a railway line to get me clear of the area; 'Bradshawing', as it was known. I set off, following my chosen track, when suddenly it disappeared into a tunnel. It wasn't supposed to do that and I realised I was following the wrong track. Back to Stoke, and with some difficulty, I found the right railway line and started again. The cloud seemed to be getting lower and when I went into cloud as I pulled up to avoid high-tension cables, I decided enough was enough. Looking at the map when I could, I saw a disused airfield at Hixon next to the railway line. As I arrived and flew over to inspect its condition, I saw that there were fences across the runways at various points, but just enough space between them to land.

I landed with some relief and taxied as near as I could get to some hangars, which appeared to be in use. Nobody seemed interested in me and when I climbed out and went to the hangars it turned out that it was an RAF maintenance unit. The airmen didn't seem too bothered about my arrival but when I asked if I could use a phone to let Bunny know what had happened, they said that was difficult, too many forms would have to be filled in. They suggested I went, via the main gate, to the first house outside, which was the local police station, where I was sure to find help. I did this, explained to the sergeant on duty my predicament, and he gave me the phone. While I was waiting to contact Bunny, the sergeant suggested he take a few details, as policemen do. I told him my name, address, aircraft registration, my airfield of departure, my intended destination and the reason for my landing at Hixon. I finally contacted Bunny and told him I would get to Leicester as soon as I could, when the weather improved.

After an hour or so, although there was not much improvement, I decided to try again. I swung the prop myself and took off. I followed the railway line again and, once past Lichfield and the high ground, the situation improved and I progressed relatively easily to Leicester. I landed and Bunny was waiting for me. Bunny was the manager of a large department store in Leicester and had come straight from his office, looking very smart in his pin stripes. The wartime airfield had three runways in a poor condition, as the only operator was the local flying club. The land between the runways was ploughed and obviously farmed. It was also now raining heavily. Bunny jumped in the left hand seat, I swung the prop and joined him in the right hand (instructor's) seat. As we taxied out, I warned Bunny that the aircraft's drum brakes, only operated at the left hand seat position, were soaking wet and even less effective than usual. Taxying on a long stretch of taxiway, the aircraft began to weathercock into wind and Bunny applied brake, ineffectively, to stop it and then decided full rudder with power might work. It didn't, and with lots of power applied, the aircraft ended up facing into wind, about 30yds into the ploughed field, sinking up to its axles in the soaking wet mud.

"Don't worry," said Bunny, typically, "I'll get out and lift the wings by the struts and you just use power to help".

This he did and we eventually arrived back on the taxiway after quite a struggle. Bunny climbed back in, now coated in mud up to his knees, and quite a few splashes elsewhere.

"This is a disaster," I thought, "and I haven't even started the airborne test yet!"

However, we took off and did the test, all at less than 1,000ft because of the cloud. After we landed, Bunny shook my hand and told me I'd passed. I couldn't believe it, what a day! I decided I'd had enough excitement and wasn't going to attempt to fly home.

Bunny dropped me off in the centre of Leicester and I found a reasonably cheap hotel for the night. He was probably glad to see the back of me! But I was on cloud nine, an instructor at last. It was the day before my nineteenth birthday. Next day the weather was the same, so I went home by train. It was four days before it improved enough for Eric Roberts and I to fly to Leicester in AK to bring PH home.

Bunny was one of the characters in the aviation scene at the time and one of the best. It was a privilege to have known and flown with him.

There was a sequel to this. A week or so later, a couple of plain clothed policemen arrived at the flying club to request from me 'a few more details'. They were very friendly and chatted for a while, asking about the club and the flying. I had already started proper instructing, although my licence endorsement had still not arrived. I had assumed that it would be dated from the day of my test. It did arrive soon after, followed by a letter from the Ministry of Aviation, pointing out the regulations I had broken by landing at a disused airfield without permission and also instructing when I was not qualified! They had validated my PPL assistant instructor rating on the day they had sent it to me, even though the GAPAN certificate was dated as the day of test.

2.   LEARNING TO FLY

When I began instructing, in January 1955, I quickly realised that the old saying, 'the best way to learn is to teach' was as true of flying as of anything else. The club developed quickly and I was getting into the routine of new pupils – some good, some average and others who ought not to have been allowed near an aeroplane – and would clearly never be allowed to fly solo. If, on occasion, I complained about the bad ones to Jack, he'd merely say, "Oh, just smile and take their money; we need it!"

As an assistant instructor I wasn't allowed to send a pupil on his first solo or authorise his solo cross-country. For these items, a full instructor rating was required. However, I enjoyed what I was doing; lots of flying with all sorts of different people to fly with and teach. My instructing style was based on Eric Minshaw's; that is, to say the absolute minimum while in the air and take over only if disaster is imminent. I thought it was better to let the student try to fly the aeroplane himself without constant interruption and the more he did himself, the quicker he would learn. Talk about it on the ground before and after the flight but in the air the student had enough to cope with, without somebody wittering on about how he should be doing it.

Some years earlier, when I had been 'allowed' to try a take-off, I had felt the controls moving without any input from me. The pilot was not just 'following through' but was actually doing it himself. My reaction was that there was not much point in my bothering, so I didn't. When instructing, I always tried to keep my hands well clear of the controls, so it was obvious (with side by side seating) to the student that he was flying the aircraft. When things got a bit hairy, a sharp word of advice usually had the desired effect, otherwise, a bit of help at the controls would recover the situation and the pupil would appreciate how far he had strayed from the straight and narrow.

I remember a tale about a wartime instructor on Tiger Moths. The Tiger had removable control sticks and this character used to carry a spare stick secreted in his flying suit. To persuade the student to try harder, he would take this spare stick out, wave it over his head in the front cockpit, or even throw it overboard, and tell the student that only he could now land the aircraft. I don't know if it worked. Both my instructional technique and the syllabus were based (on the recommendation of GAPAN) on AP3225, *The Instructor's Handbook of Flying Training.*

Part of the syllabus for the PPL at the time was a requirement to be shown the spin, and how to recover, before flying solo. As the Austers were not officially cleared for spinning, although (as described previously) they would spin and recover without a problem, we had to send students to Barton in Manchester, where they could do half an hour in a Tiger Moth to cover this part of the training. However, in 1956 the RAF decided to dispose of a large number of Tigers. They were in various conditions and total hours flown and the prices varied accordingly. They were available from £25 and a good one could be bought for £75. One of our club members, John Jones from North Wales, bought one for £75 and arranged with Jack that the club would maintain and have the use of it. It first had to be overhauled for its civilian Certificate of Airworthiness. This was done at Thruxton and when it was ready I went down by train with one of the club members to bring G-AOHC home.

I hadn't flown a Tiger before but, with my usual confidence, I didn't anticipate any problems. In fact, it all went well and we flew back via Staverton to Speke. I landed on a tarmac runway at Staverton, not the best option for a Tiger with a tailskid and no brakes, which would normally be operated from grass. Back at Speke we landed on the grass area opposite the club, as we always did thereafter. Operating the Tiger like this was a pleasant routine, mostly into wind, and saving a lot of taxiing.

Meanwhile, the rest of the flying was going well, with plenty of new students, PPL flying and the occasional visiting pilot renting an aeroplane. One rainy day, a pilot arrived with a rather dishy, long-legged blonde and asked to rent an aircraft for an hour or so. I told him the only aircraft we had available was the Taylorcraft AK and he said that was fine. I checked his licence, which was a CPL (Commercial Pilot) and, as I looked at it, and him, I thought I knew him from somewhere although his name didn't register with me at the time. I did a quick check circuit with him and he had obviously done a lot more flying than me. He went off for his flight with his lady friend and upon their return he paid me and they departed. Only then did the name finally register. He was Hughie Green of TV's *Opportunity Knocks* fame, always in the news, sometimes for his flying exploits. On one occasion, I recall, he had strayed off the corridor going to West Berlin and had been chased by Russian Migs. He had flown Catalinas and Coronados with the Atlantic Ferry Organisation during the war. I didn't even get his autograph.

Two lads whom I enjoyed teaching were Brian and Eric, apprentices at Starways, the Speke-based airline. They, like me, were mad keen to fly and, recognising their enthusiasm and lack of spare cash, I would make sure I logged the minimum time on the flight logs to keep their costs down. They both gained their PPLs. Brian went on to be a flight engineer with a Middle East airline. He had just gained his commercial pilot's licence but, sadly, died when the VC10 he was operating, with just crew on board, crashed on take-off. Brian went back into the blazing aircraft to try to rescue one of the pilots. Another apprentice at Starways was Ron, who almost finished his PPL course with us, then emigrated to Canada, where he progressed from engineering to flying Beaver and Otter amphibious aircraft on skis, floats, and even wheels.

Jim Keen was another who learned to fly with us and subsequently went on, with his wife Kath, to establish Keenair. They also started the Liverpool Flying School, a successful operation, and their son Martin became the CFI.

I remember one student who started flying with me and, after a couple of trips, booked a lesson one day for about midday. When he arrived it was foggy. A couple of other students were waiting to fly and I explained that I would have to fly with them first, if and when the weather improved. This didn't please him at all; he had a business to run and 'time was money' etc, so he stormed off. He wouldn't fly with me after that and made an arrangement with our weekend CFI, Ron Irving, who then flew with him on a one-to-one basis. He qualified for his PPL, bought an Auster and started flying all over the country on business. Some time later I heard that he had night stopped in East Anglia and had arrived at the airfield the next morning to find thick fog. Fog doesn't delay businessmen, so he attempted a take-off and wrecked the aeroplane. I didn't hear any more about him after that, so I guess he gave it up.

I was still riding my bike to get to work but during the Suez crisis in 1956, driving tests were suspended and learner drivers were allowed to drive on their own, without a qualified driver accompanying them. I bought myself a 1934 Ford Model Y for £20 from a Starways engineer friend and began to drive the couple of miles to work. When the tests were reinstated, I just removed the 'L' plates and carried on driving until I managed to pass the test, at the second attempt. No lessons, of course, which is probably why I failed first time. One of the lads who worked at Feds in the fruit side of the firm had a brother who was a driving test examiner. I persuaded him to have a run in the car with me to give me some tips for the second test, which he did, and I subsequently passed. The car ran quite well on the 80 octane fuel the aircraft used. We had our own 200 gallon portable fuel bowser.

The Ford was pretty primitive and had vacuum windscreen wipers operated by a rubber pipe connection to the inlet manifold, which meant that each time you accelerated the wipers stopped. I had a look at a club member's modern Ford and discovered it had a vacuum reservoir on the bulkhead. I thought this was a good idea and decided to make one for my car. I cleaned a one gallon oil can, soldered the lid on and two pipes into the can. I even pressure tested it. I then installed it on the bulkhead, in line with the pipe to the wipers. Quite proud of my handiwork, I started the engine to see how it worked. The can instantly collapsed like a paper bag. Very simple physics. I looked again at the modern Ford and realised that its reservoir was made of very strong reinforced steel.

My priority at the time was flying and all my money had been earmarked for reaching the point I was now at, which was flying for a living. Accordingly, I didn't bother too much about fashion, usually wearing corduroy trousers and a sweater or bomber jacket. I don't know if he was telling me something, but my boss, Jack, gave me a very smart double-breasted blazer which he said didn't fit him anymore. One of the pilots I taught to fly, Brian Wolfson (later Sir Brian, one of the Wolfson family of Great Universal Stores) who had a gent's outfitters in Liverpool, gave me an excellent pair of brogues as a present at Christmas, but clothes were obviously not one of my priorities at the time.

Soon after we started using the Tiger HC in May '56 there was an air display at Speke organised by SSAFA (Soldiers, Sailors and

Airman's Families Association). It was quite an event, with a good selection of aircraft displayed and about 120,000 people turned up on the field and the surrounding area. Air Chief Marshal Sir Philip Joubert was in charge and I was introduced to him at the briefing the day before. We did a short formation display at the end of the show with three Austers, flown by myself, Harry Knight and Ron Irving, our two weekend instructors, both ex RAF. I'd done some formation practice beforehand, formating on Eric Roberts in another Auster, and for the show Eric flew with me in the left hand seat, so I could fly from the right seat as we were the port side aircraft in the formation. Formation flying was hard work, I found, and I'd get out of the aircraft sweating like a bull. In the show, Ron Irving leading, I felt very uncomfortable on the inside of low-level turns, very close to the ground, and couldn't take my eyes off Ron to check, but we survived.

A week or two before the show, the organisers had contacted Jack to ask if we could provide an aircraft for one of the participants. This was Aleksie Dragoljub, whose act was to hang by his teeth from a ladder beneath an aircraft, without a parachute! Our Tiger fitted his requirements and we cautiously agreed to help but not without some trepidation.

In due course we met Aleksie and his personal pilot Miroslav Stoka, which thankfully relieved me of that part of the exercise. First step was for me to check out Miroslav on the Tiger, which he hadn't flown before, but unfortunately he didn't speak a word of English. Aleksie did, however, and with his help and some imaginative sign language I briefed Miroslav on the aircraft. Aleksie reassured me that Miroslav was very experienced, with thousands of hours (I only had a few hundred at the time) and was an instructor's instructor at home. One silent circuit with him was enough to show me that he was more than competent.

Next problem was to arrange an attachment for their ladder to our Tiger. The ladder was about 20 feet in length, hinged in the middle and tapering down to its end, to which was attached a light wire which held it up, folded, against the aircraft underside for take-off and lowered it when airborne. At the bottom of the ladder was a short leather strop, which Aleksie would grip with his teeth and hang from it with arms outstretched. After the performance the wire was used to retract the ladder for landing.

Cliff, at Feds, fabricated two substantial U shaped steel fittings to wrap round the Tiger's undercarriage legs, and the ladder and wire were fitted to the aircraft. Aleksie and Miroslav insisted on setting this up themselves and we didn't object, as they had done it before and had the most to lose if things went wrong.

In the week before the show the *Liverpool Echo* requested some publicity shots of Aleksie performing and one evening I set off in an Auster with an *Echo* photographer and Miroslav and Aleksie in the Tiger. This was the first time they had flown in the Tiger since I had checked Miroslav out and they had done their modifications. The *Echo* wanted pictures with the airport building in the background and so we set ourselves up in formation to fly across the airfield at about 500 feet.

As we flew around, setting up our positioning for the photos, I watched Aleksie lower the ladder, then climb out of the front cockpit, lower himself forward on the wing, onto the undercarriage and then down the ladder, which was streaming slightly aft with the slipstream. He clambered confidently down and had just reached the bottom rung when the Tiger suddenly dropped sharply down out of formation! I realised immediately that the only thing that would cause that effect was that the engine had cut out, and we were only at 500 feet. I dropped down to follow with the Auster, not that I could do anything to help (no radio). I will never forget the sight of Aleksie literally running back up the ladder to regain the cockpit and retract the ladder before the Tiger reached the ground. It seemed funny later, but not at the time. However, at about 200 feet the Tiger started climbing again, engine obviously working, and after Miroslav had flashed a big grin and given me a thumbs up, we set up in formation again and the photographer got some excellent shots of Aleksie hanging by his teeth with the airport building as backdrop.

I could hardly wait to get on the ground to find out from Miroslav what had happened. I hurried over to the Tiger as soon as it stopped and between them they explained what had caused several heart rates to increase substantially. They had routed the wire up from the ladder via the undercarriage and through the front cockpit to where Miroslav could operate it in the rear cockpit, not appreciating that it went rather close to the fuel on/off cock in the front cockpit. This was a sliding knob moving fore and aft, one in each cockpit and linked together by a rod between cockpits. When Miroslav lowered the ladder as Aleksie climbed out, the wire had, by vibration or otherwise, fouled the front cockpit knob and pulled it closed. I was very impressed that Miroslav had realised so quickly what had happened, put the fuel back on, and avoided what would have been a very embarrassing incident... or worse.

We very carefully rerouted the wire and subsequently all went well. On the day of the show, Aleksie impressed the spectators when he did several circuits hanging by his teeth from the bottom of the ladder. I suppose it takes all sorts but I can think of better ways to enjoy flying!

One participant in the show was not so lucky. Leo Valentin, the birdman with wooden wings, jumped out of a Starways Dakota at 10,000 feet, caught his wings on the aircraft and spiralled to his death; a terribly sad end to the show.

I really enjoyed flying the Tiger and it soon became my favourite aeroplane. I taught myself aerobatics, which was great fun. The Tiger had to be flown all the way round a slow roll using all the controls and, of course, the engine cut when inverted. I managed to 'grey out' for a few seconds when pulling a bit too hard into a roll off the top. On one occasion I was doing some aerobatics with Eric and as we went over at the top of a loop one side of the engine cowling undid itself and opened fully, lying across the top of the engine. I recovered and slowed down, because I thought there was a chance that the cowling might touch the prop, as when it opened normally it moved slightly forward. We were over the Wirral and I grabbed the Gosport tube to speak to Eric in the rear seat.

"I think we might have to land in a field and I'll get out and close the cowling." However, I had started speaking before I put my mouth to the tube and all he heard was "...I'll get out and close the cowling."

I couldn't understand at first why he was shouting at me not to be stupid. Having clarified the matter, I decided that the cowling seemed happy where it was and we flew slowly back to Speke, where we landed without further problems.

The flight with Miroslav was my last in HC, as the owner John Jones took it to a field in North Wales for a few days, had an argument with a hedge and HC was written off. John replaced it within a few weeks with another Tiger G-ANSX which he bought from Rollasons. He arranged for me to collect it and I flew down in Autocrat AE with one of our PPL pilots to pick the Tiger up from a farm field in Oxford-shire called Knapton's Farm.

This Tiger was a beauty and I did a lot of flying in it. However, soon after we started using it, I was up one day when it started to make strange 'clanking' noises. I slowed down, looked around the airframe, checked the mags and engine instruments, but could find nothing obviously wrong. I flew carefully back to Speke and landed. I walked all around the aircraft but nothing was apparently wrong, until I touched the propeller. It moved about three or four inches fore and aft at the tip! It was loose on the crankshaft. When we took the prop off, it was clear that the Woodruff key, which locked the hub onto the shaft, had been displaced when the hub had been fitted to the shaft. Consequently the hub had gradually worked loose. The hub and prop had been very close to completely coming off! (Thank you, Angel). The crankshaft was damaged and Rollasons very quickly sent us a replacement engine. Thereafter SX was a beautiful machine. It would get airborne in less than 100yds at about 35mph and climb steeply with the slats just opening on the top wings. This ability was to be to my benefit later.

As well as flying, I looked after the aircraft on a daily basis; daily inspections and minor snags like plug and wheel changes. Cliff and Malcolm would come to our hangar and do check 2s when required. One incident occurred which certainly taught me a lesson and was entirely my fault. PH had developed a slight fuel tank weep, causing a petrol smell in the cockpit. When I investigated, I found it was coming from the seam between the bottom and front of the tank. This was a folded joint, soldered to make it leak-proof. I removed the tank, which was straightforward enough; two steel rods passed through the tank, holding it position in the airframe. However, to get the tank out of the cockpit, one of the elevator cables had to be disconnected to allow the large yoke, to which the sticks were attached (but had been removed), to move forward out of the way. To do this, one of the kick panels covering the elevator cables on the port side of the cockpit floor had to come off, then the split pin and clevis pin holding the elevator cable to the fork on the yoke. When the area of the leak had been re-soldered, the tank was refitted. However, within a week or so, the petrol smell was back and I had to go through the whole process again. This time I thought I would speed the job by not removing the kick plate. Removing the pin holding the elevator cable was just possible, working behind the plate. Likewise, replacing it after the tank was fixed was awkward but eventually I managed to fiddle the pin through the holes in the fork and the end of the cable and fitted the split pin. I should, of course, have released the tension on the cable by unscrewing the turnbuckle and, most importantly, I should have had a dual check on the control connections. I did have somebody helping me, who'd agreed that the control cable appeared to be connected OK, but he wasn't a qualified engineer and neither was I, for that matter.

All seemed well but I decided to do a quick air test to prove it and went off with a friendly club member to try it. Five minutes away from the airfield I thought a quick stall turn would be in order but as I eased the stick back to recover from the dive, it came right back into my lap with a twang and the aircraft continued diving. I immediately grabbed the trimmer and pulled it all the way back and we slowly recovered to level flight. The stick remained fully back, obviously not connected to the elevators. Luckily, PH had a simple trim control, in the port wing root, back for nose up and forward for down, not like the Autocrat's silly rotary trim in the roof, which was not instinctive.

I now had a small problem; how to land without the help of the elevator. I experimented and found that I could control the aircraft in pitch with the trimmer right down to 40mph (flapless PH stalled at 38mph without power) and fly level at this speed, provided I kept plenty of power on to give the trim tab positive control of the elevator. I had my left hand on the trimmer and right hand on the throttle, so I briefed my co-pilot to use the ailerons as required when I told him. I decided that if I could fly it down to the runway and fly level in a three point attitude at 39/40mph, then ease the power gently off, we should be able to land OK. That is what we did and the landing was successful but, as we touched and I closed the throttle, because PH was so clean without flap and the speed didn't dissipate quickly, the tail bounced off the ground, then bounced up and down several times before the aircraft slowed down, but there was not enough speed remaining for the aircraft to leave the ground again. We taxied in to examine the aircraft and found, as I had already guessed, that when I held the end of the cable into the fork (having difficulty seeing it because I hadn't removed the kick plate) I had missed the hole in the cable end and it had just twisted and jammed, because of its shape, against the clevis pin. The clevis pin was still split pinned in place.

Another lesson learned but, thankfully, with nothing more serious than embarrassment for me and pushing my guardian angel to the limit. A disconnected flying control should have been inspected by two engineers on replacement.

A year or so later, I read of an accident to a Curtiss C46 twin-engined tail-wheeled airliner in South America, which also lost its elevator control. The pilot landed using trim and power, did a smooth wheeler landing but then the aircraft left the ground and started bouncing. The pilot couldn't control the bouncing and the aircraft crashed, killing all on board. He would have got away with it if he had landed wheels up, but obviously and disastrously thought he could save the aircraft from damage and land it intact.

We often had requests from people to charter an aircraft, which technically we couldn't do as I didn't have a commercial licence. Jack and I decided we could bend the rules slightly by asking the person to become a club member, cost £3 for a year, and then we could simply charge them the normal club rate for hiring the aircraft. We did this several times, to Exeter and similar exotic places. I remember one occasion when I took two people, bookmakers I think, to Nottingham, Tollerton. It was winter and would be dark at 1630. I explained to the passengers that we must be airborne for the return flight by 1530 at the latest for the 80 miles return trip to Speke, as we weren't able to fly at night. As the time approached, there was no sign of my passengers so I started up, taxied out, airborne at 1535 and flew across the field as I departed but with no sight of them. I didn't hear any more from them and I hoped Jack was paid in advance.

One day I had an interesting 'pupil'. He just walked in one day and said he didn't want to learn to fly, but would I let him try to land an aircraft. He had read something about flying and watched a few films and he reckoned if he was put in a position where he had to do it, he thought he would be able to get the aircraft back on the ground. No briefing, no explanations, he just wanted to be taken away from the airfield and left to his own devices. Would I let him try it? I was quite happy and told him about the circuit and height he would have to adhere to on return but, apart from that, I kept quiet.

We went off in an Auster. I took off, flew over to the Wirral and handed over to our hero. He flew quite confidently, found his way back to Speke and joined the right hand circuit for runway 35 more or less as I had told him. He flew downwind well enough and turned onto a base leg but at this point things started to go wrong. He reduced power but not all the way and to start the descent he pushed the nose down. As we turned towards the runway we were high, quite fast, still with some power on, so he pushed the nose further down to correct. Crossing the threshold we were at about 200ft and the speed was steadily increasing. More nose down was the apparent solution and we arrived at the runway with only about a third of it remaining and our speed about 130mph. He finally pulled the stick back to correct and, of course, the aircraft zoomed upwards and the runway disappeared. He then let me take over. I did a quick circuit and landed. Back at the club I offered to explain what he'd done wrong but he didn't want to know. He said he was satisfied, paid his money and I never saw him again.

By November I had more than 400 hours, the minimum for the full instructor rating, and arranged another test with Bunny Bramson. This time it was arranged to take place at Rearsby airfield, Leicester, on a Sunday, and I had to take the Tiger, as the test included aerobatics and spinning. On the day, of course, the weather was dreadful, with low cloud and rain. Nevertheless, I set off, with one of our enthusiastic schoolboy helpers, Duncan, as passenger. As we approached the high ground of Derbyshire and the Peak District, I decided to dispense with map reading until we were clear on the other side. This we did, working our way through, negotiating valleys, avoiding the bits where the ground disappeared into cloud until, at last, the ground dropped away and I could relax again.

The next job was to decide where we were and that was difficult in this area of the East Midlands. I decided that the quickest option would be to land in a field, ask somebody where we were, and then carry on. I picked out a field that looked reasonably level and had a good approach and climb out but, as we approached, I committed the cardinal sin; I changed my mind. Looking at the field beyond, I saw there was a farmhouse at the edge and, thinking to save a walk, decided to land in that one instead. I hopped over the hedge and dropped the Tiger into the second field, then realised as we slowed to a stop that there was a row of tall poplar trees directly upwind, shielding the farmhouse from the weather. I turned the Tiger to position it in the corner of the field ready for departure. When we landed I thought the area was deserted but as we stopped I could see people coming from all directions, running across fields. I immediately decided to get away as quickly as possible, as the next person would be the local policeman, asking for 'my details'. I asked the first man who arrived where we were. He pointed north-east and said "Mansfield is over there".

That was enough. I climbed in and Duncan swung the prop. The poplars were dead into wind but field length was reasonable and I thought there should be no problem. I opened the throttle but just as we got the tail up and were nearing flying speed the Tiger slowed markedly as we hit a boggy patch of ground. I kept going as the Tiger accelerated again, keeping it on the ground as long as possible then, with the poplars looming large in front, I pulled the Tiger hard up into a climb. We scraped over the trees with the slats wide open and I then eased the aircraft down to gain speed and climb away. The learning curve was showing no sign of levelling off.

We made it to Rearsby, did the test successfully with Bunny, managing a slow roll beneath the cloud, but there wasn't room for a loop, and we just managed an incipient spin. After we landed Bunny said that I'd passed and as they didn't have a Tiger at their club, would I mind if he borrowed SX for half an hour to fly with a friend. How could I refuse? One of Bunny's party tricks with the Tiger was to arrive over the threshold at about 150 feet, pull the Tiger's nose up until it was almost stalled, then sink at a high rate, slats fully out, descending almost vertically. At about 50 feet he would apply full power to arrest the descent just as the Tiger arrived at the ground, to land softly, run about ten yards and stop. Very impressive, but don't try it at home!

We climbed into our Tiger and flew back to Speke without any more adventures. I heard later that another Tiger went to Rearsby a few weeks after our visit, Bunny borrowed it to do his party trick but this time got it a bit wrong and the undercarriage was slightly bent!

I was now a full instructor and soon experienced the hardest part of teaching people to fly, sending them solo. I realised that teaching people could only progress so far when you flew with them and they needed the confidence-building experience of flying solo before they could further develop their skills. I would say to pupils after their first solo, "Now you can start learning to fly."

People varied enormously, of course; some over-confident and some under-confident. The overconfident were probably easier to handle; you could let them frighten themselves occasionally to bring them down to earth (but not literally). The under-confident needed a more careful approach, letting them learn slowly and not allowing them to frighten themselves before they gained the necessary skill to assure themselves that they could cope.

I enjoyed the work and was learning all the time.

Early in 1957 I had an incident which might have had a more serious outcome. I was doing circuits with a student who was approaching the solo stage. He had mostly flown the Autocrats (we now had two – AE and VI) but this day only PH, the flapless J4, was available and I thought it might add to his experience to fly it. We were using runway 26 and, as it was quite a distance to taxi from the club to the start of 26, I asked air traffic if we could take off from the 26/17 intersection, which was much nearer. This gave us about 400 yards for take-off and saved a lot of taxiing.

After taking off and starting the exercise, all went well, except that the student couldn't get the hang of the much flatter glide angle without flaps. In those days it was standard to make every approach a glide approach, so the throttle was closed at the point on base leg when you estimated you could glide to the touchdown point (no carb heat or mixture control to worry about). This could be modified with flaps by delaying the full flap selection until you were sure of making it. It was, in effect, a practice forced landing every time. With no radio to bother about, the only input from air traffic was either a red (go around) or a green (cleared to land) from the runway control caravan alongside the touchdown point on the runway.

The student was slow to appreciate the difference in not having flaps and on the first few circuits we ended up crossing the threshold at about 200 feet but I allowed him to continue with the landing, pointing out that on his own he would have been expected to go around from that position. Each time we landed well down the runway, so far down, in fact, that I had to ask him to open the throttle as soon as we had landed for an immediate touch-and-go and we just scraped airborne with a few feet clearance over the 08 threshold lights.

This happened several times and as we staggered across the Mersey I noted that it was a very high tide and the water was not far below runway level, which accentuated our lack of height on the climb out (in other words we were very close to the water). I didn't want to prompt the student too much, preferring that he should correct his own mistakes and thereby learn, but after a couple of hints he didn't seem to be getting the message about his approach positioning.

So, after four or five landings well down the runway in this manner, with every take off scraping over the lights (including our first take off), I decided to make the point crystal clear. As we flew downwind, I took control and told him he could modify his approach in several ways. First he could extend the downwind leg if he was consistently ending up too high or if there was no headwind component. Then, on base leg, he could assess the progress of the approach and if he still felt he was too high he could now turn the base leg slightly away from the airfield. If he was still too high he could overfly the centreline slightly, wasting a bit more height. I mentioned side slipping but that would come after his first solo.

Having demonstrated all the options available without flaps, I handed control back to him and he continued the approach. We were now, of course, a bit low and he was slow to recognise this and fed in the power only slowly. The result was that we ended up flying the last half mile to the runway rather slower than best approach speed with a lot of power on. Nicely set up for a precautionary landing in a short field but he wasn't supposed to be doing those yet.

The landing that followed was a complete mess. We crossed the threshold at about 20ft, nose high with power on and speed lower than it should have been. We touched down about twenty yards into the runway (from one extreme to the other) and, as we were slow when he took the power off, we hit the ground hard and bounced. The first bounce was high and slow, the second higher and slower and I suggested firmly that we should give up. The student correctly applied full power and the Cirrus Minor engine dragged the J4 back into controlled flight. I relaxed as we climbed away.

Then, at about 150 feet, all hell let loose. The engine began to vibrate (that puts it a bit too mildly) as though it was going to leave the airframe. I yanked the throttle back and the prop stopped immediately. We now had a real forced landing to make but fortunately had about 1000 yards of runway in front of us. I had landed before I had time to think.

The crankshaft had broken in half; not uncommon for Cirrus engines. No wonder it had vibrated! Then I reflected on what the result would have been if it had stopped on any of the previous take offs, including the first one. I reckoned we would have been swimming... if we were that lucky.

One day in April '57 I was sitting in the office when the controller in the tower rang. It was a miserable day, with cloud about 800 to 1000 feet, visibility a couple of miles, a north-easterly wind of 15 knots and occasional drizzle. A BEA Dakota had just landed on runway 04 and on final approach the crew were surprised to see an aircraft on its back in the mud and sand of the ebbing river. The pilots advised air traffic but weren't able to identify the aircraft. The controller could just see the aircraft with binoculars but also wasn't able to identify it, and was concerned that it might be a recent accident, such as an aircraft making an emergency landing in darkness during the early hours when the airfield was closed, so he asked me if I would fly over to have a look.

I went in one of the Autocrats with another pilot (there were always two or three hanging around ready to fly or just watching). When we arrived over the scene at low level it was immediately apparent that the aircraft was a Hurricane. It was on its back, undercarriage up, pointing roughly southwest, substantially complete apart from the fabric of the rear fuselage, which had disappeared, exposing the framework of longerons, ribs and stringers. I clearly remember the propeller, which didn't appear to be damaged. We flew back and I phoned the controller to tell him what we had found and, once he was reassured that it was an obviously an old wreck, his official interest in it ended.

Later that day I flew over the site again with a club member who was a freelance photographer. He sent some photos to the *Liverpool Echo* and they did an article on the Hurricane, with a photo, on April 15th. They discovered that it was a wartime accident, to an aircraft of the Czech 312 squadron then stationed at Speke. The pilot had baled out but unfortunately drowned before he could be rescued. I watched the Hurricane over subsequent weeks and it appeared that it had been exposed by one of the meandering channels (in the mud and sand when the tide was out) which had moved over the site. As the channel moved slowly away again, the wreck silted up gradually and about three months later it had disappeared completely.

During 1957, Jack suggested that I get the Commercial Pilot's Licence and the club could then apply for the ATC Flying Scholarship contract. I wasn't too keen on the idea at first, as I knew the initial medical for this licence was at the RAF Central Medical Establishment and was to a similar standard as the RAF. My previous RAF medical, as you will recall, hadn't gone well. However Jack was insistent and in April he bought a Proctor 3, G-ANPP.

I wasn't quite sure what his idea was in buying this aeroplane but it turned out to be very much to my benefit. A couple of pilots brought it up from Croydon, handed over the logbooks to me and flew home. I decided that at least I should fly it, so with Eric Roberts giving me moral support, we jumped in to try. In Wilbur's club days he had the use of a Proctor 5, which belonged to one of the members, Mr T Wayman-Hales. This meant I was familiar (at least on the ground) with the aeroplane, its DH Gipsy Queen engine and its variable pitch prop. I set off with Eric, did a few circuits and soon felt quite happy with PP. It had a full blind flying panel, radio and navigation lights, but only a single set of flying controls, so wasn't going to be much use as a training aeroplane.

In fact, as it turned out, I was the only person who flew it. Eric and I had already done the qualifying test and examination and we both had the radio licence. Next, Jack gave me his correspondence course for the CPL, which he had started but never finished. This was very helpful, except for the fact that I couldn't send in any test papers because it was Jack's course, not mine.

Jack and I got on very well and I subsequently appreciated his efforts in pushing me towards the licence. He had ambitions of becoming a commercial pilot himself, which was the reason he'd bought the course. I decided to grasp the nettle and go for the medical first. I flew down to Croydon in the Proctor, with a couple of lads from the club, the only time I managed to fly into the old airfield before it closed. After a day of medical checks at the RAF Central Medical Establishment, I went before the President of the Medical Board. It could have been the same person as at my previous medical in 1953. The office and big desk certainly seemed similar. This time the outcome was different.

"You're a bit worried about passing, aren't you?" he said.

I confirmed that I was.

"Yes, your blood pressure's a bit high, but don't worry, if you're fit, you'll pass, if not, you'll fail. You're fit and you've passed."

I didn't mention my previous medical but this experience sowed the seeds of cynicism and a mistrust of doctors which was to dog me for the rest of my flying career.

We flew home and I told Jack. I now had no excuse for avoiding the rest of the commercial licence process. I flew the Proctor frequently on 'club member charters' to various places, Newcastle upon Tyne, Bristol, Cardiff, various RAF stations in East Anglia, and also began to practice instrument flying by doing radar approaches to Speke, using their new Decca 424 approach radar which had recently been installed.

I had to do some night flying (ten hours, including a cross country) before I could apply for the flying tests, so I began to do this as well. I was never very happy flying a single-engined aircraft in the dark, but it had to be done. One night I remember I had persuaded Bernie to come with me and, after drinking tea and waiting for it to go dark, we jumped in the Proctor and taxied out. As we rolled down the runway, I thought something wasn't quite right but I was concentrating on the darkness and the runway lights. As we left the ground I realised that the ASI was still reading zero. I hadn't removed the pitot cover. I made an excuse to the tower controller and did a quick circuit and landed. Bernie nipped out to remove the cover and then we took off again to complete our planned flight. Hard work, climbing the learning curve! I also did a couple of trips with Harry Knight and Ron Irving, our part time ex-RAF instructors, to fulfil the instrument training requirement.

Bernie had gone solo in Eric's time at the club but National Service had interrupted. He was now working for Starways and did some more flying with us but he then started flying all over the world as flight engineer in their DC4s and never did complete his PPL course.

Part of the commercial flying test was to demonstrate recovery from unusual attitudes just using the basic panel, which meant primarily using the excellent large Reid and Sigrist turn and slip indicator, which was fitted in most aircraft. At the time this meant using rudder to centre the slip needle at the top of the instrument, and aileron to keep the turn needle at the bottom in the middle of its scale. I've heard different methods subsequently, using rudder to stop the turn and aileron to kill the slip and both methods work, but that was the way I did it at the time and it worked for me. This would keep the aircraft straight and level, or in a balanced turn, and the airspeed indicator and altimeter were used to climb, descend or fly level. I had been practising this in the Austers with a safety pilot, and a large map around me to make sure I couldn't see out. After an hour or two of practice I was quite happy flying this way. Not much later, something happened that made me glad I'd practised.

The day started with thick fog. Several students were waiting to fly but we spent the morning drinking tea and talking about flying. About one o'clock there was a gleam of sunlight through the gloom and I thought it could be the start of the fog breaking up. I had a good relationship with air traffic, even though we were non-radio, and they would usually let me fly in poor weather whenever I wanted to, particularly in the circuit. They would just give me a flashing white signal from the runway caravan or the tower when they wanted me on the ground if they had traffic inbound. So I called the tower and asked if I could try some circuits. They said it was still a bit thick but I could have a go, as nobody else was flying.

That should have been a warning.

As we started the Autocrat, I could see the caravan at the threshold of 08, just opposite the club, about 250 yards away, and the sun was shining above. We taxied out and I told the student I would do the first circuit to see what it was like. We lined up on 08, after our green light, and I opened the throttle. As we rolled, I reckoned the visibility ahead was about 250/300 yds. However, as I lifted off I realised it wasn't the visibility, but simply the distance from the start of the runway to a solid wall of fog. We hit the fog just as we were airborne, and I was immediately on instruments. I locked on to the turn and slip, keeping the two needles dead centre and, with the elevator, kept the speed at 60mph. We climbed steadily through the solid fog. About a minute later (and a very long minute for me) we popped out of the fog into bright sunshine and blue sky. As far as I could see there was a layer of white stratus at about 500/600ft. I started a gentle turn back towards the downwind leg, thinking frantically about what I could do next. I considered flying over to North Wales to possibly find a field on a hill above the fog, or maybe Hawarden airfield near Chester would be in the clear, but the fog appeared extensive. Then, as we flew downwind, I looked down and saw the runway control caravan gleaming in the sun. There was a funnel shaped hole in the fog, the same hole that had tempted me into the air, but the wall of fog that we hit on take-off was moving slowly down the runway and there was now less than 200yds of tarmac still visible.

As we came abeam the hole in the fog, I made an instant decision. One thing the Autocrat would do well was sideslip. I chopped the power, selected full flap, full right rudder and a lot of left aileron. Pointing the port wing tip at the beginning of the runway, the Auster went down almost vertically. As we slid down the side of the funnel and below the top of the fog, I realised I was fully committed. But it worked perfectly and at about 50ft above the start of the runway, I swung the Auster straight and landed. After rolling about 100yds we were in solid fog. As we backtracked to the start of the runway to taxi to the club we couldn't even see the caravan and the sun had disappeared. I rang the tower from the club and tried to sound casual as I told him it wasn't good enough for circuit training.

The rest of the flying continued as before. One interesting variation, which was popular at the time, was the 'whooping cough' flight. The current logic was that when a child had whooping cough, which was quite a distressing condition, if they were taken to 10,000 feet the symptoms would be eased. We did quite a few of these flights although I never heard whether they were successful.

One 'charter' with the Proctor was to Woolsington, Newcastle to pick up film of an important football match between Newcastle United and Manchester United and get it back to Manchester in time for the evening local news on TV. These trips added to my experience for the forthcoming commercial tests. We now had our own licensed engineer, Ron Ogden, who had gone to Newcastle with Dragon, but decided to come back home to Liverpool. Ron was often required to do some work in Blackpool, signing out aircraft for another company. I would take him there in the morning in the Proctor, leaving him to do his inspections, and pick him up in the afternoon, all of it good flying hours and experience for me.

Another interesting charter was when Jack rang me one day to say that a shipping agent urgently needed to get a Merchant Navy captain to a ship in Milford Haven. The weather at Speke wasn't good with heavy rain from an approaching cold front. I tentatively agreed and dashed to the Met Office. The forecaster showed me the latest chart with the front slowly moving east, but already clearing western Wales. A little happier with that knowledge, I decided to route to the west. The ship's captain arrived and we set off in the Proctor. Initially

I had to fly fairly low along the North Wales coast in heavy rain and low cloud and, although I explained the plan, I think my passenger wasn't too sure about the outcome. However, as we reached Anglesey we cleared the front and then had a very pleasant sightseeing flight in bright sunshine across the Lleyn Peninsular and along the Cardigan bay coast to Haverfordwest, where the front had just cleared. A taxi was waiting to rush my passenger to his ship and that part of the job was done.

I had to route via Cardiff to refuel, as none was available at the field, and waited an hour or so for the front to progress. Another pleasant flight along the South Wales coast in sunshine and I landed at Rhoose. After refuelling I checked the latest weather at Speke. It was still raining with low cloud but forecast to improve. I set off, routing up the east side of Wales. Fifteen minutes before Speke, I called them to find the front was still sitting overhead but they cleared me to the Whitegate NDB. This was tricky as, although the Proctor had an MF receiver, with twitcher needles, I'd never managed to make it work successfully, and in the conditions didn't feel like playing with it. I'd dropped down to about 1000ft as the weather had deteriorated, and, as I knew where the Whitegate beacon was situated, decided to find it the old fashioned way, using a map. I reported overhead and Speke asked me to hold until cleared further. After about ten minutes they cleared me to the field and I landed with some relief. The weather was as bad as when I had departed, and our engineer Ron Ogden was quite impressed that I'd flown to south west Wales and back. I basked in his admiration for a spell before I explained how easy it had been.

I really enjoyed 'my' Proctor, faster than the other aircraft by more than 50%, at 140mph, with a full blind flying panel and radio, for me it was a proper aeroplane. The last flight I did in it was another charter to East Anglia. The charterer was going to Norwich and had organised permission to land at RAF Swanton Morley. Horsham St. Faith wasn't available for some reason. However, when we landed at Swanton at about 1130, we were informed that the airfield was closing at 1200. It was probably a Wednesday, sports afternoon. We hurriedly arranged permission to use Coltishall and, while my passenger went off to his appointment by taxi, I flew across to Coltishall to wait for him to join me later that afternoon for the return trip to Speke.

One of our club members was an American, from New York, called 'Frenchie'. He was a character, always ready with a typical Yankee wisecrack. He was manager of the PX (the American NAAFI) at Sealand and arrived in the Dragon days, having previously been doing the same job in Germany. He loved flying and aeroplanes but was very critical of the finish of the paint on our fabric-covered aircraft. He told us he had a Bellanca Cruisair in Germany and also a large Cadillac. Eventually they both arrived (by road) and we had the Bellanca in Hangar 50. The Cadillac was a huge pink convertible! The Bellanca was a little beauty, low wing, retractable undercarriage (wind up like the Ansons, but not as many turns) and a paint finish like glass on the fabric, just like Frenchie had boasted about.

Unfortunately it never flew with us, needing a Certificate of Airworthiness renewal and, soon after it arrived, Frenchie disappeared overnight when he was hurriedly posted back to States. It transpired that one of Frenchie's sidelines, allegedly, was running a house of dubious repute in Liverpool, which explained why he always had a couple of pretty young girls in the Caddie every time he came to fly. Cliff kept in touch with him and eventually sold the Bellanca to the racing driver Ron Flockhart on Frenchie's behalf. Sadly, it was destroyed later in a hangar fire.

At this point I decided to get the night cross-country out of the way. As mentioned I didn't really enjoy night flying on one engine, looking down at all the black bits and wondering where I would land if the engine failed. The Proctor had good landing lights which would have helped. At least I would have seen the tree before I hit it.

As Speke wasn't a 24-hour operation at the time I decided to use Ringway at Manchester and fly to Blackbushe, just south west of London, which, at just over 130nm, met the qualifying distance requirement. I had been to Blackbushe several times in daylight, which I thought would help. Both, as major civil airfields, had the standard visual aids, of the time, of a green identification beacon, flashing a two letter ident., and also the then standard alternating white and green 'lighthouse' beacon, which, on a clear night, could be seen from 50 or 60 miles away. Similar red lights were used for military airfields.

On a fine anticyclonic August evening in 1957, shortly before it went dark and Speke closed, I took off in the Proctor and flew to Ringway. In the fifties, the passenger terminal buildings at Ringway were the old wartime buildings at the side of the hangars, which were of similar vintage. After hanging around there for a while waiting for darkness and having several cups of tea, I filed a flight plan and took off. Navigation was straightforward; a straight line drawn between the two airfields and fly quadrantal heights, 3,500ft down and 4,500ft coming back. It was a beautiful clear night, with little or no wind, no moon, but visibility almost unlimited. This was one of the reasons I was there, having waited for a suitable night for some time. I didn't intend to have difficulties with the weather on this trip.

The flight down was no problem, passing east of Elmdon airfield, Birmingham and west of Coventry, not talking to anybody except the tower on departure and arrival. I ticked off the various towns and cities as they passed on time and looked at the black bits, listening carefully to the engine. In due course I picked up the alternating white and green of Blackbushe and confirmed it when I could see the two letter flashing green. I called them, joined on left base and landed on the easterly runway. After a cup of tea and short break I filed the return flight plan and went back to the aircraft.

After take-off, conditions seemed just as pleasant but, as we progressed, I began to have problems ticking off the towns as they went by. They didn't coincide with my timing as they had done so nicely on the way down. What had happened, as I realised before arriving back at Ringway, was that I had picked up an unforecast tailwind. The high pressure was slipping away to the east more quickly than expected and the southerly wind ahead of the next low had arrived. Being higher than on the previous trip also helped. However, although this confused me for a time, the good visibility was a saviour and soon I could see the flashing beacons at Ringway. I landed slightly ahead of ETA, feeling quite relieved that this part of my commercial qualification was done. It was my first and last single engine night cross country flight. Next morning I flew back to Speke, happy that it was over.

During this summer Jack bought another Tiger Moth. He had decided that some people weren't keen on the standard Tiger (he wasn't) as it meant a flying suit, helmet and goggles and could be pretty cold in the winter. He found a Tiger in Yorkshire which had been modified with a canopy, fitted by Russel Whyham's Air Navigation and Trading at Blackpool. In September I flew to Sherburn in Elmet to collect it in one of the Austers. I wasn't too impressed when I saw it. As well as the canopy it had spats on the mainwheels. The canopy was similar in style to a Chipmunk but not of the same quality. It was hinged along one side and lifted to allow access. The perspex was slightly yellowed with age and that and the framework seriously reduced the normally good visibility from the cockpits. I was even less enthusiastic when I flew it home I found that the modifications had knocked about 10 mph off the cruise speed. It also had an old, non-sensitive altimeter with a single needle which read in 100ft increments, one revolution of the needle indicating 10,000ft. This was not impressive after being used to a three-needle sensitive altimeter. I also think the modifications may have changed its category to non-aerobatic but I never fancied trying it. However, Jack was pleased with it and, as he now had his assistant instructor's rating, he started using it to teach whoever he could persuade to fly in it. I didn't like it and avoided flying it.

Next stage of the process towards my commercial licence was to apply for the flying tests and the written exams. I had Jack's correspondence course, which was a help, so I started reading it and applied to do the written exams in December. I also applied for the flying tests and started them in November, not the best time of the year.

Meanwhile, back at the club, things were changing. Jack's brother Bert had returned from Canada, where he had been working for Avro Canada. Bert, who had a PPL, had now taken over as manager and with his rather abrasive manner was making his presence felt. He had a way of upsetting people by disagreeing with them in a way that ruffled their feathers and some club members responded by leaving. Even air traffic, with whom I had cultivated a good relationship, were treated in this way and, of course, then refused to cooperate with us, restricting our flying when the weather was marginal. I had been running the club day to day until this point, building up from one aircraft at the start to seven in 1957 and felt I was being pushed aside. Also, I would be twenty one in January 58 and my National Service deferment would end. Since I was eighteen, I had been deferred because of my engineering apprenticeship. I had been hoping for National Service to be ended, as had been promised, but unfortunately this didn't happen until after I was called up. I wasn't happy any more and began to look elsewhere.

In November I drove down to Stansted, to the Civil Aviation Flying Unit (CAFU), to start my commercial tests. The first one was a general flying test in Chipmunk G-ANWB, which type I hadn't flown before. It was a damp and murky November day, just about OK for flying, and off we went. Initially all went well, but then we started the 'under the hood' bit. The Chippie used amber screens and blue goggles to simulate blind flying. The goggles tended to mist up inside, particularly on a humid day, and also if the candidate was sweating a bit, as I was. To counteract this, a plastic tube was connected from the goggles to a tube on the cockpit side, which vented to atmosphere. It didn't work very well. The examiner, Captain Joy, briefed to this effect and said it was OK if the demisting system wasn't working to ask to be allowed to remove the goggles and wipe the moisture off.

After a few minutes of flying on a limited panel, I couldn't see a thing and made my first request. The goggles remained clear for only a few minutes and, after recovery from unusual attitudes, I had to ask again. After a couple more goggle clearing requests the examiner obviously began to lose patience and I didn't dare ask again. Subsequently I couldn't read the P type compass down between my legs, so my compass turns were done on pure guesswork. He said I would have to come back and do them again. The weather was too bad to do spinning and he said that would also require another visit. I pointed out that I had an instructor's rating and did lots of spinning, but that didn't impress.

I went back on a much drier day and flew with Captain Westgate in Chipmunk G-AMMA to do compass turns with no problem, but I didn't mention spinning, and as nobody else did, it was forgotten about.

Next step was the day cross country. I went to Stansted on a dreadful day when all flying was off and drove home again disgruntled. Next time the weather wasn't much better, poor visibility and cloud base about 800ft in anticyclonic gloom. The examiners insisted that the candidates made the decision whether to fly or not, so I weighed the weather up and, feeling annoyed I'd driven all the way down again for nothing, decided we'd go. The route was the standard Stansted–Wymondham–Stamford–Stansted. We started the Chipmunk, WB again, and taxied out. After take-off, I turned on course, climbing, and entered cloud at about 800ft. I carried on climbing and at about

2,000ft we popped out into beautiful clear conditions on top with blue skies above. I levelled at 3,000ft and continued on course for the first turning point. About ten minutes before we got there, the examiner, Captain Hale, said, "Let's assume you are on a commercial flight with a passenger who has just requested that you land him at this airfield."

He then showed me an area on the chart which was just open farmland, with no obstructions, and was about five minutes away just to port of our track. I accepted this and, a few minutes later, started a gradual descent towards the 'airfield'. We broke cloud at about 800ft and there in front of us was the area he'd indicated.

"OK," he said, "Carry on."

I climbed back on top again, levelled at 3,000ft and turned on estimate at Stamford, setting course for Wymondham. I knew that the standard routine on this cross-country was not to complete the second leg but, somewhere along it, to be asked to divert direct back to Stansted. However, after about ten minutes on this leg, he said, "This is no good; we'll have to return to Stansted."

So I set course, called Stansted for a couple of QDMs, let down through the cloud, joined the circuit and landed. Apart from map reading, I thought I'd done quite well, but Captain Hale said that he couldn't pass me on what we'd done but then, with a smile, he said I could have a free retest. He didn't say so, but I think it was a reward for my cheek. It was a month or two before I returned to do it again with Captain Joy, in MA, on a nice day, and apart from dodging snow showers, all went well. The final bit, having done the night cross country myself, was to do some night circuits at Stansted, with Capt. Hale, in WB, and then the flying tests were done.

In December I did the written exams in London and, thanks to Jack's course, passed all first time except for the easiest thirty minute paper, which was 'Rules of the Air'. This was my own fault completely, as when I read the correspondence course notes it said quite clearly that in a collision situation as they 'give way' aircraft should always turn to starboard, never to port. I considered that there could be a situation where it might make more sense to go to port, such as a close quarter meeting with an aircraft at the same level and very close to starboard but as it wasn't my correspondence course I couldn't discuss it with anybody. So of course when that very case turned up in the exam, I foolishly tried to make my point. The exam had a 100%

pass mark and so I failed. I returned the following month, curbed my contrariness and passed.

It was interesting doing the exams over four days as most of the people there had been attending the various navigation schools and knew each other. I felt like a visitor from the backwoods and kept quiet. One of the 'experts' sounded off at every coffee break about how difficult the questions were this time and everybody gathered round to hear his views. After the navigation plotting paper he said that the three point fix was most unusual in that it was so big that one of the points was off the chart and he had to use an extra piece of paper to extrapolate, off the edge. My fix had been quite small and on the chart but I didn't offer an opinion. Listening to him, I realised he'd attempted these exams on quite a few occasions and decided that he was therefore no expert in passing them.

So in March 1958 I finally had my Commercial Pilots Licence. In January I'd had enough of Bert and the flying club and had re-joined Feds, who were now sharing No.50 Hangar with the club, so I didn't have far to go. I started as an engineer, with the intention that I would fly the Anson and Rapide in due course, subject to my imminent departure to serve the Queen. Cliff was now flying the Anson and Rapide and was also embroiled in the Commercial exams. Sadly, just after I left the club to join Feds again, Jack Green was killed in his favourite Tiger Moth G-ANSA when doing circuits in poor visibility. He flew into the smooth water of the river on the approach to runway 04, hit his head on the canopy as the Tiger hit the water, was knocked unconscious and drowned in the aircraft. His student managed to get out and swim ashore. The accident was a classic 'glassy water' accident, well known to seaplane pilots and I thought that the canopy, as well as the non-sensitive altimeter, had contributed to it. Without Jack at the helm, the club's fortunes declined and, after about twelve months, it had ceased operations.

Back with Feds, I worked on the three Ansons and the Rapide. Cliff was now the only pilot, several commercial pilots having been and gone. I did some circuits with Cliff in the Rapide and a few trips in the Anson as P1(s) also with Cliff, but my impending call-up didn't allow me to settle in. I had been notified that I was due to be called up and was now just waiting for the final letter. People from the flying club contacted me to ask me to fly with them on several occasions, as the club didn't have a full time instructor. Checked out on the Rapide, I did some trips to Dublin to bring a load of mushrooms to Speke. One of the Ansons, PA, was sold to Derby Airways and Cliff and I delivered it to Burnaston Airfield, Derby.

When I had my first pre call-up interview, in 1958, to decide in which service I would do my time, it was confirmed that I would be in the RAF, because of my CCF cadet qualifications and, as I had a commercial pilot's licence and about 1,500 hours, I asked about the chances of flying. Unfortunately in 1957 there had been massive defence cuts by Defence Minister Duncan Sandys and there were simply too many pilots in the RAF looking for aircraft to fly. I was told that if I signed on for twelve years I might be considered, but there could be no guarantee. I decided that I would do my two years and no more.

One interesting part of this interview was when the Flight Sergeant in charge queried my apprentice status. When I had originally registered, aged eighteen, for National Service at the local labour exchange, I had applied for deferment because of my apprenticeship. The clerk asked me what my trade was and I told him aircraft engineer. He looked at his list and said he only had aircraft fitter (engines) or aircraft rigger (airframes). I assured him I worked on both but he told me I couldn't be apprenticed in both (his) trades. I insisted that I wanted to be registered as I had described and, after consulting his lists, he told me that the only one he could find which matched my description was aeronautical engineer. I accepted that and thought it was the last I would hear of it. However, in 1958 the Flight Sergeant picked on this rather grand job description and asked me to explain. I did, but I don't think he was impressed. He asked me a couple of questions about hydraulic systems which I had never worked on and shook his head. In August '58 I was dragged (metaphorically) screaming into the RAF and, after square bashing and trade training, qualified as a ground wireless mechanic (probably on the recommendation of the Flight Sergeant).

I did my 'square bashing' at RAF Bridgnorth, eight weeks, reduced, after about four weeks, to six weeks because of my CCF qualifications. We did some rifle (.303) shooting as part of our training and somehow I managed to qualify for my marksman badge. During this period I met, for the first time, the 'old school tie' element of the air force. Our flight commander was an education branch Pilot Officer (penguin – non flying) about the same age as me but of a particularly nasty disposition. His delight each morning was to watch us doing our drill and then walk among us, criticising whoever took his fancy. One poor lad, who couldn't march for toffee, bore the brunt of the officer's contempt.

However, another of our number, who was an old man (in our eyes), as he was in his late thirties, ex-army and grey haired, had re-enlisted in the RAF after a spell on Civvy Street. He wore a couple of campaign medal ribbons, having served in Cyprus and Suez. One day our Pilot Officer arrived to vent his spleen, as usual, and decided to pick on our 'old man'. He stood in front of him, making the usual derogatory comments about his dress and appearance and then started asking why he thought he was entitled to wear medal ribbons. At this, our man came smartly to attention, having been at ease, did a half turn to the right and marched off the parade ground with our officer shouting futilely for him to return. We were astonished but it was not until we returned to our hut that we could ask him what he had done. He told us he had gone straight to the orderly room and filed a 'redress of grievance' against the officer for denigrating his medal ribbons. It was upheld, the officer was admonished and he didn't bother us too much on the parade ground afterwards.

However, he did appear one day soon after, to tell us that he was obliged to read to us a list of qualifications and if any of us met the requirements we were entitled to apply for a National Service Commission. The list included two 'A' levels, advanced proficiency in the ATC or CCF, HNC, or a university degree. He made it quite clear that we were not expected to apply but, if we dared, to be outside his office at 0900 next day. Back in the hut we found that about five of us, from more than eighty in the flight, had one or other of the qualifications. My friend and I decided to try and next morning we were outside his office.

When called, I marched in, saluted and stood at attention in front of our charming leader. He then started reading, as he had before, the full statement and the list of qualifications. Thinking to save him time, I started to say that I had both the 'A' levels and the CCF advanced proficiency. I didn't get far, he silenced me with a ferocious glare, and, starting again from the beginning, read out the full list.

When he finished, he said,

"Do you have any of these qualifications?"

I started to reply saying, "Yes, I have the 'A' levels and the CCF..." but again was silenced with a look, from a face that was becoming redder by the minute.

He then read, from the beginning, the whole list from the piece of paper in his hand. At this point, I thought, this interview is not going well. Once again, I tried to reply.

"Yes, I've got..." and was stopped in my tracks as he shouted at me. "Yes... *what*?"

All he wanted me to say was "Yes *Sir*".

He then asked me which qualifications I had. I replied, very carefully, that I had the 'A' levels and CCF advanced proficiency.

He moved on to the next question.

"Did you go to a Headmasters' Conference school?"

At the time (a former grammar school boy) I had never heard of a headmasters' conference school (a public school) and hesitated. He repeated the question, obviously losing patience. I decided that my headmaster must have gone to a conference at some time, so I replied, "Yes, Sir".

With a face becoming a light shade of purple, he shouted at me, "Do you know what a Headmasters' Conference school is?"

I replied, truthfully, "No, Sir."

He practically screamed at me, "Get out!"

That was the end of my application for a commission. I don't think it was ever a serious possibility. I made the dizzy heights of SAC (Senior Aircraftman) before I was demobbed.

During my time in the RAF I kept my hard-earned commercial licence valid by flying the Rapide or Anson with Feds whenever I could when I was home. I had to log a minimum of five hours every six months and have a medical. I worked a 24/7 shift system, not as a ground wireless mechanic, of course, but in Leighton Buzzard, at the control centre for the RAF H/F communications around the world, managing the transmitters and receivers and their frequency changes as the earth turned and night and day chased each other around the globe. An important job but one for which there was no training course and we simply learned on the job.

We monitored, via teleprinters, the communications to RAF bases in Australia, Gan, Christmas Island, Hong Kong, El Adem, Canada, etc., and advised the relevant transmitter or receiver station when to change frequency. With the frequent postings, which the RAF favoured, this meant that we were often short of people on the watch who knew what they were doing. I actually spent 18 months there, which was unusual. At one time a new sergeant arrived to take charge of our watch and it took me several weeks to teach him what the job involved. The National Servicemen were the ones who kept the operation going, we decided. We worked five days on and three days off, so I had plenty of time at home and opportunities to fly.

One interesting diversion from my RAF work occurred in September 1959, when I was contacted to fly an Auster Aiglet Trainer, G-AOEZ, one of the latest variants. The aircraft was owned by Eric Bemrose, who owned a large printing company in Liverpool. He bought the aircraft new and was to have been taught to fly it by Wilbur Wright, of flying club days. However, Wilbur had now left the scene, for whatever reason, and the engineers at Starways, who hangared and maintained the Auster, had suggested that I could help. I agreed and first flew the Auster with Ron Ogden, one of the engineers, formerly of Dragon and the club. I discovered that it had been fitted with a Goodyear crosswind undercarriage, allegedly on Wilbur's advice. This modification was advertised by Goodyear at the time and demonstrated by their Dakota landing at Gibraltar with a 90° crosswind. No problem, I thought and we started up and set off...

As we taxied out to 26 at Speke and approached the first turn on the taxiway, I applied rudder to go round the corner, which normally would have been sufficient. With this aeroplane, the aircraft turned as expected, but the undercarriage simply castored, maintaining our track, and we continued straight ahead, albeit sideways. I had to apply differential brake to persuade it to go round the corner. Once I appreciated what was happening, it wasn't too much of a problem, but when I started flying with Eric, it was. He was just at the circuit stage and, of course, had difficulty, as most students do at first, making sure the aircraft was tracking straight down the runway on take-off and landing. With a normal aircraft, a bootfull of rudder would sort this out, but with EZ this wasn't enough, and brake had to be used, not what a student needed at that stage. It would have been much better if the crosswind gear could have been locked in straight ahead for normal operation and just released for use when required. I decided the aircraft was not really suitable for *ab initio* instruction. However, it didn't matter, as unfortunately Eric's health deteriorated and he had to give up flying. Not a reflection, I hoped, on my instruction.

One hiccup after six months at the Leighton Buzzard RAF communications centre occurred when I received notification of posting to El Adem in the Libyan desert. I pointed out that this would mean that I couldn't fly to keep my commercial pilot's licence valid and, having only just obtained it, I would possibly have to do all my exams and tests again. The Ministry of Aviation helped me by confirming this possibility in a letter. I applied to be removed from the posting, for this reason, to my Flight Commander, then to the CO of the squadron and finally the Air Officer Commanding. They all sympathised with me and agreed that it could affect my employment when I was demobbed, but said that as there was no precedent, most important for the RAF, there was nothing they could do.

I went home on embarkation leave and, in desperation, contacted the Liverpool MP, Bessie Braddock, who was a friend of my grandfather and a renowned champion of the underdog, even though, as a serviceman, this course of action for me was expressly forbidden. I explained the situation to her agent who said to leave it with him. I advised him of my imminent departure for Libya. When I arrived back at camp I was sent to London for my final jab for yellow fever. On my return I was summoned by the corporal in charge of the orderly room, who told me that my posting had been cancelled. Regarding me with obvious suspicion, as he knew of my attempts to get off the posting, he said he didn't know the reason for this and I certainly wasn't going to let him into the secret. Bessie sent me the letter she received from the Air Minister, George Ward, which said he fully agreed with my request. I completed the remainder of my time at Leighton Buzzard. After all that had gone before, I was pleased I had at last got one up on the RAF.

As we moved into 1960, I began to think about life after National Service. I kept up the flying with Cliff and Feds and by the summer I was flying the Rapide and Anson regularly. Early in the summer, the boss, Reg Gates, asked me when I was due to finish with the RAF and I told him late August.

"Oh that's no good," he said. "Cliff wants to go on holiday in August, so we'll need you before then."

He asked for my station commander's details and said he would contact him to ask for an earlier release. I didn't give much for his chances but, sure enough, in early June I was summoned to the orderly room to be told that with accrued leave, days owing, etc., etc., I could finish at the end of June. I couldn't get away quickly enough. For me, from both a career and also a personal viewpoint, it had been a complete and costly waste of time.

I settled back into a happy routine with Cliff, of working on and flying our aeroplanes. We would both start at 0830, doing whatever maintenance was necessary and every afternoon about 1300 one of us (or sometimes both) would fly an Anson or Rapide, depending on the expected mushroom load, to Dublin. A bowl of soup in the Aer Lingus canteen and the 'mush' would arrive between 1500 and 1600, we would load the aircraft, fly back to Speke and unload onto our wagon for delivery to the railway station. Finally, at about 1930, the aircraft was taxied back to, and usually into, the hangar and our day was done. The non-flying man would have finished about 1700.

The Rapide carried about 470 chips (small baskets) of mush-rooms. They were officially 2.5lbs each in weight but we discovered that the growers tended to fill them up to about 3lbs to cater for weight loss in transit, so the cargo was probably 20% overweight. The Ansons carried up to 700 chips. We loaded the aircraft ourselves with the van driver's help. The Rapide had all seats removed except one, on the starboard side, just behind the pilot and this helped keep the mush in place, as we had to leave space along the port side from the door to get into and out of the cockpit. However, if it was a rough flight they often collapsed and we had problems exiting when we landed. In an emergency it would have been just possible to squeeze through one of the triangular DV (direct vision) windows each side of the cockpit, or through the emergency exit in the cockpit roof. The Ansons, G-ALXC and G-AMBE, had a freighter cabin with the large rear spar across the middle and we would pack the mush solid behind the cockpit bulkhead, back to the door. This meant the only way into the cockpit was to climb onto the wing at the trailing edge and enter the cockpit via the large sliding DV window, one on each side of the cockpit. If we carried the occasional passenger who couldn't manage this entry, they would have to get into the cockpit before the mush-rooms were loaded.

The sliding DV window normally had a wooden stop, which re-stricted opening to about six inches, but this we removed to allow us to slide it right back and use it as a door. I discovered the reason for this stop one warm summer evening. I was on my own and had loaded the Anson, got airborne and wound up the undercarriage, all 147 turns, by which time, as I levelled at 1,500 feet for the trip home, I was sweating like a bull, so I pushed the window next to me back as far as it would go. After five minutes I had cooled down nicely and I reached back to pull the window closed. As I started to pull it forward it suddenly leapt out of my hand and I watched it spinning down towards the Irish Sea. That was why the opening was restricted to six inches! With this huge draughty hole in the side, the cockpit was soon very cold and, even though I put a jacket on, plus the heater and moved over to the co-pilot's seat to fly the aircraft until landing, by the time we landed at Speke I was shivering with the cold.

The daily mush run, sometimes with two aircraft, was often varied by the newspaper flights. As we both now had commercial licences, we had a contract to carry the excess newspapers from the early morning BEA Dakota flight, Manchester to the Isle of Man, whenever the Dakota had a full load of passengers and so couldn't carry all the newspaper load. This meant one of us leaving Speke at 0700 (we'd leave an Anson out overnight) for Ringway, picking up a small load of papers and taking them to Ronaldsway. After a leisurely breakfast, we would then fly to Dublin to wait for the mush. Occasionally another variation was to do a similar operation to Belfast on a Saturday night with the Sunday newspapers. Our day job pay was for the maintenance and mushroom flying and any extra commercial work earned us extra flying pay, so we were always pleased to do it. We also occasionally put all the seats back in the Rapide for a passenger charter flight.

We had several enthusiastic co-pilots, two or three keen school-boys and a couple of air traffic controllers who would often fly with us. They were a great help loading the aircraft, company for us, very useful for winding the undercarriage up and down, and great as an autopilot for the boring bits. The Anson was preferred for this, as it had full dual controls and a good heater, which made winter flying more pleasant. The Rapide was not favoured as a bad weather aircraft; no heater and it leaked like a sieve, however hard we tried to make it waterproof, and with its multiple leading edges it didn't enjoy icing. Certainly the pilot flying it didn't. The Anson was a better ice carrier, although we flew low to avoid it. We also used 'Kilfrost', a brown de-icing paste of revolting appearance, which was applied to the leading edges between masking tape and maintained a wet slippery surface which meant any ice formation just slid off. It was quite effective.

Cliff was now in the process of getting his instrument rating and I was thinking seriously about it. This involved flying the CAFU Dove at Stansted. Until now we'd been operating on a locally agreed 'special VFR' arrangement, which we stretched to the limit. One day I was flying the Rapide to Dublin, with Cliff sitting in the passenger seat behind me, reading a newspaper. I was practising radio range flying using the Burtonwood range, in anticipation of the rating test. I was 'bracketing' the range leg, flying from the 'A's (or 'N's, I don't remember) on the south side into the solid signal of the centreline. We were not flying airways but were at 2,500ft in cloud over Anglesey, just south of the Green Two airway centreline. As we came out of a bit of patchy cloud, Cliff spotted an airfield below and asked me where we were. I think he thought it was Valley. I told him it was RAF Mona, a satellite airfield used by Valley, more or less in the middle of Anglesey. He said he thought Mona was a just an abandoned disused wartime field, not realising it was maintained in good condition.

A few months later, Cliff was flying the Rapide back from Dublin at 1,500ft with a full load of mush and, just after passing Point Lynas fan marker on the northeast Anglesey coast, a cylinder head cracked on one engine, causing it to run so rough it had to be throttled back, no feathering being available with the fixed-pitch prop. Cliff turned for Valley, the nearest airfield and advised air traffic, but he was not maintaining height on the good engine and soon realised he wouldn't make it. He then remembered Mona – and there it was in front of him, about halfway to Valley. He made a straight in approach on the single runway and landed, with some relief. That was the problem with our aeroplanes, when fully loaded, on one engine, they had what the Pilot's Notes euphemistically described as a 'negative climb'. The engines were pretty reliable, that was only the second incident I knew of for our Rapides, the other was when Dragon had borrowed BB for a spell and Ted Dewhurst had landed on the beach at Hoylake with a cracked cylinder head.

The Anson's Armstrong Siddeley Cheetah radials were even better. We never had a complete engine failure. On one occasion I was flying an Anson back from Dublin at 1,500ft, at night, on my own, fully loaded as usual, when just about halfway across the water the starboard engine cut, just as though it had been switched off.

Looking at the engine instruments, the two pointer RPM gauge was winding backwards, but after no more than five or six seconds it burst into life again, and behaved perfectly thereafter. We examined everything next morning but could find no reason for it. But it certainly made me think. Another time, coming home again, the engines went out of synchronisation. I wasn't sure which engine had altered and just resynchronised them and carried on, all indications normal, and no mag drop. When we checked on the ground, one engine had a cylinder with no compression. We removed the cylinder and found that the piston had disintegrated and all that remained of it was a lump of aluminium at the end of the connecting rod. But the engine had carried on running smoothly on six out of seven pots. We had several brand new nil-houred ex RAF engines (bought as scrap) and we just changed the oil, cylinder, piston and con-rod, cleaned the filter and the engine was happy again.

In keeping with my routine of frightening myself every year or so, I was doing a double Dublin one day in the Rapide and, after the first trip in mostly cloud, out at 2,500ft and back at 1,500ft, our usual ice dodging, off-airways routine, I decided that for the second run I would climb to FL45, where we were on top of the cloud and just about in the bottom of the airway. It was very pleasant in the sunshine. On the first trip to Dublin I'd been having trouble with both the directional gyro and the ADF (automatic direction finder). The DG was precessing rather more quickly than usual, requiring resetting every five or ten minutes. The ADF was noisy and it was difficult to pick up and identify beacons. However, I'd managed in the morning and now, relaxed in the sunshine, I wasn't too worried.

I called Dublin and, on estimate, started my descent. I reckoned I was only five minutes away from the coast and expected to see the excellent visual landmarks of Lambay Island and Howth Head in front of me as I broke cloud, the base given as 2,000ft, but I still couldn't hear the Dublin 'Rush' beacon on the ADF. As we passed 2,500 feet, the cloud began to break and I saw land below. I wasn't expecting to have crossed the coast and was a little surprised, and then I realised that the land I could see was rather close to the bottom of the cloud. I made a 180° turn and kept my height until I could see water below the cloud, then continued my descent. As I broke cloud I turned back and saw a straight stretch of coast which I didn't recognise, no Lambay Island and no Howth Head. It was just going dark now and I was obviously either north or south of Dublin, but which?

I called Dublin but they didn't answer. I was now at about 1,500 feet and looking inland could just make out the high ground meeting the clouds. I called Dublin again and now they called, but obviously couldn't hear me. 'How far away can I be?' I wondered, 'if they can't receive my calls.' I'd decided that I must be south of track, the high ground was probably the Wicklow Mountains, and turned north. At this point an Aer Lingus Dakota, hearing what was going on, offered to relay for me. I could hear Dublin OK and he told me to climb until he could see me on radar. I acknowledged via Aer Lingus, started climbing and, as I approached 3,000 feet, Dublin, now hearing me OK, saw me on radar and told me I was 26 miles southeast of the field, a course error of some fifteen degrees from Wallasey.

Twenty minutes later I landed in Dublin and thanked the controller, who told me that I was a lucky man. Descending in cloud towards the Wicklow mountains... I could only agree with him. When the mush arrived, I flew carefully home and next day we sent the ADF away to be fixed and fitted a replacement DG. 'When,' I thought, 'does the learning curve start to level off?'

As mentioned previously, we sometimes carried passengers in the Anson, usually arranged by the boss. One time he asked me to pick up three people in Dublin. This meant one passenger in the co-pilot's seat and the other two sitting behind us on the main spar against the bulkhead, no seats and no straps. They arrived on time and I put them in the cockpit before I loaded the Anson with the mush. With some difficulty I climbed into the overcrowded cockpit past them and into my seat. I started up, taxied out, feeling quite restricted, and took off. Five minutes later, having wound the undercarriage up, nobody having volunteered, I called Dublin to report at 1,500ft on course with an ETA for the boundary. No reply, no sidetone, the VHF was dead. I had a good idea of what the problem was but in the crowded cockpit there was no way I could check. It was almost dark as I turned back and dropped below the cloud to join the circuit, hoping Dublin would guess what had happened. They were on the ball and flashed a green light from the tower as I wound the undercarriage down, landed and taxied back in. Once we had stopped, I could turn round to the electrics panel on the bulkhead behind me, asking the passenger to move out of the way, and I replaced one of the fuses, which had blown. The radio then worked OK. We then flew back to Speke and I decided I wouldn't be put in that position again.

We did fly in some lousy weather at times. In fact, while I was away in the RAF, Cliff landed Anson XC, one foggy night at Speke, when the runway was covered by about 9-10 inches of snow. He found the runway with difficulty and landed, thinking the worst was over, but as the Anson decelerated the snow built up in front of the wheels, acting like chocks, and caused the undercarriage downlocks to break and the wheels then retracted. He swung off the runway and spent the next fifteen minutes listening to the fire engines driving up and down in the fog, looking for him, until he walked to the runway and waved to them. Cliff then had to persuade the fireman not spray the aircraft with foam. He knew he had to repair it and didn't want to have to clean it as well. When retracted, the Anson wheels protruded below the cowlings, so the damage was minimal and XC was soon repaired and back in service.

Another time when it snowed, Cliff and I decided to go together in the Anson to Dublin. I don't remember the weather ever stopping us; if it wasn't good, we often would fly together. It had been snowing all day and was foggy, so there had been no movements. Just before we taxied, a Speke based Beechcraft Queenair, tricycle undercarriage twin, had departed. It was flown by John 'George' Formby, who had flown the Spitfire and Mosquito which had operated the THUM (temperature and humidity) flights from Speke for the Met Office in the fifties. I was doing the first leg and taxied out with some difficulty in 'white out' conditions, the windscreen wiper clearing just a tiny patch of screen in front of me, the rest of the windows covered in snow, blotting out the view. We made it to the runway and lined up.

We were quite heavy, having an outbound load of freight. As we lined up I saw the three tracks in the snow were still just visible from the Queenair's take off five minutes before. I thought that would be a help on take-off, as I couldn't see much else, peering through the gap made by the wiper. Runway lights and marker boards were almost obscured in the conditions. I opened the throttles for take-off and we trundled down the runway. I followed the other aircraft tracks fairly easily until – and, incredibly, this didn't occur to me until it happened – they stopped. Of course, at some point the aircraft had left the ground. I glanced at my airspeed and it was nowhere near what we required for take-off. Outside was now just a blur of white. All I had for heading guidance was the directional gyro and I carefully kept it exactly on its heading until we reached take off speed, then gently lifted the Anson off the runway and settled into the climb. It was a nice day in Dublin and by the time we returned to Speke the fog had cleared and the snow had stopped.

When fully loaded, or overloaded, the centre of gravity was so far aft that the Anson was only marginally stable, longitudinally, particularly at lower speeds, so in the initial climb it was hard work holding the speed correct with the left hand while winding the undercarriage up with the right. It was much easier with a co-pilot to do the undercarriage bit and be able to concentrate on the flying.

Sometimes we would go to Dublin with two Ansons and I would enjoy formating on Cliff en route. We didn't try formation take offs or landings.

As we moved into 1961 the future once again began to cloud over. In April the new Air Operator's Certificate was being introduced, and all commercial operators would be required to have one. The boss applied and in due course an inspector arrived from the Ministry to check our operation. He was horrified when he realised that Cliff and I were the total workforce, and we flew and maintained the aircraft. He told us we could be engineers or pilots, but certainly not both. He said we would require pilots, engineers and office staff to do our paperwork before he would even consider going further with the application. Cliff and I discussed it, but I had already decided that flying overloaded old aircraft wasn't really a job with a long term future. The boss considered buying something like a Dakota and upgrading the operation, but when he investigated the costs involved he lost his enthusiasm. His choice was to stay as a private operation, just flying mushrooms, which didn't require an AOC. Cliff and I discussed this option but I wasn't keen and convinced him that our only choice was the commercial route, but obviously not with Feds. Cliff now had his instrument rating, so was in a better position than I was.

One option appeared at what seemed an opportune moment, when Aer Lingus, the Irish state airline, announced that they required sixty pilots, having just expanded into transatlantic operations with Constellations. Cliff and I decided to apply and went for interview with the chief pilot at Dublin airport. There were two batches of thirty pilots being employed and the first thirty were notified, including several people we knew. The grapevine at Dublin had informed us that we were both accepted in the second batch but before we received our notification the Canadian Air Force decided to lay off a number of pilots and somebody in the Canadian government persuaded a friend in the Irish government to lean on Aer Lingus to employ these redundant aircrew. That was the end of our jobs.

Two of our friends were in the first intake, Ted Dewhurst from Dragon and Arthur Wignall, who had flown the Ansons with Feds. They both went on to have good careers with Aer Lingus. Much later, Arthur sadly died when practising aerobatics for an air display in a Pitts. Ted had an amazing escape when he was flying with Dragon. He was flying a Maggie one day on an army co-op exercise when he returned early, landed on the grass outside the club, taxied rapidly in and jumped out, pointing at the aircraft, unable to get his words out. When he calmed down he told us that he was flying along happily when an USAF F86 Sabre from Burtonwood came out of a cloud alongside and hit him. There was a foot square hole in the lower section of the wooden fuselage, just missing the elevator cables, and a big chunk of the lower rudder was missing. The Sabre landed with minimal damage to its fin and tailplane. Ted was called 'Lucky' Dewhurst after that. He didn't even have a parachute!

When April came, Federated Air Transport stopped operating. The boss organised a contract with Aer Lingus to carry the mushrooms. The two Ansons, XC and BE, were sold to BKS, an airline with a subsidiary company, BKS Air Surveys, which used Ansons, and Reg, the boss, decided to keep the Rapide ZP for his own use.

Later that month Cliff and I flew the two Ansons to Southend, the BKS base, and I had an interview with the BKS chief pilot. He offered me a job, initially flying Ansons with their Air Survey company and then, when I had my instrument rating, a position as first officer on the Bristol 170 Freighter car ferry service, which they had just started operating from Speke to Dublin. I would start on a retainer of £1000pa, roughly what I'd been getting with Feds doing the extra commercial work, rising to salary of £1,425 as first officer on the car ferry. He also gave me details of a Link Trainer man at Southend whom BKS used when necessary, as the instrument rating required some Link Trainer instruction and a Link test before the flying test could be taken. Another opportunity had appeared at just the right time.

I went home, trying to absorb all this and the changes to come. Cliff had already fixed a job with Starways, the airline at Speke, as first officer on their Dakotas. I contacted the Link Trainer man at Southend and booked in for a couple of days. I also began to organise the technical exam for the Bristol 170 Freighter Mk.31. These exams were conducted by the ARB (Air Registration Board), who also covered aircraft maintenance. They had an office in Liverpool where I could do the exam when ready. I'd heard of somebody called Pop Speller, who had worked for the ARB, now retired, and had collated lists of technical exam questions and answers for most aircraft, which could be purchased from him for a small fee. They were all handwritten exams then, multi choice hadn't been invented. I contacted him and soon had the list for the 170. I drove to Southend, met the Link Trainer man and did some training with him: holding patterns, procedural instrument approaches, etc. When I asked about payment, he said that, as I was with BKS he would bill them and they would adjust my pay. I was happy about that and even happier when I eventually realised that that was the last I would hear of it. I see from my logbook I did six hours with him, took the Link test in London with the Ministry and failed. I did another six hours in the Link at Southend and then passed. After learning all the questions and answers for the Bristol 170, I did the technical exam in Liverpool and passed. I hadn't even been on board the aircraft yet, so Pop Speller was good value. He even requested that if a question came up that wasn't on his list, he would be notified so that he could amend his records.

I went to the BKS office at Speke and made myself known. I knew their engineer and also one of the captains, Van den Elst, both of whom had been with Starways. I did a supernumary trip to Dublin with Van one day, to get a feel for the aircraft. It was now July and I hadn't heard a word from BKS, apart from being paid each month since April. At this point I slipped up, or, as it turned out subsequently, had another lucky break. On one occasion at Speke, visiting the BKS office, I bumped into a pilot I knew, Jim Bolshaw. He was working for Lord Derby, flying his lordship's Piaggio P166, a twin pusher, high-wing, executive aircraft. While chatting to him, I told him what I was doing and that I would be on the Bristol 170 once I got the instrument rating.

On July 21st I started my flying tests at Stansted for the rating. As I walked in to the ops room for my first test, I looked at the board with examiner and candidate's names on it and there, against DH Dove G-ANOV was my name and Captain Hunter. My heart sank. Captain Hunter had a reputation of being very difficult, short tempered, didn't suffer fools, etc., etc. The other candidates sympathised with me but were obviously relieved it wasn't them. In fact, years later, when I met Jock Hunter as a CAA flight inspector attached to the One Eleven in BA, I found him charming. But that was years away and I didn't know it then. We met, he told me what was required and we walked out to the Dove. I'd never flown the Dove. I'd sat in them when they had been hangared with us at Feds, but that was all. The rating briefing notes said allowance would be made for this, but I didn't notice. We did a pre-flight and climbed in, started up and were ready to taxi.

The first thing that floored me was the radio station box. I'd never used one. It was just an interface for all the radio equipment, which allowed you to listen to whichever radio aid or VHF you required. It confused me and I wasn't in a mood to ask questions. We taxied out OK and then the angled boards were fitted in front of me. These stopped me seeing out but allowed the examiner full vision outside. There was a small opening slide in the middle of the one immediately in front of me, so I could see out for take-off, but this would be closed after take-off so I could only see the instruments. I lined up, applied power and off we went.

As I lifted the aircraft off the runway this slide was slammed shut in front of me and it had a similar effect on my brain. The empty Dove was a performer compared with a fully-loaded Anson or Rapide and it was hurtling skywards. I was approaching 2,000ft before I remembered to retract the undercarriage and pull the power back to climb settings. Even though the brief said, 'if you make a mistake, don't assume you have failed, just carry on and keep trying,' I felt it was all over. However, I settled down gradually, followed my clearance and set off for Gatwick.

Still having trouble with this silly station box, I couldn't work out how to listen to radio aids and VHF at the same time. I couldn't even look at the station box and fly the aircraft at the same time, so I didn't know how to lower the volume of the aids. They drowned out the VHF, so, once identified, I switched them off at the box.

We were cleared to the approach at Gatwick via the Dunsfold Radio Range and I was required to do this aurally rather than being allowed to use the ADF needle. This was the famous 'cone of silence', where the note of the radio range increases in volume as you approach the overhead and, as you pass over the beacon, it drops off to nothing then rises again on the other side, something else I had never actually experienced in an aircraft. Fiddling with the dreaded station box, not knowing how to control the volume, I actually switched the range off because it was so loud, so I could speak on the VHF, missed the cone of silence and didn't realise that I had passed overhead.

"That's enough," said Captain Hunter, and he took over and landed us at Gatwick.

When he debriefed me he said I would have to do ten hours instrument training in a twin-engined aircraft before my next test. I went home thoroughly disillusioned.

Back home, I investigated the price of ten hours instrument training in a twin. The nearest option was Blackpool. Whatever it was, I couldn't afford it. The only formal instrument training I'd had was the Link at Southend, the rest was self-taught in Proctor, Rapide and Anson. However I was beginning to get annoyed. I rang Len Mooney, who had been an ATCO at Speke and I'd often flown with him on army co-ops at Wilbur's club. He was now in a Ministry of Aviation office in Liverpool, having moved up from air traffic. I told him what had happened and asked him if the examiner could demand that I did the ten hours training. Len said he probably couldn't insist on my doing it, but he thought I'd be foolish to ignore the advice. I thought about it and decided that I couldn't afford it, so I would book another test and just hope I didn't get Captain Hunter.

I was determined to enjoy my next Stansted visit, whatever. I drove down with my wife to stay overnight in the pleasant Railway Inn in Bishop's Stortford. Next day, I walked into the flying unit in a combative frame of mind, thinking that I was going to enjoy the flying, regardless of whether I passed or failed. I looked at the board, Captain Spence, G-ANUT, Gatwick to Stansted. Great! I romped through the en route part of the test with no problem, almost enjoying myself and not even intimidated by the station box, which I now understood. I did a couple of let downs OK and came to the final ILS. I suddenly realised that I hadn't done anything wrong and might actually be close to passing, so my mood suddenly changed from 'I really don't care' to 'now I really do care' and I began to try hard again. My ILS went to pieces, it was awful, from side to side on the localiser and, worst of all, just below the glideslope at decision height.

When we debriefed Captain Spence said, "Shame about the ILS, I can't pass you, as you went below at decision height, so you'll have to come back and do that bit again. You were doing quite well until then."

I was annoyed with myself but still pleased that I had discovered the secret, at least for me. Don't try too hard, it's only flying, just try to relax and enjoy it, and all will be well. It was a lesson I carried with me and I always enjoyed simulator or flying checks later. I had a partial pass and it hadn't cost me ten hours of twin flying. Next time, Captain Joy, in Dove G-ANUW, Stansted to Gatwick for an ILS with no problem. I had a pleasant lunch with Captain Joy and he told me the examiners were fed up with people who were not ready for the test just using it as cheap flying practice, as it only cost £12 at the time. On the return flight to Stansted I sat in the back, as passenger, and when we did the engine failure in a max rate climb, the Dove almost rolled inverted. I understood what he meant. The fee for the test went up to about £50 soon afterwards.

I now had the commercial and instrument rating. I still had not had any communication from BKS, apart from being paid each month, so I went to the office at Speke to try to find out when I would start training on the Bristol 170. The first thing I discovered was that a new first officer had just started. My friend Jim Bolshaw! He'd pinched my job. I rang the chief training captain at Leeds, Captain Haythornthwaite. I spoke to a girl in the office and I could hear her talking across the room to the captain.

He asked who it was calling, and when she told him, I heard him say, "Flood? He should have been stopped weeks ago!"

The girl came back to me and said, "Captain Haythornthwaite will be in touch with you."

I got the message, but at least they had employed me for six months while I got my instrument rating and it still took them about four or five weeks to tell me that I was no longer required. I went straight to the W.H. Smith bookstall to buy 'Flight' magazine. Jim stayed with BKS (later called Northeast) and when they and Cambrian were absorbed into BEA and then British Airways, he ended up about five years behind me on the BA seniority list, so I was lucky once again. Jim retired and sadly died, along with an instructor, when he was doing a flying instructor's course and they spun a Cherokee into the sea off Southport.

In 'Flight' there were just two airline jobs advertised. Both were for Dakota first officers, one with Silver City Airways at Blackpool, the other with Cambrian Airways at Cardiff. Both were the standard pay rate, as with BKS, of £1,420pa. I decided to apply for both, hoping to get the Silver City job, as Blackpool was nearer. There was one other job advert, for a pilot with Smiths Industries at Cheltenham. The position was as co-pilot on the Vickers Varsity they were using to develop their autoland system. I phoned them and quickly received an invitation to interview with a rail warrant and hotel booking in Cheltenham. I travelled down and, after the night-stop, was collected from the hotel by company car and taken to the factory. First a brief conducted tour of the factory and then I was ushered into the board room for the grilling.

I was offered a seat at a large mahogany table (once again) with six senior company officials opposite, including the chief pilot. One of the managers told me something about the company and in particular what it was developing with autoland. The chief pilot gave me more detail about their progress, asked me about my flying, and then asked me what I knew about their autoland system. Luckily, there had been a very good article about it in 'Flight' a few weeks earlier, which I had read again before coming down, so I hoped my knowledge of it satisfied him.

Another manager then explained what the job entailed. He said that flying would only take up about 25% of my time and the rest would be working in the factory, writing up reports, etc. On hearing this, my interest in the job began to decline. Next, another manager asked me what sort of remuneration I would expect. I replied, quite positively, that I assumed the job would pay a similar rate to an airline co-pilot, which would be about £1,400pa. This caused a ripple of amusement across the table and he told me that the pay would not even be half that amount. It quickly became clear that we were not talking the same language and in due course I politely bade them farewell. At the railway station, going home, I saw a bloke about the same age as me, whom I had noticed in the factory, but didn't get a chance to speak to him as my train arrived. I guessed he had been there for the same reason as me.

A year or so later, the Smiths Varsity crashed on to a house near Cheltenham while doing crew training and the chief pilot and his co-pilot were killed. I reckoned for me it was another guardian angel moment.

I had a letter from Cambrian within days of getting home, inviting me for an interview. I knew that Cambrian had a strong connection with BEA. I phoned to arrange a time and drove down to Cardiff with my wife, stopping overnight in Ludlow. Next morning, bright and early, we arrived at Rhoose airport and I had my interview with the Chief Pilot, Captain Geoff Perrott. He asked me about my flying, looked at my logbooks and chatted about Speke and people we both knew. Cambrian operated services through Speke and in the past we often had their Rapides or Doves overnight in our hangar. We returned home and a couple of days later I had a letter offering me a job. I rang to accept and Bryn Savage, the operations manager's deputy, asked when I could start. Many years later, Geoff took the edge off it slightly when he told me he only had two responses to the advert, Reg Leach and myself. As he needed two pilots, it wasn't a difficult decision.

I don't think they required me urgently but I told Bryn the following Monday would be fine. I needed to be employed.

And that was that. It was to be my last job until I retired, although I certainly didn't realise it at the time.

3.   A PROPER JOB

Although the previous chapter is titled Learning to Fly, I don't think you ever stop learning, probably just get better at covering up mistakes. The adage about 'old pilots and bold pilots etc.,' is very true, and it would be a very bold pilot who claimed he knew it all.

In October 1961 I joined Cambrian Airways as a Dakota first officer. This was never part of my plan, if I had one, but with mouths to feed I needed a job. I considered airline pilots a cut above me and didn't think I'd fit in too well. I'd met one or two who occasionally flew at Wilbur's club and they did seem almost human. On one occasion, doing circuits at Speke in an Auster, I was given a red light to go around while a BEA Dakota took off. As I flew along the runway at 1,000ft, the Dak rolled and from above I was astonished to see it go from one side of the runway to the other a couple of times before it got airborne. When I taught students I asked them to put a main-wheel each side of the centreline and keep them there during the take-off. Maybe these airline pilots weren't supermen. Cliff told me he was enjoying flying with Starways, which certainly helped.

I travelled down to Cardiff overnight by train, not sure when I was required to report, and arrived at Rhoose airfield about 0800. It was deserted. About 0900 people started wandering in and at 1000 I managed to locate Bryn Savage and reported. He showed me round, which didn't take long, the pilots' crewroom was in an unheated ex-military building by the main gate, probably the original gatehouse. Flight planning was across the tarmac, also the Met forecaster, in the RAF style control tower. The Cambrian traffic office or airport coffee bar was where we congregated before flying and got the latest rumours. Bryn suggested I organise a night stop bed and breakfast in the village for when I was overnighting in Rhoose, and gave me an address. He also gave me the technical books for the Dakota to prepare for the ARB exam. Bryn then seemed at a loss as to what to do with me, as I thought I had to be there every day, much as in my previous jobs (not counting BKS), so he suggested I catch the late afternoon Cardiff to Manchester Dakota, have an evening at home and come back on the return flight in the morning. This sounded a good idea, I was beginning to like working for an airline. I collected my ticket from traffic, met the crew of the Dak and sat on the cockpit jump seat up to Manchester. Into the city with them in the crew transport, home on the train, and realised it was good that I hadn't taken my car to Rhoose.

In fact, for the next year or so, this was my routine of going to work. I'd leave my car at the local station, train to Manchester, meet the crew in the hotel, drive with them to Ringway, jump seat to Rhoose and report for my flight. Once checked out I would usually be the operating crew into and out of Manchester, which was even better. In summer the Dakota night-stopped in Liverpool, which improved the procedure. I only had to stay in Rhoose, or later in Barry, maybe one or two nights a month. Reg Leach, who joined just after me, found an excellent B&B in Barry which we used thereafter. Mr & Mrs Roberts were very pleasant hosts and even, as they frequently went on holiday themselves, gave us our own keys and let us look after ourselves.

On my second morning, I flew supernumary back to Rhoose. Bryn ran me into Cardiff to the tailors to be measured for my uniform. He'd arranged a supernumary trip to Paris for me next day with Captain Perrott, so that night I had my first bed and breakfast in Rhoose. The following morning an early start at Rhoose and then Cardiff – Bristol – Southampton – Paris (LeBourget) – Southampton – Bristol – Cardiff. It was interesting and good fun, with a grass airfield at Southampton, learning the airline routine.

Pre-warned about air traffic control in the Paris area, it was slightly alarming being requested to climb to a higher level, then almost immediately down again to avoid aircraft, which always seemed to be last minute stuff. As the pilots told me, it was sometimes better to be in cloud, so you didn't see the ones you just missed.

Next day another supernumary trip, with Captain Ken Wakefield, Cardiff – Bristol – Guernsey then a double Jersey and back, finishing with a night stop in The Old Government House Hotel in Guernsey. I finished the following day with Guernsey – Jersey – Guernsey – Bristol – Cardiff – Manchester and three days off.

I contacted Pop Speller for the set of Dakota questions and answers but the Cambrian books were all I really needed. In fact, they were BEA books, as the fleet of eight Daks were ex BEA Pionairs, one of the nicest civilian conversions. BEA had a large shareholding in Cambrian, as an associated company, and the other major shareholder was S Kenneth Davies, a Welsh industrialist, an important and influential person in Welsh aviation, who was also on the board of BEA.

In 1957 Cambrian, like many smaller airlines, nearly went under and had to sell their fleet. BEA stepped in with backing and the aircraft, as Cambrian operated associated routes that otherwise BEA would be forced to operate. So we were effectively under the wing and control of BEA. The Pionairs were nice Dakotas. They had a full instrument panel for each pilot, unlike most Daks, which only had a full panel on the port side. This meant the co-pilot could fly the Pionair from the right hand seat (in some other Daks, the pilots had to swap seats for the co-pilot to fly). The Pionair seated 32 passengers in comfortable leather seats and had an airstair style rear door, obviating the need for steps. Another different, but nice, part of the job was that we had a hostess to look after the passengers, and she could usually be persuaded to bring us tea, coffee and biscuits or soft drinks.

Back to Cardiff for another Paris trip with Captain Bernie Sparrow and this time I was allowed to sit in the co-pilot's seat for the return legs. Another Channel Islands nightstop, this time Jersey, with Captain Ron deWilde. Back home for two days off and then at the end of the month, having taken the ARB exam, to Cardiff to do some base training with Captain Perrott, doing stalls and seven landings. After about ten days off, during which I received my Dakota licence endorsement, having done the exam and the minimum six landings, I went back to Rhoose to fly again with Geoff Perrott.

Rather just doing the minimum six landings for a co-pilot, Geoff's policy was to do the full P1 training, so we did engine failure on take-off, two single engined landings, and a single engine go-around. Good training and very enjoyable.

In October that year, the new Cork Airport was opened and we started operating a London (Heathrow) to Cork service and also Cardiff to Cork. I did some of my line training flights on Heathrow Cork with Geoff Perrott, which meant four nights in a Northside hotel.

Early November, I was on the line, and settled in to the winter routine of Manchester – Jersey and Cardiff – Paris. The only time I had to night stop Rhoose was when I did a Paris, but after I'd done a couple or three it was easy enough to organise a swap with another first officer, for me to stay on the Manchester run. There were about 22 pilots in the company at the time so I soon knew them all. I see from my logbook that the Jersey winter schedule sometimes terminated with a Speke nightstop, which was even more convenient for me.

Cambrian were always heavily involved in the 'rugby airlifts', when hundreds of Welsh fans flew to Dublin, Edinburgh or Paris to support their national team. The days before and after the matches were very busy. I was definitely enjoying one aspect of the new job, which was that when we weren't flying, we could go home, and we didn't have to work on the aircraft. About three or four weeks after starting with Cambrian, the Silver City chief pilot at Blackpool wrote and asked me to go for an interview. I replied to explain and decline, not realising at the time how lucky my choice had been.

About six months after joining Cambrian, when I was just twenty five, I remember ringing Mrs Williams in Accounts to query a deduction from my pay for 'superannuation' which I hadn't authorised. She gently explained to me that it was my (compulsory) contribution to the pension scheme, to which the company also paid a generous amount. My suggestion that I wasn't quite ready for pension contributions at that time fell on deaf ears. The pension was broadly based on the BEA scheme. Thirty years later, when I retired with a British Airways final salary pension, I realised it was probably the best financial investment decision I had ever made, albeit beyond my control!

The summer schedules of 1962 meant more flying, routes to Belfast and Dublin, and the Channel Isles schedules originated from Liverpool rather than Manchester, which suited me. We had intended moving to Cardiff when I joined Cambrian, but as time went on, with easy positioning, it became less of a requirement, and as the summer drew to a close, it became even less likely. There were rumours of an Irish Sea operation with Viscounts.

Operating the Dakota was a pleasure. Cruising at about 150kts, unpressurised of course, so we were always in the weather below 10,000ft, nevertheless it was very enjoyable. It was a delight to fly, with soft controls, the control wheel rotated a long way before it had any effect on the bank, particularly at lower speeds, and in a crosswind it was often well past the 90° position when landing. We used the autopilot as a control lock when taxiing, disconnecting for take-off of course, and the tail wheel lock helped with directional control at low speed when the rudder wasn't effective. A nice soft undercarriage improved most landings, but it would bounce, quite high, as I found out when I thought I had it taped. It was normal to do a power off wheeler, but it would do a very nice three pointer when conditions allowed. It was very satisfying to hold the mainwheels just six inches above the runway, coming gently back on the control column until all three wheels touched. We had one captain who always finished the approach with a glide and three point landing, night or day, windy or calm.

That was another interesting aspect of being a first officer, flying with different captains. Some were very good, and others not quite so good. You quickly learned who needed watching. Coming into Liverpool one night, the captain tuned the Hawarden beacon (340kcs) well before we approached it and told me it was indicating on the ADF. However, he hadn't listened and identified it, just twiddled the tuner around the 340 mark until the tuning needle moved up the scale. I listened to it and found that he'd tuned to the powerful Oldham beacon on 344kcs. I re-tuned it to Hawarden, remembering a Bristol Wayfarer (with two ex-Dragon Airways pilots) which had crashed on Winter Hill by doing almost exactly the same thing.

On another occasion, with the same captain, we were landing at Speke one night in very windy conditions. For normal landings we left the props at cruise rpm of 2050, but if a go-around was a possibility, such as low visibility or gusty wind, then the revs would be set at 2250. We had set the higher rpm on this occasion, and as we approached with the aircraft bouncing about and the speed varying by 20 to 30 knots, the captain was attempting to stabilise the speed with power. It would have been better to just leave it. As the speed dropped he'd push the throttles forward, then yank them back as the speed increased. The result was that the constant speed units couldn't keep up with demand and the revs were varying considerably. As we got nearer the ground, he increased his ham-fisted pumping of the throttles and also got out of phase with the engines, so he was increasing power just as the revs were going up. The end result was the revs varying from 2000 to 2600, with the engines howling each time he banged the throttles forward. The overspeed limit was 2700 and I was seriously concerned we would reach that point. Luckily we landed before that happened, but I wasn't impressed.

Another day, another captain, we started at Ringway on a morning of heavy snow. When we got to the aircraft, it was covered in snow and ice. The de-icing crews were very busy and we were well down their list, so our captain decided that the snow would probably blow off and we would go. I wasn't too keen on this idea and our ops manual said clearly that we must not take off with ice or snow on the wings. However, the captain said I could look out of my side window during take-off and if the snow didn't move, we would abandon. We taxied out, lined up, and at this point I had already decided that we weren't going anywhere. As we rolled and the tail came up, I set the throttles at take-off power and watched the snow. Small bits blew off, but most of it stuck fast. At about 70kts, almost airborne speed, I called 'Stop', throttled back and we taxied back in to wait for the de-icers.

Our Dak's Pratt & Whitney Twin Wasp engines didn't have hot pot oil coolers, which allowed the oil to bypass the cooler until it was warm, thus reducing the warm up time. In cold weather it could take our engines up to ten minutes to reach operating temperature, required for take-off. One particularly impatient captain would never accept this and would just line up and go when he was ready, regardless of the first officer pointing out the low oil temps.

The most serious incident was one which I considered almost put me amongst the statistics. Soon after I joined, I was having a drink on a night stop with another first officer who had started about six months before me. He asked me what I thought about one particular captain. I had flown with this captain a couple of times and said he seemed pretty good and could handle the Dak quite well, particularly in strong winds. "Yes," said my new friend, "he's quite good flying visual or doing a radar approach following headings, but just wait until you have to do a procedural ILS without radar help and see what happens." He explained that although our captain was an excellent handling pilot when visual, and competent enough when being given headings and heights to fly on a radar approach, he just could not cope with having to work out his own headings and heights on a procedural approach.

"If you find yourself with him in that situation, just give him headings and heights to fly and you'll be OK."

Quite frankly, I could not believe him, although I subsequently realised I should have done. The idea that I should tell this venerable pilot what to do was simply not acceptable at that stage of my career.

A few months later, I was flying with this captain and we were approaching Ringway on a wild winter night. The wind was gale force north-westerly and when we called Manchester approach we were informed that as the surface wind was 30 to 40kts, having an effect on the scanner, so the approach radar was out of service. We were cleared to the 06 outer marker beacon to hold and to expect a procedural approach to the 24 ILS. This simply meant doing it ourselves with no help from radar. My friend's words came back to me and a little bell began to ring, but I pushed that aside and got on with my part of the job, tuning beacons and monitoring the approach. 'Monitoring', in those days, was little more than watching.

The procedure was straightforward, to leave the hold at the 06 outer marker, then to the 24 outer marker beacon, and, one minute beyond, a procedure turn left to re-join the localiser and then the ILS approach. The ILS indicator in the Dakota was a 'raw' ILS display, with centre needles and blue/yellow sectors, and the ADF had a simple relative bearing indicator.

At the intermediate altitude of 3,000 feet, the wind was north-westerly at about 60 knots, so the drift at Dakota approach speeds, heading southwest and northeast was considerable. With the captain flying (for some captains these were still 'man and boy' days and this captain really did call his co-pilot 'boy' and give you one sector of an eight sector day – if you were lucky) I settled back to watch the approach. The monitored approach was about at this time but hadn't reached our company. As we entered the hold at the first beacon, already drifting off track, things started to go wrong. We ended up attempting to hold the wrong way round, but it didn't matter as almost immediately we were cleared to the 24 outer marker and cleared for the ILS approach. On the way to this beacon we drifted well off the approach centreline downwind, to the southeast, so as we approached the beacon our track was nowhere near the approach reciprocal it should have been. The captain then asked me for the outbound heading of the procedure turn. In retrospect, I realised that this should have been my cue to start telling him what courses to steer, but I simply could not believe that this senior pilot (flying before I was born) would ask (very junior) me what to do. So I read out the track on the approach chart and said something to the effect that, with the strong wind, a very large heading and time correction would be required. This obviously did not register because he simply steered the course I read out and, after one minute (the still air timing), started the turn to the right to regain the localiser. In fact, just as we completed the turn, we shot back through the localiser. He steadied up on the inbound heading of the procedure turn, steering the reciprocal of the outbound leg – no allowance for drift – and at this point, as we were now on a southerly heading but drifting rapidly southeast in the strong wind, I pointed out that we had flown through the localiser. This had no effect, so I said it again. Still no response, so I said, as firmly as I could, that we were now south of the localiser and should turn right to regain it. The captain commenced a turn to the right and I began to relax.

The turn continued however through west, then north and east. We were simply orbiting to the right, with undercarriage down and approach flap, at about 95kts. What concerned me was that although we were orbiting, we were drifting downwind at about 50kts, towards the high ground which started about ten miles south and southeast of the airport, and we had already spent too long on a southerly heading south of the localiser. We were now at our final approach height of 1,500ft. The situation was deteriorating rapidly and I realised that something had to be done, but genuinely believed that if I acted as I would have done in my instructing days, that is 'taken over', I would subsequently be out of work. I couldn't believe what was happening, so who would believe me later, brand new first officer versus senior experienced captain. I couldn't accept that giving courses to steer to my captain was part of my job.

At this point air traffic called and requested our position in the approach. I was doing the R/T and didn't really know what to say. I asked them to standby and looked across at the captain for a response. I didn't get one, and he just continued orbiting, now into our second 360° turn to the right. Much later, I realised he was just waiting for me to give him instructions and would have done whatever I said.

Air traffic called again for our position and again I asked them to standby, still getting no response from my captain as I looked across for some reaction. Many months later, I learned from one of the controllers what was happening in the tower. Although the wind was above the operating limit for the scanner, they did have it on and, despite its irregular gyrations, were getting a picture of sorts and were monitoring our progress with increasing alarm.

Back in the cockpit, we were entering our third 360° turn and I thought I could feel the hills feet away from our wheels. Air traffic called again, but this time it was a different voice, in fact a senior controller who had just arrived, looked at the radar screen and assessed the situation instantly. His voice was positive and urgent as he told us to steer 270° and immediately climb to 3,000 feet. My captain responded equally positively and from passing through north we rolled back to 270°, the power went on and we climbed to 3,000 feet. Apparently, when this controller came in and saw the situation he said, "Do something now or we'll have another Winter Hill!"

Thereafter it was straightforward and with a couple of more headings from the controller we intercepted the localiser and slid down the glideslope to the runway. The cloud base was about 1,000ft and we had, of course, been in cloud throughout.

The captain acted as though nothing untoward had happened and I didn't know what to say, so I didn't. I went home that night and told my wife I wasn't going back next day but when I thought of the mortgage and looked at the little tousled heads on their pillows, I went back in the morning as though nothing had happened.

When I studied a chart of the area and tried to work out where we had been, I saw that the ground starts rising less than ten miles southeast of the outer marker, but a valley runs into the hills at this point, aligned roughly northwest/southeast. The ground level in this area is up to 1,400/1,600ft, but further east and southeast rises to 2,000ft plus. We had been orbiting and drifting across at 1,750ft (1500 QFE). Crew resource management had not yet been invented.

The Dakota was good experience in many other ways. Unpressurised, we were always in the icing zone. The Dak had inflatable boots on its leading edges which worked quite well, but you had to be careful not to be too eager to put them on. The routine was to wait until the ice had built up noticeably and then switch the boots on. This would break the ice off. If they were switched on too soon, the ice would build up on top of the inflating boots and then you had no chance of breaking it off, and descending or climbing was the only option. The props had fluid de-icers but the ice would start breaking off the props even before the de-icers were switched on, and the sound of this ice thumping the fuselage was often the wake up call to ice on the airframe.

A lovely tale went around the company about a crew in the cruise one night when the first officer said he needed to visit the toilet, down at the back of the passenger cabin. He disappeared and soon after the captain noticed the speed falling off. He increased power slightly, but the speed slowly reduced. The first officer re-joined him in the cockpit and between them they decided ice must be the problem. The boots were switched on, with no obvious improvement and they ended up with climb power just maintaining a minimum cruise speed. Eventually they noticed on the flap gauge that the flaps were fully down. As the first officer left his seat he had knocked the flap lever slightly out of position and the flaps had slowly and gently moved to fully down!

Another interesting aspect of Dakota flying was landing in a crosswind. I soon discovered that the slip technique was favourite with some captains. For a crosswind from the left, this meant that, on short final, left aileron was wound on, counteracted by right rudder, and the aircraft arrived at the runway tracking and in line with the runway, wings level, but actually yawing to the left, into the wind. It worked quite well but I never liked the technique, preferring the crabbing method of flying the centre line, in trim, with drift on as required, and removing the drift with rudder just before touchdown. In fact, this was the only method recommended in the company operations manual.

One particular captain didn't like my way and told me that large amounts of rudder were only to be used for engine failure cases. I did notice that he tended to wander all over the runway on take-off, just using small amounts of rudder, much like the one I had watched in my Auster days. This captain even reported my 'enthusiastic' use of the rudder to the chief pilot. I still favoured my way of doing it. Film of certification test pilots setting crosswind limits for their aircraft shows that it works for them. I have also heard of the lazy airline pilot's way – 'kick off half the drift before touchdown and the rest after' – and that also works, particularly on a wet runway. I always remained in favour of the crab method, as described in my AP1979A Elementary Flying Training, which didn't even mention the sideslip technique, much as our ops manual.

As mentioned, the Dak could be three-pointed nicely. I always favoured a landing technique of power off and hold off, which I think works for almost all aircraft. My logic is that it's best to arrive at the touchdown point with minimum and decreasing airspeed. There are people, of course, who have a different method and viewpoint, and over the years this has been an interesting discussion point. More on this later.

I experienced just one engine failure in a Dakota. We left Cardiff one day for Liverpool, and had just settled in the cruise when the port engine went out of sync. The captain had a look at it and said it was shaking a bit in its cowlings and asked me to shut it down. I did, and we went back to Cardiff where the engineers told us we had a cracked cylinder head. It was a radial and I reckoned if necessary it would have rattled on for a few more hours if we'd needed it.

Dakota flying was relatively low level, between 5,000 and 10,000ft, or lower on a nice day, often off airways and quite interesting. Cardiff to Liverpool and Manchester was an advisory route, a sort of poor man's airway, but Bristol to Southampton and Jersey was in the FIR, and we had to keep a very good look out. South of Portland Bill were Navy danger areas, which we had to check and avoid where necessary. In Dorset we'd fly over the Cerne Abbas giant, the nude figure of a man cut in chalk, and a couple of captains enjoyed circling it and calling the stewardess to the cockpit to show and embarrass her.

Operating in to Jersey and Guernsey meant frequent landings in low stratus/sea fog and I found it strange at first to make an approach in bright sunshine only to enter a solid layer of stratus at 300/400ft. We usually managed to scrape in with a Cat 1 decision height of 170ft, and the relatively slow approach speed of the Dakota of about 80 to 90 knots. It wasn't unusual to have this stratus combined with a strong crosswind, which made it even more interesting. On one of my jump seat positioning trips from Manchester to Cardiff, where I would have started work on the next leg, due to very low stratus we couldn't land at either Cardiff or Bristol, so diverted to Jersey where most of the passengers were bound. Jersey was just as bad and we made two abortive approaches and on the second I was horrified when the captain flew the ILS down to about 40ft on the altimeter, and then flew level in solid stratus for about 15 or 20 seconds, hoping to see something. I was relieved when we diverted to Bournemouth.

One captain told me that when he was a first officer with another airline they would often land at Gatwick in thick fog when the captain would fly the ILS right down to the runway and throttle back when the tyres squeaked! This of course was before approach bans. At Bournemouth the crew positioned back to Cardiff by road and my captain came from there to join me to start again the next day. We stayed the night in Bournemouth and the next morning I had my first experience of waking up in a strange hotel room and feeling a momentary panic of not knowing where I was!

On another occasion at Jersey we taxied out in fog and sat at the holding point, waiting for the visibility to improve enough for the captain to consider taking off. While sitting there, I heard a noise outside and realised it was a Dakota of another airline landing. We couldn't see it from the holding point. We didn't take off that day, even though others were landing. At the time Jersey didn't report RVR measurements so that pilots could factor the met visibility. This allowed increasing the met vis. to obtain an equivalent RVR. So 200 or 300yds met vis. could give 600yds RVR. The stratus was usually lower, or on the ground, on the west side of the island, and the cloud base on the eastern side much higher. I heard that one airline favoured descending east of the island over the sea and, when contact, hedge hopping over the island on the localiser until the runway was spotted. There was a fatal accident when a Dakota collided with the approach lights and all on board were killed.

The Dakota was an excellent introduction to airline flying for me. However the rumours were gathering strength, and by November it was announced that we would start our Viscount courses with BEA in December. The plan was for BEA to give up all their Irish Sea services, and Cambrian to apply to operate them. This in fact was what happened in March 1963, to the consternation of the other independent operators but by then it was a *fait accompli*. Despite its BEA connections, Cambrian was considered to be an independent airline, as opposed to the nationalised corporations.

So in December 62, just after Christmas, I drove down to a hotel in Richmond, London to start the three-week ground school and then simulator with BEA. This was very enjoyable, particularly my first experience of a simulator. By modern standards the Viscount simulator was primitive, as it had no motion, but it had an identical cockpit, and flew in a very similar way to the real aeroplane. It was, I suppose, a very good systems and procedures trainer. However, this simulator was sold, with the BEA Viscount 700s that we didn't buy, to VASP in South America, and thereafter we did all our training on the aeroplane.

During the course at Richmond there was one of the last London 'pea souper' fogs. It was so bad in the evenings that we could get lost walking from the hotel to find a restaurant to eat. Heathrow had no movements for three days, except for the Smiths Varsity (a replacement for the one that crashed) which was demonstrating its autoland capability. After the course and the exam, which was with BEA, so was passed without a problem, it was back to the Dakota for a while.

In February I went to Jersey for a few days and we did base training on a BEA Viscount 701 G-AMOG, with BEA Captain Stan Nicolle. This was seven take-offs and landings and one go-around, enough for a P2 qualification. I sat in the right hand seat with one captain who always annoyed me in the Dakota as he over controlled furiously whenever the conditions were slightly turbulent. When he did this at Jersey in the Viscount, I was delighted when Stan, after a couple of circuits, had obviously had enough and reached across from his observing position to grab the control column and demand that he stopped moving it unnecessarily. I did some of my qualifying six landings with Geoff Perrott in the left hand seat, doing the necessary time for his type rating examiner ticket. After I had finished, Stan asked Geoff what he thought of my efforts. Geoff began to launch into detailed critique of my flying, which he probably thought was required of him, but Stan stopped him quickly by saying,

"No... nothing to say really, I thought it was very good, with nice anticipation."

At least one of us was pleased!

I really enjoyed flying the Viscount and couldn't wait to start operating it, although it still wasn't clear where I would be based. Eventually the Viscount positions were advertised and in addition to mostly Cardiff crews there were two crews to be based at Liverpool, one crew at Manchester and one at London. The Cardiff crews would back up at these bases, as required. Liverpool was to become the busiest base. I was still quite junior but I applied for a Liverpool first officer position and was very surprised when I heard that I was the only volunteer! The Cardiff pilots didn't want to come to Liverpool. The other three positions were filled by posting the most junior pilots from Cardiff. That didn't bother me, I was back home as a Viscount first officer at Liverpool.

On March 31st I was supernumerary on G-AMON, positioning from Cardiff to Speke to start services on April 1st. We were now operating services from Liverpool and Manchester to Isle of Man and Belfast, and Isle of Man to London. I did a couple of Irish Sea days out of Speke as supernumerary, then down to Heathrow for two days P2 line training with Captain Axelberg, and a further day as qualified P2, operating the London-Cork and London-Isle of Man services. On the April 9th I was back at my Speke base as a line pilot, and began to wear my own personal groove in the airways over the Irish Sea.

This was good interesting flying. We did between two and six sectors a day, and the Isle of Man weather, with frequent sea fog, and the odd gale, certainly ensured we didn't get bored. We had just started using the monitored approach procedure, to which BEA had introduced us on the course. When an instrument approach was required, the co-pilot would fly the aeroplane and the captain would monitor it until he became visual, when he would take over and land, or, if at decision height he didn't see enough to land, instruct the co-pilot to go around. This meant that I got plenty of instrument approaches, which I enjoyed.

The Viscount still had the basic ILS indicator, with vertical localiser needle, horizontal glideslope needle and blue/yellow sectors. In the Dakota the pilot had to interpret its indications himself, but the Viscount had an additional instrument, the Sperry Zero Reader, an early flight director. This instrument also had vertical and horizontal needles, but when switched to ILS mode would direct the pilot to join and follow the ILS. All the pilot had to do was keep the two zero reader needles centred (reading zero), vertical with bank and horizontal with pitch. Once you got the hang of it, it would direct you into a very smooth localiser intercept and ILS approach down to decision height, calculating and applying drift as necessary. It certainly made the last few hundred feet much easier. The Viscount 701 autopilot was very basic, with a pitch control and heading knob, but no height lock.

The Viscount had Decca Navigator with a flight log, which we also had in the Dakota. This was very useful, but never regarded a primary navigation aid, just a backup. Decca had competed with the VOR (VHF omnidirectional radio range) to be used as the worldwide navaid but ICAO decided in favour of VOR, which was the correct choice. VOR with DME (distance measuring equipment) became the airways standard for more than forty years. Decca was never totally reliable and suffered with interference from thunderstorms etc. It was a low frequency hyperbolic system, developed during the war and used in preparation for, and during, the Normandy landings. It was initially designed for shipping and subsequently was used widely by fishing boats. With a range up to 400 miles it was suited to ships, and although the accuracy reduced with range, its repeatability (its ability to return accurately to a position) was good and what the fishermen required.

The basic equipment, without the flight log, consisted of three deccometers showing position in zones and lanes, which we had in the Dakota, and these had to be set up before departure and constantly monitored to ensure that the flight log was accurate. If it wasn't, it was usually so far out of position that it was obvious. The Dakota's cruise speed made this system acceptable, but the Viscount's greater speed required a more automatic check which the later receivers provided, without using deccometers. Zone ident instead of lane ident, if I remember. Our Viscounts didn't have DME, weather radar or transponders.

Instrument approaches at Liverpool, Manchester, Heathrow etc., were no problem but the Isle of Man did present some difficulties. With just an ILS on runway 27 and no approach radar at that time, if the wind was easterly with a low, 600/800ft, cloudbase, our only option for landing on 09 was to do an ILS to break cloud, and then a visual circuit over the sea to the south of the airfield, because of high ground to the north. This wasn't too bad in daylight but at night it could be a bit too exciting. If the captain took over when visual on the ILS he would lose sight of the airfield downwind, being on the wrong side of the cockpit. Several captains, including the Liverpool based ones, favoured an unofficial NDB approach to 09 using the two beacons, one at Spanish Head, about five miles from touchdown, and one on the airfield. This was the easier and safer option and after some company pressure it became an approved let down procedure.

The other interesting approach was when the frequent southerly wind was too strong to land on 27 and a landing on the short runway 22 was required. With a low cloud base this again entailed a cloud break on the ILS and a slide across to the 22 approach at about 500ft.

This required care at night as the ground level on 22 approach rose to about 130ft at one mile and 200ft at less than two miles, with a hill at 350ft just off to starboard of the centreline.

One evening Captain Jimmy Jones and I were called out at Speke to take a Viscount to Cork, where one had gone u/s, to operate the delayed evening Cork to London service. By the time we were airborne from Cork, it was past midnight. As we settled in the cruise we were approaching Tuskar Rock, a lighthouse off the southeast corner of Eire, and a reporting point on the airway. A few months before, an Aer Lingus Viscount had crashed near the rock, when it broke up in flight, and the accident cause was never satisfactorily explained.

I was thinking about this crash as we cruised across St George's Channel to Strumble Head, when suddenly there was an extremely loud banging from somewhere above and behind the cockpit, as though somebody was hitting it with a very large hammer. We both jumped in our seats, checking the pressurisation, engine and flight instruments, but all appeared normal. The noise lasted about twenty seconds, then stopped as suddenly as it had started, and the rest of the flight to Heathrow was uneventful. On arrival, when the engineer came on board for the technical log, we told him about it, and he went off to get some steps to investigate. In five minutes he was back with the explanation. At the rear of the cockpit roof was a fairing in which was a tank of fluid for windscreen de-icing. The tank filler cap was beneath a removable aluminium cover which was attached by a short chain to prevent it being dropped. This cover had become detached in flight, hammered briefly in the 240-knot breeze until it detached from the chain and disappeared into the Irish Sea. Not good for the nerves!

My apprenticeship continued during that summer, the short haul operation suited me, with plenty of short sectors. The captains, particularly the newer, younger ones, were more generous in sharing the flying so Pl(s) sectors became more regular. More Viscounts were delivered during the summer and further expansion was planned for the following year, with the requirement for more crews, and thus promotions. To be eligible for a Viscount command the company required 2,500 hours total and of course an ATPL (Airline Transport Pilots Licence). I had the hours but not the licence. When I had my joining interview with the chief pilot Captain Geoff Perrott, he explained that as we worked fairly hard at Cardiff in the summer months but much less in the winter, it was usual to allow those first officers approaching command to be given three months paid leave during the winter to attend a navigation school (Avigation, Sir John Cass, London School of Navigation) to do the course for the licence exams. As it now seemed possible that I would be in line for a command the following year, I contacted Geoff to ask if I could have the time off. Reg Leach, who joined at the same time as I did and was now the sole first officer at Manchester, made the same request. Geoff replied that, as the work at the new bases was fairly constant, summer and winter, if we had time off, it would mean replacing us with Cardiff crews, at additional expense. Accordingly he could not allow us to have the three months leave.

We were disappointed and rather annoyed, particularly as several Cardiff first officers were granted leave. I decided I would have to try to do the exam anyway, while Reg decided to delay and, in fact, got a posting to Heathrow the following year so he could attend school from home. Bill Tollitt, one of the new captains, offered me his (used) correspondence course, which was a great help, much like the course from Jack Green. I also found that previous exam papers were available, and these were good value. I got stuck into the work, with help of Bill's course and notes and a copy of Bennett's *The Complete Air Navigator*, which Liverpool captain Bob Ross lent me, and I applied for the January exam, knowing that would be the only chance I would have to be ready for the March deadline.

In January I sat for the exams, not taking any notice of the 'experts' this time. A week or so later, when the results were announced, once again I passed everything except the easiest exam, which was signals. This was a half-hour exam, the last one on the second day, Tuesday. It was a hard day and I remember ending up with a headache, which was my excuse. The test was simple enough, some two letter Morse visual light signals, to simulate airfield light beacons, then two sets of aural Morse, one of two letter groups (marine), the other of three letter groups (aeronautical). I filled in all the boxes for the two letter groups with no problem, then started on the next set. I couldn't understand why the letters were coming with gaps in the wrong places until, half way through, I realised I was putting two letter groups into the boxes instead of three letter groups. Furious with myself, I put my pen down in disgust and stopped writing. Luckily, the signals exam could be done each week, unlike all the others, so a week or so later I went back to do it again. The examiner made a point of seeing me to say that they realised exactly what I had done and if only I had carried on writing the letters down, anywhere on the page, they would have passed me. As it was, I had omitted too many to pass. My second attempt was better.

However, I had the licence in time. Dakota and Viscount commands were advertised in February and I duly applied. Once again, my choice of Liverpool was fortunate, as pilots at Cardiff, who were senior to me, elected to take the Dakota at Cardiff and I was delighted to get a Viscount command at my home base.

Flying Proctor AA in 1951.

PH & I, 1952.

Nick & I, BZ & PH.

Captain Guinane, Sid, Ron, Nick, Me, Cliff M, Bernie & Ted.

Me, Bernie, Nick, Eric & Cliff M.

G-AIBZ, my first solo aircraft.

Autocrat cockpit, just like it used to be (except for starter radio and DG) G-AGTO at Duxford.

G-ANSX, my favourite Tiger.

G-ANSA [photo: Phil Butler].

PP in hangar 39, Speke c. 1958 [photo: Phil Butler].

G-AIPA with de-icing paste on leading edges [photo: Phil Butler].

G-ANZP at Speke [photo: Phil Butler].

G-ALXC [photo: Phil Butler].

G-AMBE [photo: Phil Butler].

Cliff Watson & Frenchie ZP & XC.

Rapide at Duxford (beautiful – ours were never this good).

Rapide cockpit (immaculate G-AGJG at Duxford).

Cambrian DC3 at Speke [photo: Phil Butler].

Viscount G-AMOH at Speke.

Viscount 701 – If it's dark, it must be Belfast newspapers!

Viscount and snowy day at Speke.

G-ALWF preserved at Duxford.

Cambrian One Eleven 400 G-AVOF.

BAC 1-11 400 & crew.

One Eleven Inaugural Palma from Liverpool 1970 (11000ft/2000fpm).

Peter Gates and I – G-BCPZ.

Theresa & I with PZ, Ibiza.

Aero Commander 112.

S1-11 at Speke.

S1-11 at Ringway.

S1-11 G-AVMT.

Christmas flights – S1-11 dressed up for the kids.

Christmas flights Flight Crew.

Christmas flights – with grandsons.

Christmas flights – ground crew.

Kingfisher of Hoyle.

Bulldog Ship rendezvous in Crosby Channel.

Acrosport.

Acrosport and bone-dome.

Loch Lomond for coffee.

Husky amphibian at Loch Earn.

Eurostar in garage prior to build.

Eurostar finished at Ince.

TJ & I at Southport Air Show, 2009.

Starting young – great-grandchildren in TJ.

S1-11 G-AVMU preserved at Duxford.

4. WORKING FOR A LIVING

Mid-March, 1964, I started command training on the Viscount. This consisted of a fair amount of base training and 38 line training sectors, on normal services with passengers, no simulator this time. Base training started with upper airwork, Vmca (minimum control speed in the air) work, flying on three and two engines. The cloud was a bit low for stalling the captain said, so we missed that and I never did stall a Viscount. We also did flapless take offs and landings, critical engine fail (No. 4) on take-off, and three engined ferry take-off. This item was to allow the aircraft to be ferried back to base with one engine u/s. I'd agreed with crewing that I would operate the service from Manchester for four days, in order to get my line sectors in. This was Manchester-Isle of Man-Liverpool-Heathrow, and return, six sectors a day. I decided to drive to Manchester each day, which made a long duty, particularly when some base training was tacked on at the end.

However, all went well, except for one evening base training detail at Ringway, after our six sectors. On this we did engine fail on take-off, three engine overshoot (now called go around), three engine landing and finally some night circuits. When the Viscount lost the critical Number 4 engine (starboard outer) on take-off at V1, the rudder didn't have enough control until V2, so nosewheel steering was used to help until V2 was reached and then the aircraft could be lifted off and climbed away. For training, the routine was, just after V1, to bring No.4 HP (high pressure) fuel cock right back from open, through closed, to the feather position. This would cause the propeller to auto-feather almost fully and a touch on the feathering pump switch would complete the operation.

So, on our first take off, as we passed V1, the training captain, in the right hand seat, pulled No. 4 HP cock back. The aircraft began to swing across the runway, and even with the control column hard forward, full rudder and a lot of nosewheel steering applied, I couldn't stop the swing and keep the aircraft on the centreline. I glanced down at the HP cock and realised that it was in the closed position, not in feather! This meant the prop wasn't feathered, but was still in flight fine pitch trying to maintain revs, and creating a lot of drag. I asked the captain to feather the engine and he replied that it was. I didn't have time to argue as the aircraft was getting very close to the edge of the runway, and we were soon going to be wiping out the runway lights, as we left the runway. The speed had still not reached V2, our safety speed and Vmca, but I decided that was the lesser of two evils and decided to lift it off the ground.

We got airborne just as we left the runway, still swinging slowly towards the dead engine, but as we staggered away, I fed in some bank to port which slowly stopped the swing. With full rudder and both hands on the control wheel I relaxed slightly as we reached V2 and kept climbing slowly, and only then was I able to reach across with my right hand and pull the No.4 HP cock back to the feather position. When the captain realised what he had done, he apologised. This was the same captain who nearly caused an overspeeding prop on a Dak, tuned the wrong aid, and also who wouldn't let me stall the Viscount. Some years later, on the same runway at Manchester a British Midland Viscount doing training rolled over and crashed on take-off, killing the crew. It could have been a similar incident.

The Viscount had an excellent single lever system of engine control, the propeller automatically selecting the pitch angle to suit the load and throttle setting. When the throttles were closed in flight the props would go to flight fine pitch, a relatively high drag position, but when the aircraft was landed, with throttles closed and weight on the undercarriage, the props went into ground fine, virtually zero degrees pitch, and provided excellent braking.

One enjoyable item of base training, which I think was just to show the flexibility of the aircraft, was to fly the approach, with undercarriage down and first stage of flap, level at 1,000ft until the runway threshold disappeared under the nose. The throttles were then closed and full flap selected. With the props now in flight fine pitch, to maintain 120kts the nose had to be pushed down so the aircraft was pointing at the runway threshold. It wasn't quite, but it felt like vertical, and looked impressive from outside. At about 100ft the aircraft was rounded out to land. There was no reason ever to be too high to land in a Viscount. We didn't normally plan to do this with passengers, but I remember one occasion when I was a first officer, landing at the Isle of Man on a nice summer evening and the captain got it all wrong, came in much too high on 09, and closed the throttles at about 500ft. As we pointed at the ground, the flight deck door swung open, and I looked back, up the cabin, at sixty startled faces looking down though the windscreen at the runway.

Line training continued a little more serenely, apart from an occasion when approaching the Isle of Man, with the same captain who frightened me at Manchester, and we had a flap overrun. The Viscount flaps were operated by an electric motor via chain drives. One fault to which they were prone was overrunning up. We had two warning lights, one amber which indicated a 'normal' overrun, and a red light which indicated an extreme overrun, which could possibly cause structural damage. I didn't ever see a red light. Either light tripped and isolated the electrics and then we had to use a manual system to operate the flaps. This was like a huge starting handle which one pilot (guess who – the first officer) carried to the middle of the passenger cabin above the wing, opened a hatch in the floor, and inserted the handle to wind the flaps out of the red or amber light zone. Very embarrassing with a full load of passengers. With a red light he would wind until the light went out and then a flapless landing would be made so the airframe could be checked. If it was an amber light, when it went out he could wind down flap as required. The only time it happened when I was a captain, I just asked the co-pilot to wind take off flap down and we left it like that to land. When it occurred on my line training (a 'normal' overrun) I wasn't going down the cabin, and I didn't fancy my captain doing it, so, as we were landing at the Isle of Man, we diverted to Liverpool and landed flapless, as the island runway was too short.

The long six sector day which we were doing for my line training was relieved by a lunch break in London. This was pleasant enough, but when we got airborne from Heathrow each day after lunch, my favourite training captain promptly fell asleep in the right hand seat. It was a welcome relief and just meant I had to shake him awake before landing.

During some more line training with another captain, George Keeble, our deputy chief pilot, I did something particularly stupid. We had departed Liverpool for Heathrow, cleared to FL130 (13,000ft) as usual. As I neared the top of the climb and eased the aircraft to level off, I was just about to report level to air traffic when I realised with horror I had climbed to FL140. I quickly eased the power back and gently descended to the correct level. George didn't even notice as he was writing something in his notes, probably an adverse report about me! I think there is always the chance of this sort of thing happening when two captains fly together. We should have carried a first officer to keep an eye on us. Later, on the One Eleven, there was a standard call of 'one to go' as the flight level before the cleared level was passed. The rest of the line training went smoothly and on the April 6th 1964 I did my first flight in command. I had progressed from being frightened by captains to being able to do it for myself.

Being captain, although I had plenty of P1 time in the Ansons and Rapides, required a subtle change of attitude. I noticed this on my first flight as captain, when as we settled in our seats in the cockpit, I paused for a moment and then realised the first officer had also paused. He was waiting for an indication from me, to tell him what I wanted done next. I had also paused in the same way, waiting for the same prompt, not yet appreciating that now we would go at my speed. Previously the cockpit tempo was decided by my captain, some were always in a hurry, others were more relaxed, and some wanted to talk about their gardens before they got round to the job in hand. Now I decided how the operation proceeded and I definitely preferred it that way. It was a couple of months before the next moment of truth occurred.

We were doing the first Isle of Man flight of the day and when we checked the Ronaldsway weather found that sea fog had reduced visibility to less than 100 metres, with no sig. forecast. I'd given the fuel required and burn off (fuel used in flight) figures to traffic, via ops, and could see the fuel bowser at the aircraft, and the girls were walking out to prepare their part of the job. I realised that the wheels of the organisation were turning slowly until at departure time the aircraft, full of passengers, would be ready to go. However it wasn't going anywhere because of the weather, and the only person who decided that was me. I went to ops and told them to put a weather delay on the flight. From that point on I was quite clear and happy that my aircraft did what I decided. Ah, the loneliness of command!

A few years later, I discovered one advantage of being a captain. As sometimes happens, family spending was regularly just a little more than I was earning. When it reached the point that our bank account was still overdrawn when my pay had gone in, I had a letter (not for the first time) from the manager requesting I visit him 'to discuss my account'. This was the routine at the time, and I called to see him for the compulsory chat about my 'prospects'. During the discussion, I told him that I was hoping to move type shortly and the captain's salary on the 1-11 would mean a substantial pay increase. At this point he was surprised to hear that I was a captain. He knew I had moved to the Viscount, but hadn't heard about my promotion, and now congratulated me, especially, he said, in view of my age. His attitude was now quite different and he told me he would increase my overdraft facility immediately. A few weeks later, I requested a new cheque book, and when it arrived I noticed that the account name had changed from 'Mr & Mrs' to 'Capt & Mrs'! I wasn't too pleased as I didn't want this, but decided that, rather than upsetting my bank manager, I would have to live with it.

For the next six years I operated the Viscount at Liverpool. It was a small base and we, the pilots, knew everybody, ops and traffic staff, cabin crew, engineers, loaders and fuelers, which made for a very happy and efficient operation. Our base at Isle of Man was smaller, but just as friendly and efficient. Cardiff and Bristol had Cambrian staff of course, but elsewhere BEA did our handling, apart from Aer Lingus in Eire. My school chum Bernie, after a few years with Starways as a flight engineer flying all over the world in their DC4s, including some exciting operations in the Congo, had joined me at Cambrian in Liverpool as an engineer, and Cliff was also now a Viscount captain with Starways.

I enjoyed operating through Heathrow as we did frequently, where we were handled by BEA, but we didn't get to know as many people as well as we did at our bases. Flying into Heathrow was always a pleasure, even if delayed at times, as air traffic was so slick and efficient. All the runways had ILS, but the GCA (ground controlled approach radar) was still in operation, and the controllers would often ask if we would do one, mainly for their own practise. This could be interesting, when, if you were watching the ILS, which appeared almost spot on, they would be advising that you were '30ft left of centreline', or '20ft below the glideslope'.

We were kept busy, initially being a small base, often being called out on a day off, the company preferring to do that rather than the expense of sending a pilot from Cardiff. I averaged 600/650 hours a year for few years, which is quite a lot for short haul. One year I only managed 61 days off. Flying settled into an almost boring routine, which of course is exactly how airline flying should be. I said almost, because for me flying could never be boring, I was now doing what I had always wanted to do, and often reminded myself just how lucky I was.

Soon I had a real three engine ferry, when we had problems in the Isle of man with a prop below stop light which couldn't be sorted there and it was decided to take the aircraft to Speke to be fixed. Three engine ferry take off was interesting. We didn't carry passengers of course, so were always light, usually well below the maximum three engine take-off weight figure for the runway. We had this figure calculated for all runways. As we had to cater for the failure of one of the three good engines on take-off, the procedure was to keep the aircraft on the ground until two engine Vmca (minimum control speed in the air) was reached. So on line up, the two symmetric engines were opened up to full power, brakes released, and the third asymmetric engine fed in slowly so that directional control with rudder and nosewheel steering could be maintained.

With full power on all three engines, the aircraft was held on the runway until two engine Vmca of 127kts was reached. The aircraft, at a low weight, would be trying its best to fly beyond 100kts, and it always felt most uncomfortable. On one occasion one of our Viscounts was doing some training at Belfast and an air traffic controller approached me later to ask about the take offs. He told me he had watched the aircraft with binoculars, and was astonished to see that for the last part of the take-off run the mainwheels were clear of the ground, while the nosewheel was still firmly on. I explained the take-off technique to him. It's no wonder it felt uncomfortable!

As flying with different captains was an interesting part of being a first officer, so was flying with different first officers. At a base like Liverpool, we flew with our co-pilots regularly. Although we had standard operating procedures, they were not as rigid as they were to become, so people often had different ways of doing things. Flying with people regularly meant that you got to know them well (and they you) which usually led to an efficient and safe operation. Sometimes I would fly with co-pilots from Cardiff, which was interesting. There was a little rivalry between bases, and this led to occasional differences of the 'Oh we don't do that at Cardiff' kind. Most people were flexible and it didn't usually cause a problem. I remember one first officer who came to Liverpool for a few days, and I flew with him several times. I had heard rumours about him, so was prepared. He was an ex RAF wing commander, allegedly experienced, but he had some difficulty coming to terms with the discipline of airline operation. On the first day I flew with him I had to keep reminding him to fly at a constant height and on the airway centre line.

The next day we were doing an evening Belfast. It was a beautiful day, and I thought I would let the wingco do the first leg and just leave him to get on with it and see how he did. We passed Wallasey climbing and eventually levelled at our cleared FL140. By this time he had wandered off the airway to the north, but I kept quiet. As we were so far off the airway, we were effectively flying VFR so I didn't interrupt when our cruise level varied by plus or minus 1,000ft.

Instead of flying over the southern tip, on the airway, we actually passed well north of the island, at least 30nm off track. We could see Aldergrove from about 40 miles away, and descended to land without ever regaining the airway. I was prepared for some comment from air traffic en route, no transponder, but they didn't say a word. They were fairly easy going in those days. The wingco could fly OK, but would not, or could not, knuckle down to the rigid requirements of flying airways. He left the company soon afterwards.

Another first officer, Liverpool based, was a really nice bloke, but had a tendency to fixate on particular parts of his duties, to the exclusion of others. One thing he would do regardless, was 'get the weather'. On a Liverpool to London sector as soon as we levelled in the very short cruise, he would say, "I'll get the weather", select Volmet frequency on our second VHF set, and spend the next five minutes listening to the recording to get the latest Heathrow and Gatwick weather. I'd try to explain that we'd checked the weather before we left, we'd be there in twenty minutes, when they would tell us what it was, and it was a nice day anyway. To no avail, Tom always insisted on getting the weather. Normally this wasn't a problem and it gave him something to do, but on one occasion it was.

We were doing the late evening Heathrow to Liverpool service, and at the time, we operated through Hawarden, Chester. Both airfields were forecasting fog, and I was anxious to get through Hawarden to Liverpool as quickly as possible. As we approached at Hawarden I knew Liverpool was getting close to our RVR limit, and Hawarden was also experiencing patchy fog. On the approach the RVR was above our limit, at our decision height we could see the lights and I told the tower we were visual. As the controller pushed his transmit button to reply, he paused and I heard a voice in the background saying,

"The RVR is 100 metres, do you want to tell him?"

The tower controller said to us, "You're cleared to land, the RVR is 100 metres".

We landed without a problem although our RVR limit was 600m, and the low visibility was just a patch of fog at the end of the runway. I decided that the approach ban didn't apply as the approach was over at decision height, and I was then in the landing phase. I later sent a letter to the chief pilot in case, but didn't hear any more about it. I was now concerned about getting to Speke before the fog pushed visibility below our limits, so as soon as the few Chester passengers were off we restarted the port engines and taxied out. I explained to Tom that I would put Liverpool Approach on VHF box 2 so, as soon as we were airborne, I could switch straight over and call radar for a quick approach on to runway 08. We were airborne quickly enough and I bid Hawarden goodnight and switched to box 2 for Liverpool radar. I called them and was given an intercept heading for the approach. I was just about to ask for the latest RVR when I heard the Volmet chanting the latest actuals for the northern airfields. Tom had changed frequency to 'get the weather'. I quickly changed back to Liverpool and kept my hand over the selector until I saw the lights of 08. Tom retired soon after.

A first officer joined us from Starways, John Morton, an Australian. He enjoyed taking the micky, when my landing wasn't quite as perfect as I intended.

"It's no good, Cedric, if you're going to be good, you've got to be good all the time" he'd comment in his Aussie drawl. I enjoyed flying with him, but he left us after a while to return down under and assume control of his family business. He wouldn't tell me what the business was, but the rumour was that it was a factory making lavatory seats.

About this time, three first officers came from Silver City at Blackpool, Dave Beard, Ray Atkinson and Dave Vernon. They had joined Silver City at the same time as I started with Cambrian and, in fact, I may well have been with them if their chief pilot had responded quicker than Geoff Perrott. Shortly afterwards Silver City was absorbed into British United airways. For me it had been just another lucky career move.

Several first officers joined us from BEA. They had been trained at the recently established College of Air training at Hamble, set up by BOAC and BEA to provide them with new pilots. This group had got as far as base training on the Vanguard with BEA, but had fallen foul of a training captain, who obviously had an axe to grind with the company, and he had refused to pass them. One of BEA's senior pilots was very friendly with our chief pilot, Geoff Perrot, and organised their transfer to Cambrian. They started with us and were all excellent co-pilots and eventually captains. Geoff definitely got the best of that deal, as, in due course, they probably did.

This was the period at Liverpool when there were effectively two airfields, north and south. This situation had been created when the excellent new 27/09 runway, with ILS on 27, was built to the south of Speke Hall. The original terminal was still in use on the north airfield. Whenever we could, we used the old main runway 26/08 on the north field, for convenience. In poor weather however we often had to land on the ILS runway and accept the long taxy in. It did occasionally cause problems. I remember one night coming back from London, when the visibility (RVR) on 27 was below our Cat 1 limit of 600m. However I heard a light aircraft was doing visual training circuits on 26 on the north field, which was relatively clear of fog. I asked for a runway report for 26 or 08 and was told that, due to staffing limitations, it wasn't available. They were still using the fireman counting runway lights system. After a few more urgent requests, the controller brought the relevant staff to the north airfield, and after about ten minutes I was given a runway visibility report and was able to land.

I had a significant guardian angel incident one evening flying from Liverpool to Belfast. We were cruising at FL120 between Wallasey and Spanish Head, the VOR beacon at the southern end of the Isle of Man. I heard a British United BAC One Eleven call passing Wallasey bound for Belfast at FL 240. This flight often coincided with ours on the airway Red 3. It was dark and we were in cloud. When we were about 25 miles from the island, the One Eleven called requesting descent. He was almost twice as fast as we were, and his ETA for the island was a few minutes before ours. He was given descent clearance, which was to descend to FL60 to Belfast, to cross Spanish Head above FL140, this restriction obviously was to keep him clear of us. I listened as he read the clearance back, but he read the restriction as 'to cross Spanish Head 'below' FL 140'. He also said he was leaving FL240 in descent. I reckoned he would pass us about fifteen miles before Spanish Head, and went cold as I realised he was now descending through our level. I immediately called air traffic to say I thought the One Eleven had got his clearance wrong, and there were then a couple of minutes of futile conversation between them, with the controller obviously thinking the One Eleven understood, and the One Eleven also convinced he understood correctly, but didn't. I reckoned he thought we had passed the island, and he had to be through our level before he passed it. Suddenly it was all over when he called to say he was passing Spanish Head and going through FL100. We were twelve miles from Spanish Head at FL120 and he had gone through our level, and I will never know how close he was. But he missed us and I was too exasperated to argue about it further. Dyslexia rules.

The easy routine continued with just occasional diversions due to weather. One night on the Belfast newspapers we had done the Liverpool Belfast bit and after our hot meal on the ground, (won with some difficulty after the early days of starving through the night), we set off on the return to Speke. John Barton, from Cardiff, was in the first aircraft and I was about ten minutes behind. We had some freight on board and a normal fuel to cover the flight with a diversion to Prestwick if required. The weather forecast had nothing in it to concern us. Passing the Isle of Man, Manchester control called us, unusually, to advise that both Liverpool and Manchester were experiencing rapidly reducing visibility in fog. Checking on Volmet we realised that Birmingham, Heathrow, Gatwick, and Leeds were all having the same deterioration, all quite un-forecast. Prestwick, as ever, was not a problem. As we arrived at Speke the RVR was just above our limits but trending lower, and the vertical visibility was below 100ft. John, in the lead aircraft, had decided to have a go but listening to him, and realising that I would be at least fifteen minutes later, I decided to go straight to Manchester, which was also getting close to our limits. We overflew Speke, and went to Ringway and the ILS on 24. The RVR was just above limits, vertical visibility also less than 100ft, and, after descending just a little below our decision height, 170ft Cat 1, we saw the lights and landed. We were already eating into our Prestwick diversion fuel. After we parked, we stayed in the cockpit to listen to John, now ten minutes behind us, also diverting from Speke, making his approach, having been airborne now for half an hour longer than we had been. On his first attempt, seeing nothing at decision height, he went around. On the second approach, as he told me later, he realised that Prestwick was no longer an option, and decided he had to land on this one. So, stretching his decision height even more than I had done, he landed off the second approach with some relief. This experience of a totally unforecast weather deterioration affected my decision making for the rest of my career, and I decided I would never again be caught out with less fuel than I considered necessary, regardless of the forecast.

The Viscounts were reliable, and in seven years I didn't have one airborne engine failure. I did have one engine problem however, in April 66. We were doing a four sector day to Isle of Man and Ringway. On the first flight to the island, we noticed an odd buzzing vibration which seemed to be in the roof area of the flight deck. We reported it on landing and the engineers had a good look around inside and out, but couldn't find anything wrong. On the next two legs to Ringway and back, the noise was still there and seemed to be getting slightly worse. As we had a couple of hours on the ground this time at the island, the engineers promised to do a further investigation. Shortly after, one of them came and asked me to come and have a look at the aircraft. They had opened all the cowlings on the four engines, and on one engine had discovered several faults. These faults, such as a cracked mounting of a fuel pump, were indications of vibration caused by serious imbalance. The engineers' technical books told them that the faults they had found indicated that at least one turbine blade had been damaged or lost causing imbalance and vibration. The airframe vibration we had heard was caused by the out of balance engine. That meant another three engine ferry back to Speke for an engine change.

The vagaries of the weather were clearly shown one night in May when our newspaper flights were cancelled because of snow. We weren't allowed leave during the summer in those days, May was the last month of the leave period. I had two weeks leave rostered for the end of the month, and for our family holiday had hired a motor cruiser on the Norfolk Broads. This was before I was a boat owner, and I was trying to convince my wife and kids that this was what they wanted to do. The week before our holiday, I was on five nights of

Belfast newspaper flights, which gave me extra days off. On the Wednesday night when I reported for duty it was starting to snow. A small but vigorous depression had formed over Iceland and travelled in the northerly airflow across the UK. Within the hour it was snowing heavily, and the airfield was covered by about 4 to 5 inches. When the two Viscounts were ready, the runway conditions precluded take-off. By 3 o'clock in the morning the snow had stopped and was beginning to thaw. Our take-off limit for slush was 12mm (half an inch), and the dry snow limit was 50mm (2 inches). There wasn't any snow clearance available immediately, I think the airfield had put away their equipment assuming it wouldn't be needed. At about 3.30am one of the air traffic controllers offered to take me out to the runway to assess our chances. We drove out to 09 and he put his foot hard down as we reached the centre of the runway. There must have been about 4 inches of melting slush, and the Hillman Husky wouldn't go beyond 30mph at full throttle, and created an impressive spray of slush which quickly covered the vehicle. I decided we were going nowhere in the Viscount for some time. We were stood down about 6.30am, I don't remember what happened to the newspapers that night. However, the next week we enjoyed warm and sunny weather sailing on the Norfolk Broads.

During 1965 Reg Gates, our old boss at Feds, who still had two Rapides for his own use, decided to trade them in for a more modern aeroplane. Reg had flown the Rapides himself, but not frequently enough, and, after the odd fright, decided he'd leave it to us. Cliff had done some occasional flying with him in the Rapides. So Reg, Cliff and I flew to Panshangar, a grass airfield north of London, in the Rapide G-ANZP. Here we flew in G-ARGW an Aero Commander 500, a twin engined six seater. This was a delightful aeroplane, and Reg began negotiations to buy it. A few weeks later I flew ZP to Panshangar, and Barney Potts, a Starways pilot, friend of Cliff's, flew Reg's other Rapide G-AKJS alongside. We all flew home in GW. Over the next few years Cliff and I flew in the Aero Commander with Reg whenever he required. It was usually to Dublin, made a nice change from the Viscount and I could treat my wife to lunch in the Irish capital.

It was often windy in the island, which added interest. The Viscount was capable but hard work in gusty conditions with its manual controls. One winter night I had delayed the flight from Speke because the wind was southerly, at 60/70kts. At first the cloudbase was too low to allow us to slide off the 27 ILS onto the 22 approach, but eventually, at about 2030 it was high enough for us to try. We approached on the 27 ILS bouncing all over the place in the wind, and broke cloud at about 700ft which allowed us to slide across, helped by the wind, onto the 22 approach. The turbulence wasn't too bad, as the wind, now hurricane force, was straight off the sea. The wind checks on final were all in the upper sixties, and, even though I added a margin to our normal approach speed, our ground speed was so low that it felt like we were flying a light aircraft. As we touched down the controller called the wind speed as 76kts. We taxied carefully in, backing up the good control locks of the Viscount with our hands and feet. The engineers had arranged to park us in the lee of the control tower, hopefully to reduce the wind effect.

However one problem we didn't anticipate was that when we stopped the engines, as the props were in ground fine pitch, they simply kept rotating, quite fast. The resourceful engineers solved this by one of them putting two gloved hands on the large spinners, while being held clear of the prop by a couple of his mates, gradually slowing the prop. Once stopped they lashed them together with ropes to stop them rotating again. They then needed a couple of men on the front door to hold it open while the passengers disembarked. The door had a normal opening limit of 50kts. That was it until we came to start up again. The Dart engine starter could not be engaged if the engine was rotating. The engineer in charge had a torch with red and green covers, so we arranged the start routine whereby the engineer holding the prop would release it just as the chargehand changed his torch from red to green. At the same instant the first officer would engage the starter. It worked, we started the engines and flew back to Speke where the wind was only about 45kts.

On another windy day in the island, I overflew on the morning service, and went straight to Belfast, as the wind was northerly up to 60kts. On the way back in the afternoon I didn't expect to land, but as we approached the island, it was a nice sunny day, and the wind had backed a little to north westerly, still up to 58kts, probably beyond our 30kt crosswind component limit, but I decided to have a look. I thought I would fly the approach down to the runway and see how controllable the aircraft was as I took the drift off on landing. If I didn't feel happy I would go around and divert to Speke. We made our approach and as I rounded out over the runway and kicked off the considerable drift, I thought it felt good. The aircraft straightened easily onto the runway centreline and I touched down thinking the worst was over. It wasn't. As ground fine pitch came in and the aircraft started to decelerate, it began to drift sideways across the runway with the wind. I had the nose held firmly down with the control column fully forward and steering with rudder and nosewheel, but it was still drifting to port. As we approached the runway edge I decided I had to steer into wind to prevent it leaving the runway. This meant we were now skidding sideways, increasingly so the more I steered into wind. I could feel the strain on the tyres and just hoped they would stand up to it and not burst. They survived, we slowed down and taxied in. As the passengers left the aircraft, one of our regulars, whose wife was ex-cabin crew, smiled at me and said,

"That was interesting, wasn't it".

I returned the smile and agreed with him.

Without the use of a simulator, all training, that is six monthly handling checks and annual instrument rating, was done on the aircraft. At the time it was usual, and in fact encouraged, to practice various emergencies when possible, such as when flying an empty aeroplane. In early 1966 Cambrian had negotiated a contract to carry newspapers to Belfast every night, and to Isle of Man each morning. Carrying freight gave more opportunities to do practice emergencies, and I took advantage of this. In due course, after a number of accidents, the airline industry found that this sort of flying was quite dangerous and it was discouraged, and when simulators became more widespread, it stopped altogether. I discovered myself that it didn't always go to plan. On one occasion, going to Belfast with a full load of newspapers, I had asked the first officer to stop No.4 just after V1, which he did, and once we were climbing away at about 2000ft I told him to unfeather it. When he tried the drill we discovered that the feathering pump had failed. This was required to move the blades out of the feathered position, and then the prop would rotate the engine and we could do a normal windmilling start (without the starter). This was a bit embarrassing and I didn't really want to return to Speke, so I decided to carry on, on three engines. If required, in extremis, we could have used the starter, provided the engine wasn't rotating, but this wasn't normal airborne procedure. I didn't tell air traffic at this point, and when passing the Isle of Man I called BEA on the company frequency at Belfast to advise the engineers of the problem. I was surprised when I called Belfast Approach, and he immediately advised me that he understood we had a failed engine. I reckoned somebody had been listening to our private conversation. On the ground, the engineers unfeathered the prop manually, but didn't have a replacement pump. We flew home without it, knowing that the prop, if required, would autofeather happily, the pump just being used to be sure the blades were on the stops.

On another occasion flying with a first officer from Cardiff, I briefed him as before to stop No.4 at V1, but he did exactly as my training captain had done, and just stopped the engine without feathering it. I went through the struggling routine as before, but managed to get him to realise what had happened and he moved the HP cock to feather as we staggered away. I think that was the last time I asked somebody to stop an engine for me.

We could volunteer to do five Belfast newspaper flights, some of them combined with the early morning Isle of Man newspapers, instead of the normal rostered three, and I preferred this as doing the five night flights gave us three days off before and four days off after, which meant decent breaks. I was quite happy operating five nights, usually in bed by 0600, or 1000 if doing the two flights. But this sort of flying obviously upsets the circadian rhythm, as I discovered. One night we were landing on 27 at Speke, when it was blowing up to 45kts from the northwest and snowing. We flew down the ILS, working hard at the controls as usual with the Viscount in these conditions, and broke cloud at about 500ft. As I continued towards the runway, in heavy snow, I felt very odd. I felt as though I was perched above and behind my seat and actually watching myself flying the aircraft. I felt quite detached from what was happening. At about 200ft I decided that I felt so strange that I wasn't going to attempt the crosswind landing in the heavy snow, and opened up to go around. As we flew over the river we emerged from the snow shower and I then flew a visual circuit in the clear on to runway 35, nearer to the wind direction, and now feeling quite normal. Subsequently I read that this detached feeling is an indication of fatigue. I never experienced it again, but was always on my guard whenever conditions were similar.

Operating in the early hours could create other problems of course. I remember one occasion when we had started the engines at

Speke and were cleared by our engineer outside to taxy away. We were on a slight downhill slope, and didn't usually need much power to move. However as I pushed the throttles open slightly there was no inclination for the aircraft to move. I checked the brakes were off and waved to the engineer, already having my suspicions, pointing down at the wheels, but he waved me positively away, giving me lots of 'thumbs up' signals. I increased the power gradually, and when we had a fair amount on, the aircraft, with just a little jolt, climbed over the chocks which had been left under the mainwheels, and we taxied away.

Another time when we arrived at Belfast the engineers advised me that one of the port twin mainwheels was flat. I said that we hadn't noticed anything untoward on the way over, so they rang Liverpool to tell the engineers. They checked the tarmac where we started, and found a scuff mark at the point where we had made our first turn. The wheel had obviously been flat before we started. Difficult to tell if you just kick it! The other wheel had taken all the weight for the take-off and landing. The Belfast engineers changed both wheels, which was normal practice.

Once when I was doing a week of newspapers, we carried a journalist from a local paper. He was going to write an article about the 'flying newspaper boys'. He and a photographer followed us around as we did our pre-flight duties, then the photographer went home and the journalist flew with us to Belfast. He chatted away as we were having our meal in the crewroom, making notes all the time. He asked if I took my family on holiday by air (at the time we favoured farm holidays, the canals or Norfolk Broads) and without thinking, I replied flippantly,

"Oh No, much too dangerous".

When the article appeared in print, he, of course, quoted me verbatim. My flight manager wasn't impressed with my 'lacking a sense of humour' explanation. I was very careful with journalists after that.

My guardian angel was in full control in July 1965. One lovely summer evening I did the service through the Isle of Man to Belfast and back to Liverpool in Viscount G-AMOL. Next day was different, it was cloudy with rain and drizzle. Viscount OL flew a freight service to the island in the morning, and was returning to Speke late afternoon, when, at about 200ft on short final to runway 26, it rolled over on to its back and crashed into a factory at the edge of the airfield, killing the two pilots and two women in the factory. It was a shock to everybody in the company. At the time I was the BALPA (British Airline Pilots Association) pilots' local council chairman, and as soon as I heard about the accident I went to Speke. Another captain, Howard Benton, also a pilots' representative, and I went to the crash site, but there was little to see as the aircraft had caught fire and there was hardly anything recognisable as part of a Viscount. When the fireman working in the wreckage found and began to recover a body, we decided to leave. Next morning Howard and I were at Speke, to do what we could. I was not impressed when one of the official investigators arrived, obviously in a foul mood, and told everybody that as this was the third independent airline crash in twelve months, there would have to be a full public inquiry (there wasn't). I thought he was jumping to conclusions rather prematurely.

There was little we could do, but Geoff Perrott had asked Bob Ross, who was the senior pilot at Liverpool, to visit the families of the two women killed in the factory, to offer condolences. Bob wasn't too happy about this, so I offered to go with him to give some moral support. It wasn't very pleasant, but had to be done. We met the husband of the younger woman, who, although very upset, did talk freely to us and made our task easier. He showed us a postcard with a photograph of a Cambrian Viscount, in fact G-AMOL. He asked us if that was the aircraft which crashed, and we confirmed that it was. He then told us that it was the same aircraft in which he and his wife had flown to the Isle of Man the previous year on their honeymoon. Truth is often stranger than fiction. When we visited the family and friends of the other lady, (she wasn't married), nobody would speak to us. It was a very difficult ten minutes or so before we could politely make our excuses and leave. I also went with Bob to the digs of the two pilots, to collect their belongings and to make sure that there was nothing that would embarrass or upset their families (there wasn't). Bob told me that this was standard RAF practice in a similar situation.

In due course the accident report was published, without reaching any conclusion as to the cause. It said that flap asymmetry was a possibility, but there was no mechanical evidence. Speed was good, the control column was hard over against the turn, and the flaps had been selected up. A BEA Viscount G-ALWE had crashed at Ringway in the fifties due to flap asymmetry, but that was proved with clear evidence and additionally the flap failure had caused the aileron lock to engage, and modifications had cured both defects, making a similar accident very unlikely. I thought it was a structural failure of some sort but as the fire had been fierce there was little of the airframe left to show it. There were several Viscount crashes caused by structural failure, in extreme turbulence, or overstressing for another reason, and indeed some time later, one of ours had a bent fuselage after a heavy landing and was written off. We were all asked if we had any thoughts about it, and I reported that OL had one idiosyncrasy, which was that as you rounded out on landing it would swing slightly to starboard. We used to joke that it was auto correction for a port crosswind. It was a subjective comment and couldn't really help, but it could possibly have been an indication of a structural weakness.

The loss of a Viscount left us short of an aircraft for the summer schedules, so the company chartered a DC4 from Aer Turas of Dublin, which then operated for us on the Irish Sea routes over a period of several weeks. I managed a trip in this aircraft just once when I was positioning back from the Isle of Man. I sat on the jump seat in the cockpit, and was impressed when the captain, an elderly American pilot (probably a contemporary of Ernest Gann) who had obviously been flying the DC4 for many years, flew the aircraft round the circuit at Speke like a Tiger Moth, sliding on to the 26 approach at about 200ft. I was very pleased to have experienced this legendary aircraft.

During the early sixties, the approach ban had been introduced. This was an RVR (runway visual range) minimum reading, below which we could not attempt to land. In the fifties the RVR was calculated with the help of a fireman who sat at the end of the runway and reported how many runway lights he could see. By mid-late sixties, tranmissometers had taken over. These were two units at the side of the runway which transmitted energy (laser) to each other and calculated the visibility. They were much more accurate than the firemen. All our approaches in the Viscount 700 were Category 1, flying the aircraft manually, and nowadays these are standard at 600m minimum RVR. At the time however, the minima were calculated according to a formula which used the quality of the approach and runway lighting to arrive at the approach minima. So during this time, the runway minima, which had started around

600m (initially 600yards), were revised and ended up as low as 350m at airfields with good lighting, such as Heathrow and Liverpool. I remember some interesting landings during this time, as 350m is quite a low visibility for a manual approach in a Viscount, even though the decision height remained at the Cat 1 limit of 170ft. In fact the 350m RVR limit was mentioned as a contributory factor when a BEA Vanguard crashed on the runway in fog at Heathrow. Soon after the Cat 1 minimum was revised and set at a minimum of 600m.

As previously mentioned the Viscounts had Decca Navigator with a flight log. I always liked this system, which pre-empted GPS pictorial navigation by about fifty years but maybe with not the same accuracy and reliability. It was a good back up to VOR and NDB (our Viscounts didn't have DME), but occasionally the flight log pointer would be observed to be tramping off across country, and then had to be manually restored to our approximate position when it would hopefully proceed correctly again. Accordingly it was not approved as an approach aid.

I managed to confirm this for myself when I was doing a week of five night newspapers to Belfast. At the time Liverpool only had one air traffic controller on duty overnight, which meant that he couldn't use the approach radar, as he was required to be the tower operator. The weather was settled anticyclonic gloom with a fresh easterly breeze. This meant landing on 08, the old airfield by the terminal, or 09 the new runway. Each of these runways required a radar approach as the cloudbase was about 800ft. The only official option in the conditions without radar was to do a procedural ILS (no radar) on 27 to break cloud and then a visual circuit below cloud to land on 08. This is what we did the first night, which added almost fifteen minutes to the flight, which at three o'clock in the morning wasn't our preferred choice. The next night, similar conditions, I told the first officer I would give him a Decca approach from Wallasey. We advised the controller we would make our own approach and left Wallasey descending from 2,500ft to 1,500ft heading for a six mile final on 08, just as we would have done on a radar talk down. The flight log pen moved across the chart in little spidery jerks as it always did. The chart even had the approach centre line with marks at each mile from touchdown. At five miles I told the F/O to start his descent and continued heading instructions and height checks at the mile points. We broke cloud at about 700ft over the Mersey and there in front of us was the runway. We were pleased with our Decca approach, and, as the weather was the same all week, the next two nights we did the same 'monitored' approach successfully. By the last night I was fairly relaxed about it and started the talk down from Wallasey as before. This time the flight log didn't twitch about as it usually did, but was quite steady and followed our track with apparent confidence, which should have triggered suspicion. I continued the approach until, as before, we broke cloud at about 700ft over the blackness of the river. This time, however, I couldn't see the runway, although the lights of the east bank were quite visible. We were obviously over the river so I told the F/O to continue descent while I tried to work out where we were. At about 300ft and theoretically a mile from the runway, I switched the landing lights on. Ahead I immediately recognised Otterspool promenade, which put us just over two miles north of the runway centreline. I called for the go around and we then did an ILS on 27 and, as the wind was under twelve knots, a downwind landing on the long runway. I hoped we hadn't disturbed too many courting couples in their cars on the prom, but my confidence in Decca was slightly dented.

Another incident about this time occurred when an ATCO (air traffic control officer) at Speke, who, due to illness, had stopped controlling and had been given a job in the landings office, where we filed our flight plans. He used to check the plans with meticulous, but pedantic, care, which inevitably upset some of our pilots. The local pilots understood the situation, and diplomatically bit their tongues. I was quite surprised when he informed me one day that he had filed a form 939 with the Ministry reporting me for landing 'below limits'. When I asked him to explain, he told me that I had landed on runway 08 on a day when the RVR was 700 metres and our minimum was 800 metres. This was at a time when, due to the RVR calculation previously mentioned, the runway limits had been changed. I told him that on the day in question our limit for 08 was 600 metres, so it was quite legal to land, but he wasn't happy about this, saying that he should have been advised. I thought no more about it, until, a few months later, he told me he had had to file another 939 about me, once again for landing below limits. Again I asked him to explain, and he told me I had landed on the ILS runway 27 when the met actual was giving the cloud as 8 oktas at 100ft. Our minima for the approach gave a decision height of 170ft. I tried to explain that when the met actual gave a cloudbase of 100ft, it was often possible that at 200ft the pilot would see the lights and be able to land, and in fact the 8 oktas at 100ft was not an approach ban. My explanation didn't convince him, and he said he would file his report anyway. At this point I decided that arguing was pointless, and decided to write to the relevant department of the Ministry to complain about being reported twice for landing below limits, when I clearly had not. I did this, and soon after had a phone call from Geoff Perrott asking what I was doing stirring things up at the Ministry! Having explained to Geoff, shortly afterwards I received a letter from the Ministry, assuring me that there was no problem, and that was the last I heard of it.

One day I brought some interesting passengers back from the Island. We had positioned to the Island to collect some retired sea captains and their wives who had chartered the St. Trillo, a small passenger ship which operated day cruises between Liverpool and Llandudno, on the North Wales coast. Their charter was a day trip from Llandudno and back in the evening. However an increasingly strong northerly wind meant that the ship couldn't berth on the pier at Llandudno and they had diverted to Douglas in the Isle of Man. We picked them all up in the island and flew them back to Speke, where coaches were waiting to take them home. I was in the cockpit doorway when one of the old mariners came to me as he was disembarking, and said,

"Captain, thank you for a pleasant flight. I didn't feel you steering once." I thought that was a nice compliment.

Late '68 we began to get rumours of new aircraft, and early in '69 it was confirmed that we were buying four BAC 1-11 400s from Autair. Autair, later renamed Court Line, had bought the aircraft as a stop gap while waiting for new 1-11 500s ordered from BAC. Three were delivered to Cambrian for the 1970 season and the other for 1971. Cambrian had started doing inclusive tours (ITs) with the Viscounts from Cardiff and Bristol to the Mediterranean for Hourmont Travel, a local agency. It was intended to expand this business with the 1-11s, bringing Liverpool into the operation, and also use them on the scheduled services. Two captains, Ken Wakefield and George Keeble were seconded to fly with Autair for the '69 summer season to gain experience on the aircraft, so they could do the training of our crews. My seniority put me in line for moving to the 1-11 when it arrived, but later that summer Geoff Perrott approached me to ask if I would consider staying on the Viscount as Flight Manager of the fleet. I told him I'd think about it, but almost immediately decided I would rather go on to the new aircraft. Before I could tell Geoff, he contacted me to say that a Cardiff pilot had accepted the position. I guessed I wasn't first choice. No matter, I'd had enough of the Viscount after seven years and was ready for a change.

Just after Christmas '69 several of us from Liverpool drove down to Bournemouth to start four weeks of ground school at the BAC factory. During the course we had factory visits, to see the Court Line 500s and also the BEA 'Super One Elevens'. Despite the order for eighteen 510s, the BAC people were not too impressed with BEA. The 1-11 was designed with a standard cockpit layout for all the variants, allowing pilots to fly all of them without the need to check out on a different type. All the switches in the cockpit were forward for take-off, American style, so on the instrument panel they were up for on, and on the roof panel they were down for on. BEA decided that they wanted all the switches to be up for on, and also wanted the excellent Collins flight director and HSI (horizontal situation indicator) replaced with the Smiths flight system, as in their other aircraft types, Trident and Comet. They also decided that they didn't want the forward door airstair, which retracted into the fuselage, as their other aircraft didn't have them. Unfortunately removing it upset the centre of gravity limits and a lump of concrete had to be installed in its place. Subsequently the BEA 1-11s were such hybrids that pilots flying them couldn't fly any other marks of 1-11 at the same time, as could pilots flying all the other 200s, 300s, 400s, and 500s.

The course was enjoyable and an interesting insight into the air-craft manufacturing industry (them and us), apart from this particular difference of opinion with a customer, and it was clear that the manufacturer considered that they built excellent aircraft which the airlines criticised and didn't really know how to operate. It was a feeling that increased when we sampled our lunch arrangements. We were shown to a bare room with scrubbed wooden tables, a bit like being back at school. There was a minimal choice of menu. On the first day, one of our pilots accidentally wandered into the 'pilots' restaurant' nearby, which was very pleasant, with waitress service and tablecloths, only to be redirected to our canteen. When we mentioned this to the manageress who organised our meals (and did treat us rather like schoolchildren), she said,

"Well, when you boys have done the course and are qualified, you'll be able to use the pilots' restaurant whenever you come back here".

Some of our 'boys' were World War 2 veterans. We weren't impressed and after a couple of days organised a lunch allowance from the company and thereafter we went to the local pub. This did make staying awake in the afternoon more difficult. After the airframe course we had a few days with Rolls Royce in Derby doing a course on the Spey engine. This also was enjoyable, but I still noticed a 'them and us' attitude to the airlines. We were all conscious that we were going from four engines to two, and frequently plied our instructors with questions about failures which might leave us with just one engine. They usually dismissed the thought that a Rolls Royce engine could fail. We did our ARB technical exams in Liverpool without problems, and then it was back to flying the Viscount for a few weeks before starting training on the 1-11.

5.   ONE ELEVEN

Late January 1970 I started training on the 1-11, having done the airframe and engine courses. The first stage was over to Dublin, to use the Aer Lingus simulator. An hour or so in a D4 link trainer to be introduced to the Collins FD108 flight system, and then we did twenty hours in the simulator. This was my first experience of a proper simulator with full motion, and it was very enjoyable, even though there was some work going on in the building, and it did take the edge off an ILS approach, when, above the hammering, Paddy shouted across to his mate to pass him a screwdriver. This was the only time we used the simulator in Dublin, as for the next few years we went to Aylesbury where Redifon, the simulator manufacturer, had a 1-11 simulator in a large hangar, on one side of which was a huge three dimensional relief map of an airfield and several miles around. Above this was a camera mounted on a gantry which moved in unison with the simulator and the picture from this was projected onto a screen on the simulator windscreen, giving the pilot a reasonable daylight visual display.

I then started training on the aeroplane. After the Viscount, for which strong arms were required, and with so many window surrounds that it was difficult to see out of, etc., the 1-11 was a delight. Superb visibility from the cockpit, beautifully balanced and relatively light (compared to the Viscount) powered flying controls, two engines down by the tail that most of the time you couldn't hear, etc., etc. Initially, it was odd when moving the throttles to have no noise indication of the power change. You had to use the engine instruments to gauge the power. It soon became second nature. Although the Viscount was a big step up from the Dakota, after seven years of flying it I was ready for a change, and although I was to fly the 1-11 for the next 22 years until I retired, I still really enjoyed flying it then and could happily have flown it for another 22 years. It was that sort of aeroplane. When I started flying the aircraft, I was talking to a neighbour and he asked how the two aircraft compared, and without thinking, I said it was like comparing a tram with a Rolls Royce. That summed it up for me.

My base training, all at Speke which suited me, was with Ken Wakefield, and I really enjoyed it. We started with upper airwork, approach to the stall, or as far as stick push, a comprehensive stall recognition and prevention system resulting from the deep stall accident to an early prototype 1-11. Emergency descent, used after explosive decompression, was great fun, throttles closed, spoilers out, then roll the aircraft on its side and pull back into the dive, at 90º to the airway. No good just pushing the stick forward as all the passengers would hit the roof. So maintaining positive 'G', into the descent at max speed, autopilot and speed lock in. The 1-11 400 would fly up to FL370 (37,000ft) as it had full drop out oxygen for the passengers. At that level it lost a bit of its sparkle, although it would make its VMO of 0.78M. After five days of circuits at Speke, doing all the variations, engine fail on take-off, flapless landings, emergency elevator landings, single engine go-arounds as well as normal take offs and landings, and an instrument rating, totalling nearly 12 hours flying, I was ready for line training. This was completed on scheduled services between Liverpool and Heathrow, with a few Cork and Dublin trips thrown in, and one IT to Palma de Mallorca from Cardiff and back to Bristol, twenty-five sectors, including five in the right hand seat to gain an understanding of the first officer's job.

For a relatively small company, the training was excellent, and certainly not skimped. Before we started on the 1-11, the usual frightener 'hot ship' rumours circulated, 15% failure rate expected for example, but once we started flying most people enjoyed it, and just one or two didn't make the grade. Reg, who joined Cambrian with me, flew Mosquitoes and Spitfires during the war, and told me he wasn't happy not having propellers, but he got used to managing without them until he retired. His feeling emphasised the major difference between the Dakota, Viscount and the 1-11. The slow response of the jet engine and complete lack of slipstream effect. Applying power in the Dakota meant an instant increase in lift due to the airflow over the wings from the engines. This effect also applied to the Viscount, with four engines covering more than half the wing area, even though the engines were prop-jet. In the 1-11 however these benefits were lost, and with the acceleration time from idle to full power of 6 to 8 seconds there was no point in relying on power to rescue a low speed, low power situation. Once this became part of your thinking, it ceased to be a problem.

Line training went well, apart from one copybook blot for me when, in the cruise on a London to Liverpool sector, the training captain, Dennis Paines, pulled the circuit breaker on one of the engine vibration indication gauges. This gauge, which normally had a very low reading and which never varied, was nicely hidden behind the spoiler lever from the captain's seat viewpoint, which, of course, was why he did it. I didn't notice it and he suggested that I improved my instrument scan. A very valid point which I accepted and made sure I did in future. This gauge, while seeming not too important at the time, became a focus of our attention later, which I will describe in due course.

The 1-11 was certainly a step up from the Viscount, cruising at 7 or 8 nm a minute, and you learned quickly that you always had to be ahead of the aeroplane. In 1970, before the fuel crisis, the company's operating policy was to keep time in the air to a minimum, which meant going as fast as possible for most of the time. I remember, on a line training flight into Heathrow, starting to slow down on the approach, and being urged by the training captain to keep the speed up as long as I could, which resulted in my arrival at ten miles on final still doing more than 300kts. At six miles, spoilers out, still about 240kts, I had no chance of getting flaps and wheels down before the runway and had to ask the tower for permission to do a 360° turn to give me more time. They agreed and we landed. Not much chance of getting away with a request like that nowadays. This was before compulsory noise abatement procedures, and speed limit of 250kts below 10,000ft, etc.

Once we settled on the aircraft, it became routine and enjoyable to operate like this. Howard and I had an unofficial contest to do Liverpool to London, or vice versa, in the shortest airborne time. 25 or 26 minutes became the norm, and anything less justified a bit of ribbing. I think I may have claimed the best effort one night when I did it in 22 minutes. We were doing the last Heathrow to Liverpool service and there was a strong southerly airflow. Taking off from 27R we had flaps and undercarriage cleaned up by 500ft and accelerated quickly in the climb to our maximum IAS of 353kts. As we turned on course I asked radar for a direct routing to Lichfield, which was given immediately. We levelled at FL140 for a short cruise where the tailwind was probably 80 to 100kts, then called Manchester radar for a turn before Lichfield direct to Whitegate beacon for Liverpool. The approach was always the key to success, slowing down as late as possible, which usually meant a power off approach with the speed reducing until, with luck, power would be restored at about 200ft to stabilise the approach. Of course it didn't always go to plan, and sometimes we would land with speed just reaching target threshold and the throttles closed. On this occasion we made our 22 minutes airborne, which I don't think Howard ever bettered, 475kts average ground speed, even with the slower bits at the start and finish.

Although we had a noise abatement procedure, it wasn't compulsory anywhere at the time. At Heathrow there were noise monitoring points around the airfield which we could call after take-off to see how many decibels we had recorded. This was the thin end of a wedge, of course, which led to standard compulsory noise abatement procedures everywhere. The 1-11 was a noisy aeroplane, externally, which eventually led to its retirement when it couldn't meet the stage 3 noise requirements of the nineties, without expensive modifications. If the 1-11 had been developed, as the DC9 was, it could have been a world beater.

Once on the line, we settled to a nice mix of scheduled services, London, Cork, Isle of Man, Dublin, Glasgow, and inclusive tour flights from Liverpool to the Mediterranean, the three Balearics, Palma, Menorca and Ibiza, plus Barcelona, Gerona, Valencia, Malaga, Alicante, Corfu, Rome, Genoa, Rimini, Venice etc., etc. We also went to Tenerife, just about the limit for the 1-11. To make Tenerife from Liverpool direct, there had to be no more than 10kts headwind, and a passenger load which allowed us to have full tanks, or we had to make a tech stop to refuel at Faro in Portugal. The first time I did this flight we climbed to 37,000ft, found that there was little or no headwind, and, having full fuel, decided to go direct. This meant using long range cruise speed of 0.72M rather than normal Vmo of 0.78. The cabin crew didn't enjoy this as the aircraft was flying in a nose up attitude, and the bar trolleys had to be pushed uphill and ran away downhill. The forecast for Tenerife was CAVOK (ceiling and visibility OK), and the same for our only alternate, Las Palmas on Gran Canaria, seventy miles away. The flight took about four and a half hours and we landed after a short air traffic delay, eating into our holding fuel, with just minimum fuel remaining. There was no radar, so we had to be able to see conflicting traffic to descend, or remain high and descend in the hold on arrival, which is what we did. We were using the old airfield at Tenerife, Los Rodeos, now called Tenerife North, at 2,000ft on a col between two mountains, the one to the northeast just a bit higher than the airfield, but El Pico to the southwest rises to 12,000ft. The sky was clear as we landed, but looking northwest over the sea there was a solid layer of stratus. We parked, and as I finished filling in the tech. log, still in my seat, I looked up and thought the windows had misted up. They hadn't, but the visibility outside was about 50 yards. After about fifteen minutes, it cleared and we were back in sunshine. Apparently this often happened, as a lump of stratus from the sea to the northwest detached and drifted over the field, but they didn't bother mentioning it on the forecast. I wasn't too happy that I'd arrived with minimum fuel on the basis that both islands were forecast CAVOK. This 'temporary' fog effect was a factor in the worst aviation disaster some years later when two 747s collided on the runway.

Next time I went to Tenerife, we had a full passenger load and couldn't take full tanks, so we flight planned for a refuelling stop in Faro, Portugal. We flew at normal max speed, Vmo, much more comfortable for the cabin crew. The two sectors worked out about four and a half hours and with a twenty minute fuel stop our total elapsed time to Tenerife was almost the same as going direct. It was a more comfortable flight and we had much more fuel on arrival to cope with ATC delays. I didn't bother going direct afterwards, but always managed to do the return trip in one.

One day, I was operating a Liverpool, London, Isle of Man, London, Liverpool schedule. After the first leg to Heathrow, we had a long lunch turn round. I knew the weather in the island was windy, south westerly about 45/55 knots, and checking it when we arrived from Liverpool, found that it was going to be well above our crosswind limit for landing on the main 27 runway. It was almost straight down the short runway 22, but that runway wasn't covered in our Volume 3 of the Ops manual, which gave us landing and takeoff weight figures for all temperatures and winds for all the runways that we used. I knew that this was produced for us by the BEA operations department at Heathrow. I rang the department and explained the situation to them and asked why we didn't have figures for that runway. I was told it was simply that they hadn't been asked to provide them. After a quick check they said that, with the wind, the runway was useable and said they would happily produce some figures within half an hour and bring them to me. I then rang our main base at Cardiff to get the OK to use the short runway. I discovered that all the senior pilots, chief pilot, his deputy, and the 1-11 flight manager, were either on holiday or in America or somewhere, but all quite beyond contact. The duty ops manager didn't have the authority to give me the go ahead, but thought it a good idea. When the BEA ops man brought the new page for the short runway, he explained that there was no problem operating from it with the strong wind, the only caveat being the fact that there was no LCN (load construction number) for the runway. However he said that wasn't a problem for the airline, rather a consideration for the airport as to how many landings they would allow on that runway. I decided to use my initiative and operate. We did, landed and departed on the short runway with no difficulty, to the delight of the Isle of Man staff, who fully expected the flight to be cancelled. However a week or so later, I received a letter from the 1-11 flight manager, although accepting my good intentions, reprimanding me for using that runway without authority, and pointing out that it was not company policy to use runways without an LCN, or glideslope guidance. I suppose you can't win 'em all.

When we started operating the 1-11, the company decided that standard operating procedure on landing would be to use 'normal' reverse thrust. There were three settings for reverse, idle, normal and full. We would select normal reverse on touchdown, with full spoiler and lift dumper, idle at 80kts, and cancel idle by 60kts. Normal reverse equated approximately to a normal climb power (max continuous) setting, ie: quite a lot of power. Twin engined aeroplanes are effectively overpowered, to cater for the engine failure just after V1 case. Losing 50% of power just after V1, means that the remaining engine has to be capable of accelerating the aircraft through VR and V2, taking off and climbing away, meeting all the climb profile requirements. To meet these engine out requirements, a four engined aircraft would only lose 25% of its power. So the 1-11 usually didn't normally require the engines to be at full power on take-off. There were two settings for take-off, normal take-off thrust, which was still less than full power, and reduced thrust, used on most runways where the take-off weight was 2000kgs less than the maximum for that runway, with regard to the ambient conditions. The only time full throttle thrust was used was when an engine failed and the remaining engine would be opened up to full power. This limited power procedure improved engine life and so produced a greater time between overhauls.

So, back to the use of reverse, I think engineering persuaded the company that using normal reverse thrust on all landings would save on wheel braking and reduce costs. I didn't like this routine, as normal reverse was noisy and unpleasant for the passengers, particularly at the rear of the aircraft, and, at an airport like Heathrow and most of our destinations, quite unnecessary.

As mentioned, one of the 1-11 engine instruments was a vibration indicator, at the bottom of the engine panel. This had a scale of one to five, and normally indicated a low value, round about one. Each engine had a datum figure established when it was fitted and shown next to the gauge. Our operating manual gave figures which, if an indicated rise above datum by a certain amount occurred in flight, meant an entry in the tech log, and a rise to a much higher figure would call for an engine shut down. In the first year of operation the vibration indicators didn't ever move much and so were not regarded as a problem. However, as we moved into 1971, there was a gradual increase in tech log entries of readings which had increased above the datum. These entries became so numerous that we had a notice from engineering which effectively told us that as there were so many instances of increase we shouldn't be too concerned about the indications for the time being until they determined what the problem was.

During the summer season of 1971 the reason eventually became clear. My contribution to the story started on a day in June. We were operating a service from Liverpool to Corfu. We left Speke in the torrential rain of a summer thunderstorm and when we arrived at a hot and sunny Corfu, we couldn't open the forward passenger door. The rain at Speke had frozen in the door seal at height, and it was ten minutes before it melted and the door could be opened. The rear airstair was no problem so the passengers left without any delay.

For the return flight to Speke, we were close to the limiting weight for the runway, which meant we had to use 8° flap, rather than the normal 18°, which gave us an increase in the allowed take-off weight (and a higher V2), in the hot conditions of a Corfu afternoon in June.

The light southerly wind meant we were using runway 18, which is extended to the south on an embankment into the sea (in fact a lagoon). There's a hill, with hotels, and a pretty photogenic island (featured on many postcards) just off to port. We lined up and, cleared for take-off, accelerated down the runway. I was flying this leg, and at VR I rotated and we were airborne at V2. At about 150ft I called for undercarriage up and, as the copilot moved the selector to the 'up' position, there was a dull thump from somewhere behind us. We were carrying an engineer on the jump seat on this flight, to help with refuelling etc., and I heard a brief profanity from him. From a very positive climb with increasing airspeed, the aircraft stopped going up, swung to port and then started a gradual descent, even though I instinctively pushed both throttles fully open.

My immediate thought about what had happened, associating the performance change with the undercarriage selection, was that maybe a wheel had fallen off and bounced back to hit the aircraft, damaging the tail. The aircraft was descending slowly at about 100fpm indicated on the VSI, I was holding the speed marginally above the V2 of 146kts, and looking ahead, projecting the flight path, as in a landing, trying to decide where we would hit the ground, or sea. I thought that we would just miss the end of the runway and touch down in the water. I had full right rudder to keep the aircraft in trim, still thinking about airframe damage, but as we skimmed past the end of the runway and arrived over the water at about 70/80 feet I heard the undercarriage doors finally slam shut. The descent stopped and we slowly began to climb away.

Until then I had been fully occupied with flying the aircraft and trying to decide where we would touch down. The first officer and engineer hadn't spoken, but, as they told me later, were watching our progress, or lack of it, with increasing alarm. Now, as the aircraft began to steadily climb away, I had time to look at the engine panel. Number 1 engine indications showed that it was winding down with the hot end temperatures off the clock. It was 'only' an engine failure. I called for a shut down and the drill was completed. From that point on the day improved, and, almost relaxed, we did a left hand circuit, carefully avoiding Albania, and landed back on runway 18.

We discovered (much later) that a compressor disc rim on number 1 engine had broken into three pieces and destroyed most of the engine as it departed rearwards, but being Rolls Royce built, all the damage was contained within the casing. Several American engined aircraft had accidents when a similar failure resulted in serious airframe damage, as debris broke through the engine casing, damaging flying controls. There were lots of bits of our engine on the runway, and a British Caledonian 1-11 crew who had been watching from the apron told us that there were flames about twenty or thirty feet behind the engine before we shut it down. They said it was very impressive and asked us to do it again. Our hostess sitting in the crew seat at the back by the engines wasn't in the least worried, she told us she heard a bang but thought it was a toilet seat falling down.

Number 1 engine provides the hydraulics for undercarriage retraction, and, on take-off, to cater for its failure, the No. 1 AC (electric) pump is always switched on. However the engine pump is higher capacity, and it will retract the undercarriage in 10 to 12 seconds. The AC pump takes about 26 seconds to do the job. So for nearly half a minute all the undercarriage doors were open, with considerable drag, as the legs slowly retracted. We might have been better placed initially if the undercarriage had been left down, as with all the doors remaining closed there would have been much less drag. Undercarriage up or down, the doors are fully closed. Later I tried several times to replicate the take-off in the simulator, but never got it to behave as the aircraft had done. However many years later, just before I retired from British Airways, there was a very similar incident at Zurich with a London based crew flying a S1-11 when the aircraft behaved in an identical fashion. We had a safety notice from the company which advised us, if in that situation, to avoid ground contact it would be preferable to fly the aircraft down to stick shaker speed.

Considering it later, I realised that, on that runway, I had little choice but to try to fly the aircraft. I wondered what my reaction would have been if it had happened at Heathrow, with a mile or more of runway remaining. I thought that there was a distinct possibility that, believing the aircraft was not going to climb, I may have decided to close the throttles and land ahead, undercarriage up. In fact, I later read of an accident in the USA in 1970, when the captain of a United Air Lines Boeing 737 in a very similar situation did just that and landed straight ahead, wheels up. The aircraft was wrecked, everybody survived, but the investigation showed that it was 'only' an engine failure, and he was castigated, of course. Maybe I was lucky, once again.

The company decided it was cheaper to leave us, two pilots and an engineer, in Corfu until the engine was changed and then we could fly the aircraft home. Our passengers were accommodated on a BEA Trident to London next morning. A freighter aircraft was chartered to bring a replacement engine and engineers to do the job. The cabin crew, three girls, were expecting to go back with the passengers, but at the last minute ops decided to leave them to come back with us. Hotel accommodation was tight in Corfu, but the agent found us space in a brand new hotel down the coast, which hadn't quite opened, and for three days we were the only residents. The girls were delighted to be staying and dashed into town to buy bikinis (none of us had night stop kit) but as the first officer had wisely packed swimming trunks in his briefcase, we three sat by the pool during the day, shirts off, uniform trousers rolled up to the knees, and using his costume in turns when we felt like a swim. The first evening in the hotel, after a meal, we all spent an hour or so on my balcony, chatting, sipping our drinks and watching the moon rise over Albania. I felt extremely warm and contented as I reflected on the day, and how near we had been to a totally different outcome. We then had three relaxing days before the aircraft was ready to fly home.

Three months later, to the day, in the same aircraft, we had just levelled in the cruise en route to Liverpool from Majorca when number 2 engine, after a light thud, ran down. I briefly thought about trying a relight, then dismissed that idea, and we diverted to land at Barcelona, just 40 miles away. The Spey had an automatic shutdown system when the ratio of the speed of the two separate rotating elements of the engine altered, indicating a problem. We decided that this must have been what caused the shut down, and it was confirmed later that it was a blade failure.

My third engine that summer, this time firmly on the ground, was when an aircraft landed at Speke and was snagged for a fault when power was restored on the approach. I was waiting to fly the aircraft next. The pilot wasn't too sure what happened, but my mate Bernie was duty engineer, and, as he had a good idea what the problem was, asked me if I would ground run it to be sure. We taxied over to the far side of the airfield away from the terminal building, and with the brakes firmly on, increased power on the engine at Bernie's request. As we reached about 95% thrust there was a very loud bang and the aircraft lurched from side to side, the engine continuing banging and shaking until we throttled back. It was a compressor stall, caused by a missing turbine blade, with an effect which was like switching the engine off and on. Another engine change. I was quite pleased I had experienced this, and years later when it happened just after take-off with the same effect on the aircraft, I was in no doubt what it was.

Those three were some of the dozen or more engines which were prematurely changed that year. The vibration indicators hadn't lied. It eventually transpired that the cause could be traced to using normal reverse on landing. The early 200 and 300 series 1-11s had spoilers, but our 400 series (like the 500 series) also had lift dumpers, which were positioned on the top surface of the wing more or less in front of the engines. They were activated by the spoiler lever, but, while the spoilers operated at all times, the dumpers only operated on the ground on landing. American Airlines had the same 400 series 1-11, and they had discovered that when using normal reverse on the short fuselage aircraft fitted with lift dumpers, the airflow to the engine was disturbed, causing temporary overheating, and eventual damage. The longer fuselage of the 500 series eliminated this problem. American had told both Rolls Royce and BAC about their findings, but the information hadn't filtered through to us. Another example of the manufacturer's 'them and us' attitude. Our procedures were changed to using just idle reverse when landing on most (long) runways, and that was the end of our engine problems.

The vibration indicators had another benefit. For several years the copilot had to watch the gauges as the engines were shut down. As they ran down the indicator would rise up the scale and he had to log the peak value on a small form. Sometime later I was speaking to an engineer in London, who told me he was responsible for collecting and collating these figures. He said that when they were put on a graph for each engine, at a certain point the readings began to rise, and when they reached a predetermined value, it was time to remove the engine for overhaul. He said it certainly prevented engine failures and associated damage.

Subsequently, the 1-11s were largely trouble free. The air conditioning and pressurisation packs did give some trouble. There were two systems, fed by each engine, or alternatively by the APU (auxiliary power unit), a small jet engine mounted in the tail of the aircraft which was normally switched off after take-off, and restarted before landing. The APU was used for pressurisation and conditioning on the ground and for take-off, so, in the event of an engine failure, full power would be available from the remaining engine. The usual aircon faults were auto shut downs, caused by an overheat from a ducting leak somewhere in the pack in the centre section. The system could be reset when it had cooled and often would work normally thereafter, but if limited to one pack cruise level had to be reduced, which could be a problem on a long sector.

One evening I arrived at Speke to operate to Lourdes (Tarbes) in southern France. The engineers told me there was a problem with the aircraft and they were waiting for spares. The fault was with a rotating collar attached to a main undercarriage leg, which operated several micro switches linked to retraction. One of these switches sensed that the undercarriage leg (compressed on the ground) had extended after take-off. If the leg didn't fully extend, it wouldn't fit precisely into the bay in the wing, and could possibly damage airframe structure or the pipes of the hydraulic system. If this switch didn't operate as normal, the undercarriage lever could not physically be moved to retract after take-off. There was a small lever under the large one which could be held to allow the undercarriage lever to move, but this was solely for use in an emergency situation, such as engine failure, when it was essential to raise it. However, the engineers explained to me, if the faulty collar was positioned correctly by hand before take-off, the undercarriage would retract normally, but the collar would not reset itself after landing. They could do this at Speke, and if I took an engineer with me to do the same at Lourdes, we could operate on schedule. I agreed to this arrangement.

We took off from Speke and, as promised, the undercarriage retracted normally. We flew to Tarbes and after landing our engineer did the pre-flight and fuelling, saving us a job, and also reset the faulty collar for take-off. Assuming all was well, we took off again, but this time the undercarriage lever wouldn't move. The engineer thought the collar may have vibrated out of position, which it probably had, and suggested that we could pull a circuit breaker on the panel behind my seat, which would isolate the circuit which was stopping the lever movement. I decided not to do this, as we now had no guarantee that the leg had extended. We were now climbing on course, and I didn't fancy going back to Tarbes and maybe going through the whole routine again. There was no speed restriction with the undercarriage down, as the undercarriage limit speed was solely for retracting and lowering, and applied to the operation of the doors, which were now all closed. Icing might have caused problems, but it was a clear night, so I decided to carry on. We had plenty of fuel, but when we reached our planned cruising level, we found that our speed was well down due to the extra drag, and the extra power and increased flight time was eating into our reserves. We asked for, and were given, a higher flight level, which improved our fuel consumption, but didn't help our speed. We were down to about M0.68/M0.69, and as we crossed France the controllers kept asking us to confirm our aircraft type. We made it back to Speke with a reasonable (legal) amount of fuel remaining, where I was glad to find that the engineers had the spares to fix the snag.

Later that year '72, I took an aircraft to Corfu to operate Corfu Gatwick next day. When we arrived at the airport in the morning I found we had been flight planned (by operations in Cardiff) Corfu Gatwick via Brindisi. As we only had half a passenger load, we could carry full fuel, enough for Gatwick direct, and so I assumed that we would be picking up more passengers in Brindisi. It was not possible to check with operations in Cardiff from Corfu, as, hard to believe nowadays, it could take anything up to an hour, or more, to connect by phone from Greece. I had discovered this the previous year when the engine failed at Corfu, and it was very frustrating. The weather at the military airport at Brindisi wasn't good, with a strong southerly wind, rain and broken cloud down to about 500/600ft. The only instrument approach was ILS on runway 35, which meant a downwind ILS to break cloud and a low visual circuit to land on 17. No radar, and as we commenced our procedural approach, we could hear an aircraft talking, in Italian, to the controller, who told us it was a training aircraft. We started our final descent towards runway 35, and reported at the outer marker, confirming that, when visual, we would break off to land on 17. We were now in and out of cloud and, at about three miles from the runway, a DC8, opposite direction, suddenly appeared out of a patch of cloud directly in front of us. I pulled up to make sure we missed him, as he turned hard to port to fly downwind at about 500ft. This was the training aircraft, an Alitalia DC8 doing visual low level circuits on 17. We followed him downwind, above the lowest bits of cloud, to land after him as he did a touch and go. To cap it all, we taxied in to find that there weren't any passengers for us, and the Brindisi landing had been planned in case we needed fuel, but that hadn't been made clear to me.

As we moved into '73 there was a complication for our flights to the sun. French airways air traffic controllers went on strike. This meant, as far as we were concerned for overflying, that France was closed. To get to the Mediterranean we could route east via Belgium, Germany, Switzerland and Italy, or go west over the Bay of Biscay, flying down longitude 8°W, which was just outside French airspace. For British airlines this was the preferred routing, as the eastern option was longer, very busy and delays were lengthy. However the 8°W route was outside VHF coverage, and to go this way aircraft had to have HF radio, which has a much longer range. Our 1-11s were so equipped, and so we began operating this route, down to Lands End, then a southwest heading to 8°W, down this line of longitude by dead reckoning, and when just northwest of Spain, turning southeast to rejoin the airway system at Santiago. We communicated with Shannon on HF for our clearances. The HF worked quite well on three out of four of our aircraft, but one of them, 'BL, often didn't perform as it should.

I did a trip for BEA one day during this period, unfortunately in 'BL. The Vanguards were the only aircraft in the BEA fleet which had HF, and, like us, were able to operate via 8°W. This trip was London to Lisbon and return. We made it to Lisbon without a problem, HF working well, but the return flight wasn't so straightforward. Once airborne we tried, without success, to contact Shannon on HF for clearance to our cruising level as we were flying north over Portugal and Spain, and as we crossed Santiago and headed northwest for 8°W we were still at FL180. The Spanish controller on VHF couldn't help us further and suggested we continue to call Shannon on HF to get clearance to a higher level. We did this immediately but still couldn't get a reply from Shannon. After several abortive attempts, a BEA Vanguard heard our calls and, possibly helped by our Bealine callsign, offered to relay to Shannon for us. This he did, and after a time, managed to get a climb clearance to FL240 for us. This was better, but we were hoping for FL350 or, at worst, FL310, and FL240 meant a much higher fuel consumption. We had set off with a full load of passengers and less than full tanks, but an amount which gave us adequate fuel, with Gatwick diversion, for the planned flight at FL350. We worked our consumption at FL240 against time and found that we had no chance of making London with any reserve, and would be looking at St Mawgan, or Cardiff with no reserves at best, not really an option. We slowed down to long range cruise and reworked the figures which were better, but still only giving us Cardiff with not much reserve. I then decided to ease the power back to a consumption figure which gave us a chance of getting to London with Gatwick diversion. This gave us a speed even lower than long range cruise speed, but at least a chance of getting to our destination. As we progressed and our weight reduced the figures slowly improved, and instead of routing via Lands End, we managed to reroute along the Channel over Jersey and the Isle of Wight. We finally had fuel for Heathrow with Gatwick diversion. It was a lovely clear summer evening and we thought our problems were over until we called Heathrow Approach for our descent. They advised us of at least thirty minutes holding before our approach. I immediately told them that we were on minimum fuel and, rather than holding, I would like to divert directly to Gatwick. Typical of efficient and helpful Heathrow, they immediately started giving us radar headings for a straight in approach. We landed at Heathrow just a few minutes late on schedule.

Another 8°W trip which was interesting, was an overnight Liverpool to Palma and return. Routing via 8°W meant that with a full load we didn't have enough fuel for Palma, so had to tech stop in Madrid on the way to refuel. At this time only a few flights were allowed into France. Some London Paris flights were operating, and I knew that they had to have specific diplomatic clearance for each flight. When we started at Palma for our return we were very surprised to be given a clearance across France, instead of via Madrid as we had flight planned. I insisted to the Spanish controller that we couldn't fly over France without diplomatic clearance for our flight, but he was just as insistent that we could. Unknown to us the French government had introduced a temporary arrangement using military controllers to operate the airways system, and had removed the overflying ban. I decided to accept the clearance and set off. As we reached French airspace, the controller cleared us to FL340, a level not normally used, as with 2000ft separation above FL290, the usual levels were 310, 330, 350, 370. I felt uneasy about the situation, and the French military controller was obviously very limited in his command of the English language, as became clear quite quickly.

About ten minutes ahead of us was a British Caledonian 1-11, also at FL340. Soon after passing over the Pyrenees, this aircraft called to say he had lost an engine and was requesting an immediate descent. The response from the French controller was to tell him to 'standby'. About half a minute later the 1-11 made the same, but more urgent, request for descent, saying that he wasn't able to maintain FL340 on one engine. He received the same 'standby' response. Shortly after the 1-11 announced to 'all aircraft' that he was turning 90° to port, commencing a descent and diverting to Bordeaux. After a couple more futile attempts to get a sensible response from the airways controller, the 1-11 announced to all that he was calling Bordeaux. We switched to our second VHF to listen to his progress, heard him call Bordeaux, and receive clearance to approach. The airfield controllers at Bordeaux were not on strike, and were the normal staff. The 1-11 was downwind when the controller asked him the reason for his diversion. The 1-11 explained, but obviously the airways controller hadn't even understood the problem.

We continued to Liverpool without any more excitement, but two days later there was an accident when two Spanish aircraft, an Iberia DC9 and a Spantax Coronado, collided over Nantes. The DC9 crashed but the Coronado managed to land with half its port wing missing. The fault was attributed 90% to air traffic, but the ramifications regarding responsibility went on for many years. A few days later we reverted to routing via 8°W.

In these busy IT times, delays were starting to be a problem. Palma was particularly bad, and initially they didn't have radar. We would often join the hold on arrival at anything up to FL200, and then let down slowly as each aircraft was cleared to approach as it reached the bottom of the stack. This could be frustrating on a clear night, but the German aircraft had their own solution. They were legally allowed to fly VFR at night, which we weren't. So on a clear night they would, on occasions, call air traffic to cancel IFR, leave the hold at FL180 or wherever, descend visually clear of the stack, and then call to join the circuit at 1500ft. This didn't impress the rest of us, stuck with IFR and the holding routine.

The next problem at Palma was getting out. When calling for start-up clearance it wasn't unusual to be given anything up to two hours delay. Pilots began to beat this by calling on ground frequency for start-up clearance on the approach, before they landed! When air traffic realised what was happening, they decreed that you couldn't call for start until the passengers were on board and the doors closed. This of course meant that the poor passengers could sit in the aircraft for all of the delay, up to two hours, before taking off.

During this time, I had landed and called for departure just a little before the passengers had finished boarding. I was very surprised to be given start up clearance immediately. I asked the traffic officer to hurry up with the loading, signed the papers, all the doors were closed, and we started up and called for taxi. As we called for our departure clearance, the controller told us we had to return to the ramp. Puzzled, I asked him the reason.

"You don't have any baggage loaded!" was the response.

Luckily we weren't delayed on our second attempt, twenty minutes later.

The 1-11 fleet generally had good serviceability, just occasionally letting us down. A slightly embarrassing incident was when taxying out at Jersey for London one day. As we followed the curved taxiway around the similarly shaped terminal building, we felt a slight thump, as though we had taxied over something. Almost immediately the Tower controller called to say,

"Speedbird 5423, one of your wheels has fallen off!"

We stopped and waited for the engineers to come and tow us back in, after we had disembarked our passengers, in full view of all the other passengers in the terminal. One of the mainwheel hubs had cracked centrally around its circumference, and half the hub plus the tyre had exploded off the axle, taking a couple of aerials under the fuselage with it. When it was investigated by engineering, it transpired that the crack had been developing for some time, but had not been picked up during routine maintenance. I was just glad it didn't happen on take-off. That could have been interesting on the relatively short Jersey runway. It would have been just as interesting if it had occurred when we were airborne.

A similar incident occurred at Heathrow to another airline, one day when we had just pushed back from the alpha stands. We were pointing at runway 28R waiting for the tug to clear and the engineer's OK to taxy for 28L departure. An Air India Boeing 747 was landing on 28R and, as we watched it touch down, one of its mainwheels detached from the bogey, moving ahead of the 747 as the aircraft decelerated, and then started bouncing, getting higher with each bounce. We watched, fascinated, as the wheel crossed the runway, ahead of the aircraft, and disappeared, bouncing, higher with each bounce, in the direction of the many car parks on the northside. We didn't hear any more about it, so, even if it dented a few cars, at least it didn't kill anybody.

I once worked out which type of incident was most prevalent during my flying career, and it appeared to be the air miss. I had several over the years, the one in a Viscount with a 1-11 being the worst so far. I'd had another in an Auster when I was instructing, when three Meteors in formation, from Hooton Park, went over the top of our aircraft from astern, missing us by no more than a hundred feet, and we were deafened by the noise of their engines.

Back to the 1-11, I was flying from London to Liverpool one day, we had passed Lichfield and were given a clearance by Manchester Control to descend to Whitegate at 3500ft. This was the usual clearance and we started down at maximum speed as ever. We were passing through bits of cloud, but mostly visual, and as we went through about 9000ft I spotted an aircraft ahead. It was opposite direction, at about FL70, and just about where we would pass through that level. It was very slightly to our starboard, so I edged a little more to port and we passed it at the same level about half a mile away to starboard. It was a Bristol 170 with roundels which turned out to be those of the Royal New Zealand Air Force. As we passed through its level I called Manchester, saying,

"Manchester, Cambrian 123, do you know about this Bristol 170 that we have just passed?"

There was no reply. We continued our descent and levelled at 3500ft and, as we were approaching Whitegate, I called again,

" Manchester, Cambrian 123, level at 3500ft. Did you know about the Bristol 170 we passed? "

A different voice to the one which had issued our clearance replied,

"Cambrian 123, call Liverpool now on 119.85, and would you please phone me when you land."

We landed at Liverpool, and I called air traffic at Manchester. It was the watch supervisor who had replied to me and he told me that when I called passing the Bristol 170 the controller on my sector was so shocked that he couldn't speak. He had been relieved at his position, and was still in such a state that he couldn't get a word out. The supervisor told me that somebody had 'wiped the 170 from the board'. I replied that we could have wiped him, and us, off the face of the earth. He asked me what I wanted to do about it, this being before the air miss and air prox routine was firmly established. I said that luckily we were visual and totally in control of the situation all the time. The poor controller was not likely to need further emphasis on what had gone wrong, and, as I was sure the supervisor would know how to handle the situation, I would leave it to him. He thanked me and that was that.

Another type of incident that occasionally reared its ugly head was 'turbulent wake'. In the flying club days my first encounter was when I had taken off in the Proctor one lovely calm evening behind an Aer Lingus Dakota. As I passed about 200ft climbing out, the aircraft began to roll quite positively to starboard. Full aileron to correct had no effect and I reached a bank angle of about 70/80º before the aircraft dropped out of the vortex and I regained control. It certainly made me think.

We were landing one morning in a Cambrian 1-11 on 28L at Heathrow behind a DC8. We had the required separation but there was a very light wind and as we passed about 300ft, with the DC8 just turning off the runway, we obviously hit one of his vortices. The 1-11 rolled gently but positively to starboard, as I fed in aileron to counter it, ineffectively. Again, luckily, and before we reached a dramatic angle of bank, we dropped out of the vortex and just managed to 'S' turn back to the runway. (My references to the runway numbers at Heathrow are as they were then, 28 and 10, not as they are now 27 and 09 due to variation changes)

On another day, coming back from Cork into London, we had started descent when air traffic asked us to increase our rate as an opposite direction heavy 747 was climbing ahead. We did as requested and soon saw the 747 well above us. However this meant that, at maximum speed, we managed to coincide with his climb out track. We went through his wake with a bang, and I was grateful that we were in a 1-11, built like a battleship. The cabin crew number one was in the cockpit almost immediately, and I went on to the cabin address to explain and reassure the passengers that all was well. These sort of things were just part of airline flying, and I was happy that they were incidents that I was able to talk about afterwards.

One small childish pleasure we managed to extract from the flying was when operating the London Cork service. Having just flown down from Liverpool and established that there was a fairly level cloud top at about 6 or 7,000ft, when climbing out of London for Cork and cleared up to a higher level, we would reduce the climb rate and increase to maximum speed about 1000ft below this level. Then at max speed the pitch wheel on the autopilot was wound gently back so that the aircraft rate of climb increased to about 4,000fpm and we popped out of the cloud like a cork out of a bottle. Very satisfying.

One day, flying from Aberdeen to London, we had one of our helicopter division pilots on the jump seat. I had recently been watching a helicopter at Cork doing training, and it had been landing on the grass by the runway, just like a light aircraft, rather than hovering. I didn't quite understand why, and asked our passenger. He explained that when operating commercially, they had to cater for the engine failure case, just as we did. So when they were fully loaded, they had to take-off and land with some airspeed in hand, in case one engine failed, if they were not capable of maintaining the hover on one.

We had a duty which involved positioning from Heathrow to Gatwick, and this was normally done on crew transport. At the time, BA had a helicopter shuttle service between the airports, which was operated by a British Caledonian S61. Whenever we could we'd arrange to use this service, if seats were available. I was intrigued the first time we did this, when the helicopter taxied from the central area, across the south runway, to take off from a parallel short grass runway. At Gatwick, we landed on the main runway and then hover taxied at a couple of feet to our stand. Our passenger's explanation made it all clear.

My wife and I flew to New York from Manchester in the Tristar for a holiday. To her surprise after arriving at JFK, I dragged her across to the TWA terminal where I knew there was a helicopter service to Manhattan. They charged us crew rate of $10 each and we piled into an ancient S61 (ex-Vietnam I reckoned), with several of the Tristar cabin crew. With every nut and rivet vibrating, we staggered across to Manhattan, but the view as we arrived was spectacular and well worth it, and we landed on one of the piers at the south end. The helicopters had previously landed on the heliport on top of the Pan Am building, but this was closed in 1977 when an undercarriage collapse caused the rotors to hit the tarmac and several people were killed.

About this time I almost made long haul. Ops in Cardiff rang me one day to say that they were negotiating a charter to Canada. A piece of machinery was required to be delivered to an airfield in central Canada, we had got the job, and I had been pencilled in for the flight. The freight weighed only a few tons, so we could have full tanks giving us range for the operation, via Iceland and Greenland. The idea of operating into Narsarsuaq, Bluey West One, was appealing. However the company licence to operate didn't cover that area, so we had to apply to the CAA for a special dispensation. I then heard that the CAA required us to have HF radio capability, which we had. The next problem was that they decided we needed a dedicated and qualified flight navigator. Ops duly arranged with BAC to borrow one of their flight navigators. Nevertheless the CAA finally decided that they wouldn't grant us the clearance to operate the flight, and that was the end of my North Atlantic ambitions.

During these years I had occasionally been flying with my old Feds boss, Reg Gates in his Aero Commander 500 'GW. Reg used the aircraft for business trips, mostly to Dublin to meet the mushroom growers. Cliff did most of this flying, but when British Eagle folded in '68 Cliff had to find a new job. Eagle had taken over Starways in '63. Cliff started working as an executive pilot for a civil engineering company, initially flying a Piper Aztec, and later a Cessna 401. This meant he couldn't fly as often with Reg, and late in '69 Reg contacted me to say that wanted to fly more frequently, maybe two or three times a week, and would I be able to do it. I explained that I couldn't possibly manage that amount of flying in my spare time, but suggested that I check out several of our excellent Cambrian first officers on the Aero Commander and he would then have a pool of pilots to call on. Reg agreed and I initially checked out three of our lads on the aircraft and this arrangement worked satisfactorily for a while. However they flew only very occasionally over the next year or so, as I did, and Reg's optimistic requirement of several times a week didn't materialise. In fact, due to ill health, Reg began to relinquish control of the business to his son, Peter, who had been at the Liverpool Institute when I was there.

Peter had worked for his father after leaving school, but then moved on to other things. He now came back into the business and developed the firm, from being just an importing business, into a transport operation with a fleet of lorries. He also learned to fly, getting his twin rating soon after his PPL, to the dismay of his instructor at Oxford who thought he was running before he could walk. In fact, Peter was an excellent pilot, also doing the full instrument rating soon after, and he would have made an airline pilot with no problem. He started flying 'GW, the Aero Commander, as soon as I'd done some training with him. He then flew it frequently, but after some winter flying experiences, told me that when he had arranged a meeting perhaps four or five days ahead, he would then spend a lot of the time worrying if the weather would be OK for the flight. So he decided that if he could arrange the meeting for a day when I was not working and could go with him, he could relax and concentrate on other things. This worked well and over the next few years we flew a lot together, often combining business with pleasure, taking our wives with us, such as one trip via Brussels, Paris, and Perpignan to Ibiza for a few days, then home via Bordeaux.

One trip with Peter I remember was on the bread and butter run to Dublin. When we went to the Met. Office at Speke we found the Dublin weather was foggy. Also in Met. was one of our Cambrian first officers, Joe Hall, who was operating our service to Dublin. When he heard we were also bound there, he couldn't resist a bit of leg pulling, telling me that they would give us twenty minutes start and still get there before us. We set off and, sure enough, the 1-11 passed us when we were halfway there. However when we arrived at Dublin the RVR was 130 metres, and the 1-11 was holding at the beacon waiting for an visibility improvement to their Cat 1 landing limit of 600 metres. We, however, being a private flight, had no laid down limit (at that time), and I said we'd try an ILS approach. Peter did a very competent ILS and at about 150ft I told him to look up and land as I could see the approach lights. We learned later that after holding for half an hour Joe's 1-11 had diverted to Shannon. I made the most of it next time I saw him.

On our way home from Dublin on a fine day, Peter suggested some sightseeing over North Wales. We cleared off airways and descended, avoiding Valley. As we passed over Caernarfon, I said the Llanberis Pass was pretty so we turned to fly along it. It was a nice clear day with a very light northerly wind, and we flew into the Pass at about 1,000ft with the hills above us on each side. About halfway along, we suddenly hit the most severe shock like turbulence, banging the aircraft from side to side. The Aero Commander is a tough well-built aircraft (ask Bob Hoover) but I didn't like it and asked Pete to pull up quickly. We zoomed above the level of the mountains and all was smooth again. Don't trust mountains was the lesson.

On another occasion I went with Peter in the Aero Commander to collect his in laws from Sunderland. Shortly after taking off, one engine ran down (the fuel pump drive had sheared), so I feathered it and Peter turned back to land at Speke. The aircraft performed well on one and was quite capable of a single engine go around. Air traffic asked if we were declaring an emergency, but I declined the offer, explaining that we were quite happy. Nevertheless when we landed, I was surprised when we were followed to the hangar by no less than fourteen fire engines. This was probably the start of what I considered was the overreaction to anything which might be classed as an emergency. I remember in the fifties whenever a 'standby' occurred at Speke the two airport fire engines would position themselves halfway down the runway, and that was the total response.

On one occasion a BEA Dakota landed with an undercarriage problem, and as it slowed, the port side retracted and as the wing touched the aircraft swung gently off the runway on to the grass. There was no fire and the two fire engines monitored the situation happily. Incidentally, I remember the replacement wing sent up from Northolt had the registration G-AGIB on it, which was the reg. of a Short Sunderland, instead of the Dakota reg., G-AJIB, but I'm sure somebody noticed before it was fitted. I remember particularly because that was the Dakota in which I made my first flight.

The Airwork Sabres often had similar problems and whenever we saw the two fire engines 'standing by' we would all leave the hangar to watch the ensuing drama, such as a Sabre landing with its undercarriage up. The policy changed in later years so that whenever an 'emergency' was a possibility, the airport called on all the surrounding fire stations for extra support. When the Sabres first started arriving at Speke, they were positioned by RAF crews direct from Germany. The first batch of four arrived and decided to make a formation landing. They were probably used to two or three miles of runway, rather than Speke's just short of a mile. They made a beautiful formation touchdown on 08, about halfway down the runway, and all four continued off the end of the runway, still going quite fast, crossing the dual carriageway of Speke Hall Road, and stopped in the field beyond. This incident prompted the installation of traffic lights on this road to be used when aircraft were landing. After another incident when sixteen aircraft arrived in bad weather, low on fuel, and had to be rescued by Manchester radar, landing at Manchester, Speke, and some, if I remember, at Burtonwood, Airwork started using their own pilots to bring them over individually.

When Peter took over the business from his father, he inherited the Aero Commander 500B GW. After flying this for a while, he decided to update. In August 74, we flew down to Staverton, where the Aero Commander dealer Glos Air was based. After a demonstration flight in the latest variant, a 500S Shrike, Peter began negotiations to buy a new aircraft. This was a few months after we did a trip over a few days to Menorca in GW, via Jersey and Zurich outbound, and Bordeaux coming home, mixing business with a bit of pleasure, and I think Peter decided he wanted an aircraft to his own specifications. In December we flew to Staverton again to deliver GW and to fly, for the first time, G-BCPZ, Peter's new Shrike Commander. As PZ was not fully fitted out Glos Air lent Peter G-ASYA, a 560F Commander, for a few weeks. This was slightly different to the others, with a MTOW 340 kgs higher, and geared Lycomings. These geared engines had something of a bad reputation, but provided they were operated in accordance with the manual there wasn't a problem. For example, it was important to keep the engine driving the prop, rather than reducing power to the point where the prop was driving the engine.

We did half a dozen flights in YA with no problem, before we flew it back to Staverton to pick up PZ. This Aero Commander, PZ, was a beauty, and my favourite of all of them. It had a leather upholstered interior, six seats and a toilet (a legal extra seat). The cockpit was well equipped for IFR and Peter had decided to fit, as an extra, a King KNS-80 RNAV. This was a fairly new piece of kit, which allowed the pilot to 'move' a VOR/DME to anywhere he wished. Thus an RAF airfield in Norfolk, which we occasionally used, could have Clacton VOR repositioned on it. We could then navigate to that field using VOR/DME. It was simply a matter of putting the relevant bearing and distance in and the set did the rest. I was sceptical when Peter first told me about it, but once I had used it a few times, I was convinced. It could even be set up to give ILS indications to a runway. That depended, of course, on being able to receive signals from the distant VOR if necessary down to the ground, but we used it mainly to position to final or downwind at about 1,000ft, and for this it worked well.

On one occasion visiting Glos Air, we were sitting in their office discussing the new aircraft, and outside the window on the tarmac was a single engined Aero Commander 112A, N1221J. I casually mentioned to the dealer that I particularly liked the look of the aircraft, which I thought was one of the nicest of the current singles, with retractable undercarriage, constant speed prop, air con., etc., etc. He asked me if I'd flown one, and when I said I hadn't, he threw a set of keys to me across his desk, and suggested I go and try it. Peter came with me, and I did a couple of circuits in it, confirming my view that it was indeed a superb little aircraft.

Shortly after PZ was delivered, in February 75, after a few bread and butter runs to Dublin and Hull, we did another business/pleasure trip to Ibiza, via Paris Le Bourget and Perpignan outbound, and Bordeaux coming home. We landed at Perpignan outbound to fill up with fuel, as there was a possibility of a tanker driver strike in Ibiza. Over the next year or two, I did quite a bit of flying in PZ with Peter. Although he now had his instrument rating, he still reckoned it was more relaxing for him to fix an appointment ahead, and let me worry about the weather.

Back on the 1-11, I was enjoying the nice mix of schedules and IT flights. One night we had been to Ibiza, and on the return, with a full load of passengers, had fuel for Liverpool with just a Manchester diversion. As we crossed the Channel, both airfields were forecasting deteriorating visibility, and as we passed Cardiff, which was wide open, they were both giving about 800 metres and trending (within two hours) down to 400. Our Cat I limit was 600 metres. As we continued north, I was reminding myself of my promise not to be caught out again short of fuel. Just past Brecon, we got the latest actuals which, as before, had the pessimistic trend, and I realised that if we continued and, on arrival, both went below Cat 1 limits, we'd have nowhere else to go. We turned around and landed at Cardiff, refuelled with enough to hold for an hour or two up north and still get back to Cardiff. When we arrived at Liverpool the RVR there and at Manchester was still just above Cat I. Once again, you can't win them all.

Most of the added interest to the routine flying was from the weather, of course. One of our regular schedules was the early morning Liverpool to London, followed by a London to Cork and return, then a few hours lunch break at Heathrow and finally a late afternoon Liverpool. Cork, in the southwest approaches, was generally relatively warm, but with frequent gales, rain and low cloud. It was a pleasure operating there, being a quiet corner of our world, and on a nice day, when we could see all of the southern Irish coast, Cork would clear us in visual, and we'd descend early and fly along the coast at 1,000ft and max speed. One morning we'd done this and at about twenty miles out the approach controller told us to call the tower for landing clearance. I was flying, relaxed and happily enjoying the day (or fat, dumb and happy as it's known), and I called,

"Tower, Cambrian 601 joining left base visual for 17."

He replied that we were clear to final and gave us the QFE. This didn't agree with the QFE numbers we were expecting, and as we were trying to resolve this, he asked where we were from. That didn't make sense either, as our 1-11 came to Cork every day at this time, and I told him from London as usual.

His reply explained all,

"OK, this is Shannon Tower."

The Shannon QFE was about 20mb different to Cork. We apologised, changed to the correct frequency, just one digit different, and quickly called Cork for a landing clearance.

Another Cork trip in February '73 was unusual in that it was snowing. As we set off from Heathrow the runway report from Cork wasn't good, deep snow and braking action poor. We fully expected to divert to Shannon, which was clear. Cork airfield is at 600ft which made the difference. En route we called Cork to get the latest information, and they told us that the Aer Lingus flight had just diverted to Shannon, but they had snow clearance in progress and were hoping to have the runway ready for us. As we arrived it was still snowing heavily, with low cloud, but we were advised that the runway had been swept and the braking action was 'good'. The visibility was just above limits for a Cat 1 approach, so we were vectored into the ILS. I briefed the first officer, Terry Morgan, that I would just request idle reverse initially on landing, and then assess braking and decide if more was required. This was because the ops manual warned that if reverse came in asymmetrically on a slippery runway, due to one engine opening up in advance of the other, it could cause the aircraft to slide sideways, and possibly off the runway.

Down the ILS on 17, and at about 200ft we could see the approach lights. That was all we could see, with the heavy snow it was almost a 'white out'. As we came over the threshold and landed, everything was white, including the runway, and I called for idle reverse and applied the brakes positively. With the screen wipers thrashing away, in the poor visibility and heavy snow it was difficult to be sure of our progress along the runway, but shortly after touchdown, I was aware of objects passing on our port side, which were, in fact, the snow ploughs waiting at the intersection of the short westerly runway. I realised at that point we were about halfway down the runway, I had the brakes hard on with absolutely no effect, and we were still doing about 120kts. Deciding I didn't have time to talk about it, I grabbed the two reverse thrust levers and pulled them both hard back against the stops. The engines seemed to take an inordinately long time to wind up, but finally they did, and we could hear the roar from the back end. We stopped about 100 metres from the end of the runway as I pushed the levers back to cancel reverse. Normally this was cancelled by 60kts. We turned around to backtrack, taxying gingerly on the slippery runway, the braking action was poor at best, and as we passed the point where we had stopped there was a big patch of clear runway where the reverse had melted the snow. I guess somebody was just trying to please us with the 'braking action good' report.

One of our IT destinations was Porto, in Portugal, and we usually arrived there between midnight and one o'clock in the morning. Porto was prone to fog overnight, but had an ILS on the southerly runway, and three NDBs, positioned at the outer marker for the ILS, about four miles out, and at the middle marker points for both runways, at about half a mile. The problem was that I can never remember the ILS being operational, it was always 'on test'. There were two Cat 1 instrument approach procedures, one an NDB with a decision height of about 400ft, and the ILS with the height at 170ft. Of course when the ILS was 'on test' we couldn't use it. I did a couple of trips when the conditions were good, and also when an NDB approach was required. We had the ILS on to see how it behaved, and it always appeared to be working OK. In fact on one occasion we landed in poor visibility from an NDB approach and while we were on the ground the visibility dropped even further to well below our landing limits, but an Air Portugal Boeing 727 on training was doing circuits happily, obviously using the ILS. Another time I stretched the

NDB limit down to about 250ft, not something I would normally do, but 400ft is quite high, and with the ILS indicating, the approach lights glowing through the cloud from 400ft, we managed to land OK on our second attempt, not enjoying it. The agent was delighted to see us. His delight was mainly that he didn't have to send the passengers on a seven hour coach journey to Lisbon, and wait for the outbound passengers at Porto. I only diverted to Lisbon once, and the delay waiting for the passengers meant we had to do a 'split duty' to be legal, and spend six hours resting in a hotel. The chief pilot, Geoff Perrott, rang me after this trip to ask me how I had managed it legally. I explained to him, slightly peeved, as I had very carefully checked the regulations, and made sure that we had six hours off duty in the hotel, to comply with the split duty requirements, and completed the schedule legally with minimum disruption for the company.

Another trip was Liverpool Genoa Rome Liverpool, and on schedule we always transited Genoa in the early hours when it was dark. I landed there several times in the dark, fully aware of the high ground to the north, but it was only when we were delayed one night and landed in daylight that I really appreciated the impressive mountains on the northern side as we made our approach.

In April 76, a trip with Peter and our wives, in Aero Commander PZ, was to Ibiza, via Chambery southbound, and Bordeaux on the return. Chambery was interesting. Peter had been sent a brochure of the airfield, and decided it would be worth a visit. Situated in the French Alps, at the time it was a mountain rescue helicopter training base. It had an ILS, but the glideslope was 6° instead of the usual 3°. We positioned for the approach in cloud, negotiating the mountains on either side, and once established on the ILS approach, found we were doing 120 kts with the throttles closed and full flap to maintain the glideslope. We broke cloud and landed with no further problem, and after a coffee continued on our way.

Meanwhile, as I was enjoying the flying, things were moving elsewhere. Consequent upon the Edwards Committee recommendations, in May 73 the government announced their intention to merge the two nationalised corporations, BOAC and BEA. The two smaller companies Cambrian and Northeast (formerly BKS) were effectively owned by BEA, and were thus included. Although several of our pilots were averse to this development, I regarded it as a move which assured our future, even though we weren't sure what that future held. British Airways was established in September 73 and in March the following year the four constituent airlines were dissolved. The first change was the creation of divisions within British Airways, Overseas, European, Helicopters etc., and ours, which was Regional Division, comprising Cambrian, Northeast, and the Channel and Scottish units of BEA, with all the Viscounts, 748s, 1-11 400s, and Northeast Tridents. The integration began, but only very slowly at first, and it would be years before it was complete.

Our division was used to start the initial operations on routes such as London to Lyons, until the route became established and profitable, at which time European Division would take it over. We were now part of a nationalised organisation and the problems soon became evident. The desire to operate profitably was not very evident, and as each year produced another operating loss, various attempts were made to improve the situation. One clever plan was to introduce 'profit centres'. This meant that each operating unit was responsible for its own profit and loss account. It led to some strange anomalies. For example, we, as Regional Division, were charged by European Division for our handling at Heathrow when we passed through. This charge became so high that our management sought competitive bids from other operators to provide this service, and found that Dan Air would do it for a third of the price. This would obviously mean money leaving British Airways, so the European Division charge was sensibly renegotiated and reduced.

The total futility of this profit centre logic was demonstrated to me when I was having lunch one day in the BEA (European Division) pilots' crew restaurant in the Queens building at Heathrow. We were joined at our table by a Trident 3 captain, who told us an almost unbelievable tale. He said he was on Shuttle back up that day. The Shuttle service from Heathrow to Manchester, Glasgow, Edinburgh and Belfast was operated at the time by the Trident 1 fleet, and the backup service (the extra flight guaranteed if the scheduled service was oversubscribed) provided by the Trident 3 fleet. He told us that he had been called to operate an extra Belfast back up service that morning. When he asked how many passengers he had, he was told about thirty. Being an intelligent, thinking pilot, he quickly realised that the Trident 1 was going full, with 100 passengers, and his Trident 3, with more than 140 seats, would be going with 30 passengers. He made the fairly obvious suggestion that he could take all the 130 passengers in his Trident 3, and save operating two flights. He was informed that was not possible as the shuttle back up was contracted from Mainline by Shuttle, and, as such, paid for. If he operated the frontline service that would be considered an extra charter for which Shuttle would have to pay Mainline an additional charge, and so it was cheaper, for Shuttle, to operate two aircraft. So he went to Belfast with thirty passengers, and returned empty. As he said, you couldn't make it up. The profit centre experiment didn't last long.

Having worked for a private airline which became a nationalised airline and was eventually privatised, there is no doubt for me that nationalisation doesn't work. The morale in the airline, when profit is not a priority, definitely suffers. It's much nicer to work in an organisation which is efficient and depends on maintaining that efficiency for its secure future. The airline's regular annual losses led Margaret Thatcher to appoint Sir John King (later Lord King) in 1981 as chairman with a brief to turn it around. With Colin Marshall as his right hand man, he did just that. A reduction of 40% in staff numbers, without strikes, and many other improvements meant we were soon back in profit and by 1987 were successfully privatised. My job didn't change in any way, so flight operations must have been fairly efficient.

One aspect of the initial integration was that we, as Cambrian, were effectively absorbed into BEA, and it was decided that 'we didn't do inclusive tours'. So our IT operation was slowly wound down, and, by 1976, we had stopped doing them. The pilots at Liverpool had a company pep talk from Bryn Savage to explain (as is usual in these situations) that nothing would change, despite our changing working pattern. Reg Leach summed up our feelings with his analysis that we would be doing 'more and more of less and less'. The effect of all this on the Liverpool base was to dramatically reduce our workload, and we spent half our time on home standby. So much so that I remember on one occasion being on home standby for four days, and spending it sailing my boat along the North Wales coast. The chances of being called out were negligible, as there were several captains on standby, as well as me, all of whom would have been glad to fly. We were gradually integrated into the BEA Birmingham 1-11 400 operation and often found ourselves operating on their routes. However during this slack period I managed to do a lot of flying with Peter in PZ, so 'it's an ill wind'.

This couldn't last of course, even in a nationalised outfit, and the end result was that in March 1977 we were given about ten days' notice that the Liverpool 1-11 base was closing and from April 1st we would be based at Birmingham. The edict also applied to the Cambrian 1-11 bases at Cardiff and Heathrow, and so, on April 1st, the Birmingham base at Elmdon became home to all the British Airways Regional Division 1-11s and crews. We were given fairly generous disturbance allowances, and temporary hotel provision while flying from Birmingham but for me, with no intention of moving there, it meant a lot of driving to work.

Just after we started at our new base, Peter decided to change PZ for a Cessna 402B, G-BENE, which disappointed me, but I didn't pay the piper. He decided the Cessna was roomier and more economical. It had a lower MTOW than PZ, but being lighter had a bigger payload but, for me, lacked the solid feel of the Aero Commander, which gave me a very secure feeling, whatever the weather. Bob Hoover's demonstrations proved my point. Both had boot de-icing, but the Aero Commander was much better in icing conditions, as we found later.

In April 77 we picked up the Cessna from Westair at Blackpool. Denis Westoby asked if we'd like a check ride with him, but we graciously declined and said we'd be fine, working it out as we went. With Peter flying, I was reading the checklist and we started the engines. When we reached the point of taxying, we couldn't find the parking brake to release it. We looked everywhere you would expect to find a parking brake, to no avail. Denis was watching us depart, and so we called him over, and sheepishly asked him to show us where the parking brake was located. He pointed it out, hidden under the edge of the instrument panel, hugely enjoying our embarrassment. Thereafter the flight proceeded to Speke without a problem. I flew NE with Pete over the next few years, notably twice to Corfu, about eight hours flying each way. The second time we went, Peter decided he'd like to fly overnight, so we routed via Nice to refuel, with our passengers, Peter's wife, three children, and my wife sleeping most of the way. On the return flight via Marseilles, we picked up ice on the corner of the Alps, tried going up to FL120 to beat it, but had to descend eventually before landing at Marseilles. The Cessna didn't cope with these conditions as well as the Aero Commander did.

Cliff, meanwhile, was still flying for a local construction company. Initially he had an Aztec, which I tried briefly with him, then changed to a Cessna 401B, G-AZRD, similar to Peter's 402B. I did some circuits in RD with Cliff in 1975, to cover me flying it if necessary. A few years later in 82, Cliff rang me to say that he had a trip on, but also had just had a hiccup with his medical, was temporarily unlicensed and could I help. I agreed of course and together we flew from Speke to Luton, with Cliff's boss, John Finlan and his wife, to collect their children, then via Dinard for customs, on to Laval, the nearest airfield to John Finlan's in-laws' residence. After a quick meal, Cliff and I flew back, via Dinard, to Speke. A nice day out, and Cliff soon had his licence sorted.

It was a fairly pleasant summer operating from the new base at Birmingham, but another aspect of the integration was seniority. The BEA pilots had decided unilaterally that as some of us, in Cambrian, had enjoyed a relatively quick progression through the ranks to command (I had been a first officer for just two and a half years) we should be 'adjusted' in seniority to equate with their time to command. Their unilateral decision was that Cambrian captains should lose nine years of seniority to join the combined list, and this was accepted by the new company, BA. We, of course didn't accept this arbitrary decision, and, not getting a lot of support from BALPA, decided to challenge it in the High Court. We all chipped in £100 to brief a QC and elected Jimmy Jones to be the test case. It went as far as the steps of the High Court on the morning of the hearing before the company backed down and offered to negotiate a more reasonable arrangement. This effectively tied our seniority to somebody in BEA with a similar date of joining. It meant I lost about four and a half years of seniority, (ie: making it the equivalent of seven years to command) but it didn't affect my pay. Some of our captains lost a few increments and their pay stood still for a few years, but overall it was a reasonable solution. It also meant that we were entitled to bid on the annual BEA (BA) bid for base and type.

When this bid list was published in September, there were some positions available on the Super 1-11 fleet at Manchester. Howard and I as captains, and Ben Casey and Dug Davidson as first officers, were successful in a bid for Manchester. We were pleased to be moving back north, but didn't appreciate what a hornets' nest we were about to disturb. At the end of November, I did my last 1-11 flight from Birmingham and moved to the Manchester base.

6.   SUPER ONE ELEVEN

First we had to do a 'differences' course on the Super One Eleven. Being a hybrid, just for BEA, this aircraft was quite different from all the other 1-11s. It had a Smiths flight system, the same as the Trident, and all the cockpit switches were 'up' for 'on'.

All the other One Elevens had the Collins FD108 flight system and American style switch arrangement of 'forward' for 'on', which meant the roof panel switches were 'down' for 'on'. The hydraulic panel had been moved from just in front of the throttles to starboard side of the roof panel, and its place taken by the Decca Harco flight log, the latest, and hopefully best, of the line. Weights and speeds differed in various ways, but after some classroom work, and time in the S1-11 simulator, we were ready for line training.

One thing it did have, which the 400 1-11s didn't, was autoland, just Category 2 at the time, Cat 3 came later. This was interesting. As mentioned, my preferred way of landing an aircraft was to close the throttles at about 50ft and then progressively raise the nose to arrive at the touchdown point nose high with speed reducing positively.

There was another popular method of landing the 1-11, both 400 and Super, known as 'tweak and push', which meant maintaining approach attitude, power and speed right down to the runway. As the aircraft hit ground effect, which was quite noticeable on the 1-11 with its low wing, power was chopped and with a quick backwards tweak of the elevator, and then a slight push, the aircraft arrived very smoothly on to the ground. I didn't favour this method, as deceleration didn't start until after touchdown, and the aircraft landed in a more nose down attitude, whereas I preferred it to be nose up, using aerodynamic drag, and decelerating.

There were some good exponents of 'tweak and push' and one first officer in particular at Manchester, Francis, enjoyed making me squirm as I thought the aircraft would thump on to the ground but he always ensured it didn't and made a very smooth landing instead. However I was delighted when I did my first autoland in the simulator. At 50ft the autopilot closed the throttles, then progressively raised the nose to reduce the descent, arriving at the runway for a smooth touchdown, with the nose high, throttles closed, and the speed reducing positively. It landed the aircraft just like I did.

At the start of 1978 we arrived at Manchester to start line training. We very quickly became aware of a strong undercurrent of resentment to our presence. It wasn't universal, some pilots were quite happy to accept us, but there were a few who didn't. One first officer told me quite bluntly that, as far as he was concerned, BEA should have taken over our routes and aircraft but should have sacked all our pilots, as we were not needed. However, after a year or so, he thawed and became quite friendly. Another simply refused to engage in any conversation with me when we flew together, apart from the communication required during the operation of the aircraft. Rumour had it that his wife once hit him with a hammer, so maybe it wasn't just me who caused resentment. I flew with him once with my wife on the jump seat, and with her he was charming and chatted happily. Apart from his lack of social communication, he did his job, so I couldn't complain. They simply regarded us as intruders who were taking command vacancies which they thought should have been theirs, by right. Not an altogether pleasant working relationship.

Some first officers indulged in a slightly childish habit, which, giving them the benefit of the doubt, I accepted magnanimously. When doing the instrument checks during taxying, they would say, when checking the turn and slip in a right turn,

"Needle's to me, and ball's to you!" The apostrophe made all the difference. Anything to make them happy.

The BEA pilots numbered approximately 2000, BOAC about 1000 and Cambrian and Northeast together about 240, so the BEA pilots were a vociferous majority. They called the BOAC pilots 'Vulcans' and Cambrian and Northeast 'Klingons', after the Star Trek tribes. I remember an occasion when I walked into the crewroom at Tegel, Berlin, and said 'Good Morning' to the London captain who was the only person there. He studiously ignored me, got up, and walked out. It was just as well I wasn't sensitive.

The Sl-11 fleet of eighteen aircraft were based at London, Manchester and Berlin, six aircraft at each base. Crews were based at London and Manchester, and the Berlin operation was covered by night stopping crews, usually doing six day tours, flying the German Internal Services from Berlin mostly to Hannover, Cologne, Dusseldorf, Bremen, and Stuttgart, along the three corridors over Russian controlled East Germany. Pan Am operated 727s on other routes, such as Frankfurt, which was their prime route.

I started my line training with a Berlin tour. We positioned as passengers out to Berlin via Dusseldorf, a training captain, first officer and myself. At this time I was involved in buying a new boat. I had just sold my first boat, a Westerly Centaur 26ft sailing cruiser, and was awaiting delivery of a Westerly 33 Ketch. Talking to the training captain en route I discovered he also had a sailing boat, a Macwester 26, similar to my Centaur. We chatted about boats and sailing and I thought because of our mutual interest I was in for a relaxed few days. I was wrong. We were doing an evening Dusseldorf service when we arrived at Berlin and the training captain told me I was to do all the paperwork, navigation logs, runway calculations, etc., which normally the first officer did. He then wandered off to chat to the ops staff. Graham, the first officer, one of the more pleasant ones, said to me, "Here, don't worry, let me do it".

The first officers knew the paperwork routine off by heart and it would have taken me three times as long to work my way through it. When we got to the aircraft I was instructed to do the engine start, taxying and do the R/T as well. This was quite contrary to our standard operating procedures, which split the duties between the two pilots, which was how we had been operating in the simulator. After take-off we continued in a similar vein, and I was doing all the flying and the R/T, not a problem, but quite contrary to SOP. When we arrived at Dusseldorf I was told to fly a manual ILS approach using autothrottle. This was a combination never normally used, autothrottle was used for an automatic approach, and normally for a manual approach the pilot would handle the throttles. However, I did it, without complaining, and this irregular routine continued back to Berlin, but when we arrived there a Cat 2 approach was required due to the visibility, and I had to vacate the left hand seat as I wasn't yet qualified.

This non-standard operating routine continued for the next couple of days, and I realised that I was being put under extra pressure quite deliberately. I discovered later that this training captain was one of the anti-Cambrian brigade. On our last day together we operated Berlin to Cologne then Heathrow. After a lunch break we did the final sector to Manchester, and when my captain checked the weather for me he told me, with some ill-disguised pleasure, that there was a crosswind component for landing on runway 06 varying above and below our 30 knot limit. Our first officer had been allowed to go home early the previous day, and the captain was operating in the right hand seat. We also had another training captain positioning to Manchester, and as the aircraft was full, he was sitting in the cockpit jump seat.

As we made our approach at Manchester, air traffic were calling the wind, northerly about 35/45 knots, and with each call my captain would convert it from the chart into a crosswind component for me. He was reading out, "32 knots" then "29 knots" and "34 knots". I was quite happy and fully intending to land, but I wondered what his attitude would be if it was decided I had landed above limits. However, at about 150ft, the last wind check came and he said, "30 knots". To my delight, I then made the smoothest crosswind landing I had ever made, it was just not possible to feel the aircraft touch the ground. I waited for a comment, but there was absolute silence as we taxied in. I decided later that the crosswind component routine had just been a little bit more pressure to see what I would do.

The rest of my line training with a different captain was much more relaxed and I enjoyed it. After a very pleasant final line check, Berlin Dusseldorf Berlin, with Arthur Parkinson, whom I remembered from when he was flying BEA Rapides and Dakotas at Speke in the fifties, I was finally cleared on the line. Even though I had flown the 1-11 for eight years, and been a captain for fourteen years, I was treated like a new captain, and I had to do 70 sectors (including training) before I was allowed to let the first officers fly Pl/s, or I could do Cat 2 approaches. In fact I was on a Berlin tour when I completed this requirement, and the next day a Cat 2 approach was a necessity for us to operate to Hannover. However I didn't have the necessary piece of paper confirming my Cat 2 capability. We were on the early Hannover flights, and as our Manchester flight manager was also in Berlin I decided to ring him at the hotel (probably in bed) to obtain authorisation. I did this, and after being asked if I was sure I could cope, he gave me the OK.

It took a while to settle in at Manchester, mainly because of the negative attitude of some of the pilots, and for a time I just put my head down, and escaped to my boat whenever I could, which provided a nice release from the pressures at work. Gradually, after a year or two, things improved, pilots came and went, more ex Cambrian colleagues joined us, and we were finally accepted, as British Airways became the standard rather than BEA. It was a difficult couple of years and at least one of our number succumbed to the pressure and took early retirement, but I gradually settled into enjoying flying again. It was a nice mix of flying at Manchester, one Berlin tour each month, and then European schedules the rest of the time. Paris, Amsterdam, Geneva, Brussels, Nice, Milan, Rome, Copenhagen, Stockholm, Frankfurt, Dusseldorf, Munich, etc., as well as the domestics, Glasgow, Edinburgh, Belfast, Aberdeen, Dublin, Jersey, and of course London very often.

The S1-11s, as mentioned, had the latest Decca Navigator equipment, Harco. This was a flight log system as we had in the Dakotas and Viscounts, but, allegedly, to a more advanced standard. However it was still the same low frequency system, subject to the same interference from thunderstorms etc., and also its own little foibles. It would occasionally simply give up and the pen would go wandering off the chart with a mind of its own. Several first officers hated it, and when this happened, would just switch it off. I didn't go along with this, and insisted on it being kept on, and I actually enjoyed trying to get it to work again, which it usually would. When it worked, it was great, and well worth the effort.

The Decca company had protected their monopoly by not selling their receivers. They would only rent them to customers, and provided a maintenance service using their own engineers. Decca, of course, owned and maintained the chains of transmitters which the system used. I remember that fishing boats paid about £1,000 a year for the privilege. However, in the early eighties, several electronic companies, such as Philips and Shipmate, decided to challenge Decca's position and began producing solid state receivers for the yachting (and fishing boat) market. The Decca company wasn't pleased by this development and started a futile battle in the courts to stop it. I had recently bought a new Westerly 33 yacht, so I bought one of the Shipmate Decca receivers and found it remarkably accurate and reliable. It cost just under £1,000 and it was no wonder fishing boats began to buy them. It intrigued me that the set in my boat was the size of a book but it was just as good as, or better than, the equipment in our S1-11s, which comprised three large boxes, each about one metre square, which needed fans to keep them cool. It was basically wartime technology. The Shipmate set didn't have a pictorial display, of course, but, using waypoints and routes, it was extremely useful. Decca eventually gave up the battle in the courts and introduced their own small solid state receiver for yachts (and fishing boats).

Manchester was a pleasant operation, and the base was favoured by people from the area, who had no desire to move to Heathrow. Consequently there were quite a few senior pilots, some of whom had been there for years. When the profit centre logic was in vogue, we were barraged by management rumours threatening various measures, as (they said) we were such an expensive operation having so many senior pilots on high pay, whereas, if we all went to Heathrow, and Manchester was crewed by junior pilots, on lower pay, the base could be more profitable. We pointed out the lack of logic in this argument, as we would all still be being paid by BA, wherever we were, and moving lots of pilots about in this way would simply create additional costs in disturbance and resettlement allowances. The rumours slowly dissipated. It was clear however that the company wanted to be Heathrow Airways, and the outstations were a nuisance.

We were always told that our operation wasn't profitable enough to justify the cost of new replacement aircraft, even though the fares at the time were relatively high, and generally fixed via cosy agreements between governments and the national airlines, BA, Air France, KLM, Lufthansa, SAS, Swissair etc. It intrigued me that a few years later the low cost carriers could operate the same routes with new aircraft and also slash the fares. Beyond the comprehension of a simple pilot, I guess.

When I first moved to Manchester, we still were paid on a BEA arrangement, which had two jet pay scales, narrow and wide body aircraft. There was a strange anomaly in this agreement, whereby pilots on narrow body pay could, when their seniority allowed, bid to fly the Tristar, the wide body, knowing that the company may prefer to post a more junior pilot on to it, such as a first officer on Tristar, saving training costs. This could also save pilots moving base, with all that additional expense. So the agreement was that if a pilot junior to me went on the Tristar, I would get wide body pay. I had done this and all was fine until the company decided that they wanted me to move to Heathrow to go on the Tristar. At that point I had to choose which option I preferred, and if I wanted to stay at Manchester then I would lose wide body pay. This happened to me a year or so after starting at the base, and I told the flight manager that I wanted to stay and would accept the pay cut. Fortunately, within months a new pay agreement was finalised with BALPA, and narrow and wide body scales disappeared, and a single pay scale for all aircraft, including Concorde, was introduced. This helped the company by removing the motivation for pilots to move base or type to maximise their pay. As I had now reached the top of the captains' scale, even after our seniority penalty, I was more than happy. Another lucky break.

Soon after I arrived at Manchester, the computer program SWORD (system for worldwide operational route data) became our main source of flight planning. Putting our flight number into the teleprinter produced reams of paper with all the information we needed. Route, time, fuel, weather, TAFS, NOTAMs, bulletins etc., etc. It was quick and efficient, but it was a shame to lose the old personal touch which we had when we went to the Met Office in each airport to talk directly to a forecaster (I remember Bill Giles at Aldergrove) and also be given a hand written forecast for the flight. We had started using the BEA plogs (prepared nav log) in Cambrian. They were produced for each sector, each pilot had one, and it provided all the nav information we required, tracks, distances, radio aids, and diagrams of the departure and arrival. With our Aerad let down charts for all the airfields we would need, we were fully equipped. More about SWORD later.

Once settled in at Manchester, flying continued in a pleasant routine. The variety of routes and weather, from snow in Copenhagen to fog in Milan, made for an interesting operation, with little chance of boredom. The main runway at Copenhagen, the approach to which was over water, had a warning on the ILS chart of a marine foghorn. This was situated on an rock about a mile from the threshold, and operated in fog. It was very loud and could be heard clearly in the cockpit, and would have been alarming on a Cat 2 or 3 approach in fog if not forewarned.

One change during late 78, early 79, was the fitting of ground proximity warning, GPWS. This provided an automatic warning of unintended approach to the ground, and was set to operate, by an aural warning announcing 'Pull up, pull up!' when ground contact was twenty seconds away. The problem was that when we started flying the 1-11, the company policy was to keep the time airborne to the minimum. This meant flying as fast as possible, for as long as possible, and this became the standard way of flying the aircraft. Although a 'stabilised' approach was technically standard procedure, it was a point of honour to reduce speed at the last possible moment on the approach, and establishing final approach power at 300/400ft was not unusual. This could, of course, lead to some slightly hairy situations when it didn't go completely as planned.

I discovered the new routine according to GPWS one night when landing at Berlin. Radar had positioned us behind a PanAm 727 and kept us rather high as we turned final. They cleared us to join the ILS, but we were well above the glideslope, at 2,500ft in cloud, as we turned on to the localiser at about seven miles. At about 900ft, still slightly above the glideslope, I increased the descent rate to recover the slope, but at about 700ft, as we came out of the cloud and arrived on the slope, the GPWS demanded 'Pull up, pull up'. The standard operating procedural response to this was to go around, and this, reluctantly, was what I did. I had to put in a voyage report, but the company accepted that the situation had occurred from poor radar positioning. I decided that I needed a quick rule of thumb to avoid this happening again, and, reading the GPWS description again realised that the twenty second rule simply meant that whenever the rate of descent was three times the actual height the GPWS would operate. So on my approach at 700ft I must have briefly reached 2100 feet per minute rate of descent. This was nothing unusual in an old fashioned 1-11 approach, but thereafter I used this rule and it never happened again.

The Sl-11 fleet had been fitted for some time with an 'event recorder'. This recorded all the flight parameters over a period of several hours. We had no control over it, and occasionally we would see an engineer replacing it when it was full. When it was downloaded, it was operated at high speed, but if one of the parameters had gone over the prescribed limit, it would 'squeal', and it would then be downloaded at normal speed to record what had actually happened. It had originally been fitted by agreement with BALPA that the information would be anonymous, and pilots would not be identified or reprimanded. Every month or so we had a document circulated showing all the 'events', operating flaps or undercarriage above limiting speed, approach with throttles closed, etc., which was intended to show if there was a trend to unsafe operation. I remember one occasion, before GPWS was fitted, when the flight manager at

Manchester told me about an event he knew about when a Manchester Sl-11 was descending from the east at night, over the hills, and had gone through its 3000ft clearance, and down to a few hundred feet above ground before the crew had realised and recovered. I think the flight manager knew who the crew was and was furious that he couldn't do anything about it.

My flying was fairly uneventful, apart from a brake failure taxying in at Sylt, a German island holiday resort in the Friesian Islands. Operating from Berlin Tegel was usually a pleasure. Our aircraft were parked just outside our offices, operations and crew room, and the routine was normally Teutonic clockwork efficiency. We also had a crewroom on the top floor of the Berlin Hilton hotel, as there were normally at least a dozen crews staying, and the British Officers club was a favourite haunt in the evenings. I would often take my wife with me on a tour, preferably when I was on earlys, finishing by mid-day, and we would enjoy exploring West Berlin, the Zoo, Tiergarten, shops in the Kurfurstendamm (Ku'damm), Checkpoint Charlie into East Berlin, etc., etc.

Operating along the three corridors across East Germany from West Berlin to West Germany was interesting at times. The corridors were ten miles wide and limited to 10,000ft. The Russians were on the edge of hostile, and didn't approve of any deviation from them. We would occasionally see the Migs flying just outside our territory, apparently waiting for us to slip up. During the summer, when cunim build up could be dramatic, it could be difficult to stay within the corridor and avoid the worst of the weather. Eventually it was agreed with the Russians, as tensions eased, that if we declared a 'weather emergency', it was permissible to deviate slightly outside. On a cold clear winter morning it was intriguing to see a steam train chugging its way across East Germany. The RAF kept several Transport Command crews current on our aircraft so that, in the event of an escalation of the Cold War, they would fly our aircraft (empty of course) along the corridors. It never happened.

We were now Cat 3A capable, and during winter, when foggy days were frequent over Europe, we could often spend a week when almost every landing was either a Cat 2 or 3. On one occasion operating a double Hanover with a first officer who had been on the Sl-11 for about eight years, I did the first couple of Cat 2 landings, for which the standard operation was for the first officer to do the approach and the captain to monitor until he was visual to land or call for a go round. For the third landing, at Hanover, I suggested we swap around for a change, quite unapproved of course, so I did the approach and let him monitor until he saw enough to land, which he did. He enjoyed the experience, saying it gave him quite a different view, literally, of the operation.

The Sl-ll only had one autopilot for its autoland system, unlike the Trident which had three. This meant it had to be closely monitored during the final approach, by the pilots and its own self-monitoring system, which would disengage the autopilot if there was the slightest unexpected divergence of any parameter. The final part of the approach was consequently a quite intense operation, checking for lights going on and off at various points, and any divergence from the required indications called for a go around. As we didn't have an auto go around facility, this meant a manual go around, almost always carried out by the first officer. On one occasion landing at Berlin in limiting Cat 3 conditions, my wife was sitting on the jump seat between us, as the aircraft was full. For Cat 2 or 3 landing we transferred to the accurate radio altimeter for the last few hundred feet, and our decision heights were bugged on that instrument, 60ft for Cat 3. As we passed about 250 feet, the tensest part of the approach, my wife leaned over to me, and asked,

"Why does that altimeter have a different reading to the other one?" referring to the approximate 50 ft discrepancy between radio and static instruments.

My immediate response, not wanting to enter into a discussion about it at that point, was short and sweet.

"Shut up!"

Fortunately she understood the purpose of my precise reply, and didn't enter into an argument about it, as she would have done under normal circumstances. We auto landed successfully, and as we taxied in I explained the reason for the difference. I didn't think she even noticed such things.

The automatics were great, but not, as some people would think, allowing us to sit back and watch. In fact, as in the autoland operation, it meant an increased amount of monitoring to ensure the automatics were doing what they should. It was interesting when we had visitors to the flight deck, they would often see us sitting there, apparently doing very little, and they would say,

"It's automatic, is it?"

We would confirm that it was, they would nod, obviously thinking that there were buttons marked 'Start', 'Take-off' and another marked 'Land', and that's all there was to it. In fact the autopilot was great in the cruise, navigating the airways and maintaining height allowing two pilots to monitor its progress. We would occasionally be asked (never told) to operate with an unserviceable autopilot. On a short sector, such as Manchester London, this wasn't a problem, and I would always agree. Soon after we started on the 1-11 with Cambrian, I was asked to take an aircraft, sans autopilot, to Palma. I agreed. However once we settled in the cruise we realised how difficult it was to fly. Accurate flying at height required the total attention of the handling pilot, and a couple of seconds diverted attention would result in a climb or descent of 2,000fpm or more. The handling pilot was therefore out of the loop, and not available for normal monitoring. I didn't volunteer to do a longer trip like that again. It was interesting to watch an extremely competent first officer do a manual ILS approach. However good he was, and some were very good, the ILS needles would move very slightly. Whereas in an automatic coupled approach the two needles would be locked in the centre all the time.

The co-pilots at Manchester were mostly excellent, just one or two didn't qualify for that description. One, ex-RAF, whom the flight manager told me was an ace, was pretty good, but had one habit which always niggled me. When he was flying, regardless of the weather conditions, as he lifted the aircraft off on take-off, I noticed he always dropped his head so he wasn't looking out, but transferred straight to flying by instruments. He would hold the runway heading, which meant, if there was a crosswind, we drifted away from the centreline. He would then follow the standard departure accurately. I preferred to fly visually if possible immediately after take-off, with reference to the instruments of course, and make allowance for drift to track along the runway centreline. Looking out also meant that you would be aware of hazards such as birds, and, if unfortunate enough to meet a flock of them, you had the chance of trying to avoid them by a slight variation of the climb angle. You couldn't do that on instruments.

Another first officer was John Puddle. It never really struck me as interesting until, on a very wet rainy morning, I listened to the one of the girls doing the cabin address welcome announcement to the passengers. With great delight, she said, "You probably won't believe this, but the flight crew today are Captain Flood and First Officer Puddle!" I'm sure the passengers were amused, if they believed it.

Cabin crew, without exception, were very good, both in Cambrian and BA. They were well trained and knew their jobs inside out. There was usually an excellent working relationship between flight deck and cabin, with occasional liaisons of course, some which even led eventually to marriage. I liked to maintain a relaxed atmosphere on board, which I considered was the most efficient. However I remember on one occasion being taken to task by a route check captain. Before departure, the CSD had come to the flight deck to check on our coffee/tea requirements. I'd flown with him for years, enjoyed several meals together on night stops, and we exchanged pleasantries before he left to arrange our drinks. The check captain was horrified that the CSD had greeted me using my first name, Cedric. I assured him that we were friends, I knew he would always address me as 'Captain' in public, and didn't see a problem. However he said I should 'establish my authority' when I was on the aircraft, and suggested asking the cabin crew some emergency procedures each time I came on board. I replied that I didn't consider my authority was ever in doubt. I didn't say so, but I thought the cabin crew must have loved flying with him.

Winter ops from Berlin meant plenty of flying in snow conditions of course. However the European airports were very well organised for this, and when it started they would immediately start sweeping the runways, and for most of the time there wouldn't be a problem for us. Occasionally the weather would beat them, and I do remember diverting to Cologne on one occasion when Dusseldorf was closed by snow. It was at Dusseldorf that Howard had an interesting experience. He was landing in heavy snow when the runway was being swept between flights. He descended on the ILS, cleared to land, and as he arrived at the runway the visibility was about 600 metres. Just as he touched down, he spotted a line of snow ploughs across the width of the runway coming towards him. He slammed the throttles open and pulled the aircraft off the ground, missing the snow ploughs by inches. After profuse apologies from air traffic, he came round for another ILS and landed. He and the first officer were shaken by the incident, and the company sent them off to a hotel to recover. He did well in the circumstances, but was very lucky.

With Cat 3 capability low visibility wasn't the problem it had been in the past. The BA fleet was one of the earliest to be so equipped, and it was nice in the early 80s when London was foggy and they would only allow UK departures to Heathrow for Cat2/3 aircraft. The 1-11 had a very strong airframe, its theoretical fatigue life was well beyond what any aircraft reached. One of the S1-11s was caught in a violent thunderstorm over the Alps, experienced golf ball sized hail, and for the rest of its time proudly displayed its mottled leading edges, with the many dents carefully repaired with filler. Our monochrome weather radar, not as good as later multi-coloured ones, was nevertheless good enough, with careful adjustment, to show the way round the worst of the weather. It showed the cells OK, but often, when the way ahead looked dreadful, we'd slow down and strap the passengers in, but after a few minutes of turbulence we would burst out into clear conditions. Conversely when the radar didn't show anything too bad, we would encounter some nasty stuff.

I reckoned to be struck by lightning about once every two or three years. You could often guess when it was coming when St. Elmo's fire on the windscreen was more than usual and the static noise in your headset steadily increased until finally there was a loud bang as the aircraft was struck. On one flight I did from London to Liverpool in thundery conditions, Reg Leach was a passenger down the back, and he told me, after we landed, that in the middle of it all a blue ball of static, about two feet in diameter, sailed down the middle of the cabin and disappeared out of the rear door. On another occasion we were descending into Manchester in daylight, going blacker outside by the minute, with St. Elmo's and static noise as ever, when we had the almost inevitable loud bang. The first officer, who had been on the S1-11 for about eight or nine years, visibly jumped in his seat. When I mentioned it after landing, he told me it was his first lightning strike. He'd been lucky. On the 1-11 it didn't usually cause a problem for us, but the engineers would find the odd small hole on the airframe in known places where it discharged.

I remember once when sailing my yacht in thundery conditions I heard a strange noise, went on deck to investigate, and realised that the mast was 'hissing' with static. We weren't struck by lightning, but the advice in those conditions was to earth the mast and rigging by attaching a short length of chain to it and trailing it in the water. I never did this, and never had a strike, but yachts occasionally were struck, usually with devastating results.

Another incident I remember was when we were landing one day at Belfast. The first officer was flying and as we passed about 300ft on finals, the master warning lights started flashing. I looked up at the roof panel and saw that the number one hydraulic system had lost all its pressure. The undercarriage was obviously locked down, and I decided that I would land rather than go around. I told the first officer to carry on with the landing, the runway length was more than adequate. We stopped easily, using a bit of reverse thrust, and turned off the runway to stop and await a tug to take us the rest of the way. One of the hydraulic pipes in the undercarriage bay had broken, and there were pools of fluid all over the runway.

During my airline flying (pre 9/11) the cockpit was always available for passengers to visit. We were not strictly allowed to have passengers in for take-off or landing, but could carry staff passengers on the cockpit jump seat. I frequently bent the rules to allow passengers to join us. It was quite usual for cabin crew to bring me a passenger's PPL (Private Pilot's Licence) before take-off with an obvious request, and I was always pleased to accommodate them. For a private pilot it was very enjoyable and, I hope, instructive to sit in for the take-off and landing. It was also good customer relations as far as I was concerned. Once when doing the last Heathrow to Manchester flight of the day, the dispatcher came to the cockpit to say that the aircraft was full but there was a regular passenger who was desperate to get home and would I possibly let him use the cockpit jump seat. I was delighted to agree and the passenger joined us.

When we arrived at Manchester he thanked us and said how interesting it was, as a regular, to fly up front and actually see what was going on. Another happy customer. It wasn't always completely under my control however. I remember a similar last flight from London, the aircraft was full, I'd given away the cockpit and extra cabin crew jump seats. One of my friends from Cambrian days, Captain Dave Williams, who had moved to the London base and commuted, arrived at the last minute with a jump seat request. I explained and apologised to him, and he said he understood and disappeared. Shortly after take-off, Dave appeared in the cockpit and, surprised, I asked him how he managed to get a seat.

"Oh, I just sat in one of the toilets" he told me.

I left it at that. A few years before I retired the company changed its policy and we were allowed to carry passengers on jump seats if 'it was in the commercial interest of the airline'. The decision to carry, and whom to carry, was always at the discretion of the captain of course. This led to some interesting conflicts. Another last flight of the day to Manchester, and a long haul 747 captain had approached me earlier to request use of the jump seat if necessary. I assured him that it was his. Just before departure, with the captain installed on the seat, the dispatcher arrived to see me (late as ever) and advised me that a London based cabin crew member had to position to Manchester to operate the Tristar service next day, and he had given her the cockpit jump seat. I explained as gently as I could that the decision as to who, if anybody, could travel on the cockpit jump seat was mine and mine alone. He had no authority to pre-empt my permission and would have to make alternative arrangements for the cabin crew member.

On another occasion I was taking my wife out to Berlin and we were operating via Heathrow and Dusseldorf. The flights were mostly full but I had assured her that she was first choice for the cockpit jump seat if required. We parked at Heathrow and she went off through passenger channels to join us on the Dusseldorf service. As we prepared to leave for Dusseldorf, the cockpit door opened and the Sl-ll flight manager came in.

He said, "Hello Cedric, sorry I didn't get a chance to let you know, but the flight is full, so if it's OK I'll join you on the flight deck".

He was horrified and embarrassed when I told him of my promise to my wife, but as he had to get to Berlin (flight managers were always running late) he dashed off to arrange with the check-in staff to put my wife on the next 737 service, an hour later, but direct to Berlin. He realised he should have contacted me before he did. My wife arrived OK, quite happy, and said she preferred travelling with the passengers as she had much more interesting conversations.

Another aspect of customer relations was the nervous passenger. The cabin crew were used to dealing with them, and could usually reassure them and settle them down, but occasionally they would ask for our help. I would always suggest that the passenger was brought up to have a chat with us, which would often be all they needed to be reassured that everything was under control and they could stop worrying. In the Viscount days we often had the disc jockeys from the pirate ship Radio Caroline which was anchored just off the Isle of Man. I was never too sure whether Jimmy Saville and Co. were nervous or just wanted a bit of privacy from their public.

One passenger in particular I remember was on a 1-11 night flight return to Liverpool from Majorca. One of the girls came up to tell me that a male passenger was literally shaking with fear. She'd tried the standard couple of whiskies routine. So as usual I suggested she bring him up. He arrived a few minutes later, in quite a state, and explained how he felt. I asked what the problem was, and he said he was frightened of crashing. He told us he was on his honeymoon, and it had been ruined by his fear of flying home. I tried the usual, explaining the instruments and what we were doing, flying is safer than the motorway etc, all to no avail. I told him that we were not going to crash, but he replied,

"They all think that, don't they?"

He finally left us, saying that he would definitely never fly again.

The other extreme came many years later, on a flight from Geneva to Manchester, the CSD (Cabin Service Director) came up to say the usual. A young lady passenger, in her twenties, travelling with her mother, was, as ever, shaking with fear. I suggested the cockpit visit and she duly arrived. After chatting to us for about five minutes she visibly relaxed, and so I showed her the cockpit jump seat and suggested that after her meal she could come back and join us for the approach and landing. This she did and, secure in the jump seat between the pilots (which, as I told her, had the best view in the aircraft) as we started our descent, she was smiling and asking questions about all sorts. She became so chatty in fact that, as we turned finals, I had to gently remind her that we had a job to do, talking to each other and air traffic. It was a nice day and she really enjoyed the approach and landing, and went back to the cabin happily after thanking us. As the passengers disembarked, her mother came in to the cockpit to thank us and say that she couldn't believe the difference in her daughter, who had told her that she would never be worried about flying again. We were delighted and it showed the power and benefit of the cockpit visit, at least on this occasion.

Occasionally of course we carried celebrity passengers. Football teams often, Juventus, from Birmingham to Turin, the Liverpool team several times, (and I'm an Everton supporter). I 'won' a china cup and saucer which Bill Shankley used on one flight, (he wouldn't drink from plastic). I kept it for a few years before I gave it to an uncle who was an avid Liverpool supporter, and he really appreciated it. Pop stars, politicians etc., and, shortly after he resigned the presidency, Richard Nixon. He was on the early Berlin London flight one morning, and when I walked out to the aeroplane I was surprised to see several G-men stationed around it. I ignored them and did my pre-flight walk round. Normally in Berlin we had local German cabin crew, but on this UK bound flight we had a Manchester crew. As I climbed on to the pier to enter the forward door, our CSD, a lovely little Lancashire lass, was berating the G-man who was standing in the galley.

"Look, chuck, I can't do my checks with you standing there. Go and sit down."

The 6ft 6inch G-man touched his forelock, and with a 'Yes, Ma'am', obediently moved into the passenger cabin. Shortly after, half a dozen black limousines arrived at the aircraft with Nixon and his entourage. Even a deposed President was given the full treatment. George Bush senior visited Berlin while he was President and stayed in the Hilton. He had one complete floor and the place was overrun with G-men. A no-go zone was established for 100 yards around the hotel, and we even had to disembark from the crew bus, and walk this last bit with our bags. Everybody entering the hotel was checked but we were generally left alone.

In the Viscount days, I had Sir Alan Cobham as a passenger from Liverpool to the Isle of Man one day. He didn't make a fuss, and I spoke to him just briefly as he disembarked. Afterwards I regretted that I hadn't invited him to sit up front with us. I'm sure he would have enjoyed it more than sitting down the back.

Every six months we did our simulator checks, and once a year we had a route check. This was a flight accompanied by a route check captain, who checked that we were operating in accordance with the company standard operating procedures. Route check captains were different to training captains, and were ostensibly there to make sure that the training department was doing its job. I remember one had the nickname of 'Smiling Assassin'. We had a similar system in Cambrian, but the route checks were done by the training captains. When I started at Manchester, the first officers explained the (BEA) system to me, saying that on this annual flight it was important to operate precisely to the book, dotting the 'Is' and crossing the 'Ts'. They said as long as you did this, it was acceptable to be a bit more flexible the rest of the time. I didn't agree with this, my view was that on a route check I should fly exactly as I did every day, and if there was something in my operation of the aircraft which didn't meet with approval, then I should be told, and I would change it. I'm afraid my rather relaxed attitude to these checks wasn't exactly what was required. Much later, just before I retired, I did a route check with a London based captain. We were going to Geneva and just before departure one of the girls brought us a selection of newspapers to read on the turn round. Settled in the cruise, FDH (fat dumb and happy) as usual, I picked a newspaper up to show the others a headline, then dropped it back by my bag. Nothing was said at the time, but when I was debriefed, I was astonished when the captain told me that this action constituted a failure, and would require another check flight. His demeanour indicated that if I had slow rolled the aeroplane it wouldn't have been much worse. Eating a three course meal from a tray on my knee during the flight was acceptable, but glancing at a newspaper was not. I did another check a few weeks later to satisfy the system. I still maintain my attitude was correct.

Another aspect of these checks was opinions of the best way to fly. On the Sl-ll we were encouraged to use 26° flap for landing, rather than full 45° flap. As long as the runway length was acceptable, more than 2500m, and no tailwind, it meant less power on the approach, and so quieter and more fuel efficient. Landing speed was higher, about 8-10 knots, and the aircraft had a more nose up attitude, which I liked. I used this technique whenever I could, although not all pilots favoured it. On one of my route checks, all had gone well, and landing back at Manchester, I decided on 26° flap. As we touched down, I did as always with this flap setting, and gently applied the brakes, holding the nose up with elevator against the nose down pull from the brakes to use aerodynamic drag as long as possible. Nothing was said until debriefing, when the check captain could hardly contain his displeasure. He told me he had never seen anything so dangerous. Astonished, I asked him what he was talking about. He said applying brake while the nosewheel was off the ground. When I asked him how that was dangerous, he said that if one brake had failed I would have swung off the runway. I assured him that I was using the brakes differentially and, if one brake had failed, then I would simply have stopped using the other one. This didn't make him any happier however, and, although he passed me, we parted without coming to any agreement. I didn't consider him a particularly good pilot anyway, and he'd obviously never flown aeroplanes without a nosewheel (tailwheel aircraft), if he thought one was essential for directional control.

Next year I flew with a London route check captain (a sailing man). The landing was almost an identical situation to the previous year. I wondered as I approached whether to modify my technique (I hadn't changed anything in the intervening year), but decided to do it exactly as I usually did. The captain was positioning back home on Shuttle shortly, so he asked if it was OK to debrief me in the cockpit, alongside the co-pilot. I agreed happily.

He said, "That was absolutely fine, Cedric, no problems whatsoever. I would like to make just one comment, however, about the landing".

This, I thought, is the punch line.

He continued, "I thought the landing was excellent, that's a really nice technique, holding the nose up against the brakes".

Which just shows you can please some of the people, some of the time.

The 1-11 was a delightful aeroplane to fly and I never tired of operating it. We always tried to fly manually whenever we could and do a visual approach if possible. Even at Heathrow it was occasionally possible, on a quiet evening, to ask for, and be given, a visual approach from the Bovingdon beacon. At Manchester, as the local airline, air traffic were usually co-operative in acceding to our requests. One lovely summer evening I had been to Belfast with a London based first officer. I was flying the leg back into Manchester and as we crossed the Wallasey beacon on the Wirral coast we could see the airfield clearly. The controller cleared us visual, and once we had passed over Liverpool airport, cleared us to the approach. I lost height to about 1,000ft, throttles closed, spoilers out to kill the speed, and downwind abeam the threshold of 24 started a descending turn to finals, dropping wheels and flaps, aiming to hit the approach at about 400ft. It worked out beautifully and, with just a bit of power for the last few hundred feet we touched down. As we did, I realised that my co-pilot was grinning like a Cheshire cat. Not too sure, I asked him what was so amusing.

He replied, "Oh, I really enjoyed that, it was poetry in motion".

His pleasure and appreciation made me equally happy.

The 1-11s spent a lot of time in and out of Heathrow and we had a few of our own short cuts to beat the system. One favourite was when parked, as we often were, on the alpha stands just south of 28R, we would ask the ground controller, when we had pushed back, if there was any possibility of departing from block 16. This was a taxiway connecting strip about halfway along the runway, directly opposite the alpha stands. If we were lucky, the tower controller would clear us to use this block to line up, saving us taxying to the holding point and joining the queue. This way we could often be airborne three or four minutes after pushing back.

With their frequent movements in and out of Heathrow, the 1-11 pilots tended to be slightly irreverent. One apocryphal tale (from Roger Bacon's 'Straight and Level' in Flight magazine) illustrates this. There was the usual queue for take-off at the 10R holding point. The controller was advising each aircraft of the usual 'line up in turn' procedure. He lined up a Pan Am 747, and told a KLM City Hopper Fokker F27,

"After the Pan Am jumbo departs, line up and wait".

The KLM aircraft acknowledged the clearance.

The next aircraft was a BA Concorde, and the controller called him,

"Speedbird Concorde 01, after the City Hopper departs, line up and wait".

The Concorde replied, in a slightly superior voice, "Roger, Speedbird Concorde 01, to line up and wait when the City Hopper departs. Is that the dumpy little pale blue one?"

The controller confirmed his aircraft recognition. Next in turn in the queue was a BA S1-11, and the controller called him,

"Speedbird 783, after Concorde departs, line up and wait".

The 1-11 replied,

"Roger, Speedbird 783, after Concorde, to line up and wait. Is that the long thin white one?" Enough said.

I always enjoyed the simulator. The S1-11 visual was an early computer generated light display, which meant we always flew in the dark, but it was very effective. I heard that in the database was a simulation of Manhattan, and it was possible to fly down Seventh

Avenue below the level of the skyscrapers, banking to miss the buildings, but I never saw this bit. We did sim as a crew and a few first officers hated it and were worried by it. It showed in their performance, as one or two whom I knew were excellent in the real aircraft didn't do as well in the sim. My attitude was that the worst that could happen was a retest and I'd have to do it all again, which I didn't mind. Of course, that never happened. The spring check was one day, four hours in the simulator, and after the compulsory base check items were done, engine fail before and after V1, single engine approach, go round, and landing, there was time for some training exercises, usually several devious failures one after the other resulting in one of us sitting with the book on our knee working things out. I enjoyed it as good practice and review of aircraft systems which we didn't normally have to think about. Reading the manuals wasn't the same as doing it in the simulator. If there was time available after we had done what was required, we had the chance to try anything of our choice. Sometimes I would choose to do some aerobatics, but they weren't quite the same on instruments. The autumn check was two days, eight hours sim., and was extended to include the annual instrument rating renewal.

One early S1-11 sim check was with a London training captain. I had heard that he was anti-Cambrian, but he seemed amenable enough as we briefed. I did the first detail, my instrument rating. As we got airborne, I thought something wasn't quite right, and quickly realised the simulator motion wasn't operating. This made flying more difficult without the usual feedback from the movement of the sim., but I said nothing and did the test OK. When it was over, the captain, with a smirk, asked me when I noticed and I told him.

'Oh yes, I noticed as you rolled on take-off, but didn't want to disturb you at that point by switching it on', he said.

After we finished the day's work we had some time to spare and he asked if we wanted to do anything. I said as my single engine ILS approach wasn't spot on (although it had passed) I'd like to do another one. I did this, but when I countersigned my form at the end, I noticed he had included it as a retake. Cheeky, I thought, but par for the course at that time, and not worth an argument.

One strange thing about the instrument rating in the simulator was that we had to do it, effectively, as a single pilot operation. The other pilot would do whatever we asked, tune beacons, undercarriage, flaps etc., but nothing more. This meant it was nothing like our usual routine of a shared and monitored operation. I believe it changed, after I retired, to a more realistic two crew test. One odd, but useful, particularly in training, ability of the simulator, was 'freezing'. The trainer could stop, or freeze, the sim at any point, and then we could discuss whatever was happening. Having chatted about it and sorted any misunderstandings, the button would be pushed again and we would continue from where we left off. A bit surreal maybe, but quite useful.

In my first year at Manchester the pilots had a one day unofficial strike. I've forgotten what the dispute was about as it had started well before we arrived. It was a purely local disagreement and BALPA didn't support the action. In the event, it was supported 100% by the local pilots, and unfortunately I was flying that day. My first officer was Tony Hughes, also ex Cambrian, and he rang me the evening before to decide what we would do. We had no inclination to strike, but realised that if we, and only we, didn't, it would probably increase the alienation we were experiencing from some pilots. Accordingly we kept our heads down and supported the action by refusing to fly. I was disappointed that I didn't stick to my principles, but sometimes cowardice is the better option.

The S1-11 maximum cruise level was FL350, rather than FL370 which the series 400 could use, because the aircraft didn't have drop out oxygen for the passengers, as did the 400. The cabin crew had a number of plug in masks for passengers, and the plan was that, in the event of a loss of cabin pressure, they, equipped with their portable oxygen sets, would go round the cabin plugging in these masks for those passengers who needed them. All this while we were carrying out our emergency descent to 10,000ft. We practised our part of this routine on most simulator checks. While in the cruise at 35,000ft, (37,000 in the 1-11 400), there would be a bang from behind us, the cabin height warning of above 10,000ft would light up, and the cabin rate of climb indicator would show a maximum climb. This indicated explosive decompression, and so each of us would knock off our headset, put on our oxygen mask (pulled out from the roof above us) as quickly as possible, and replace headset. We hurried in the knowledge that we had less than thirty seconds before we would be affected by hypoxia. The aim was to be on oxygen within twenty seconds. The drill then was that whichever pilot was first to establish on oxygen would take control of the aircraft, close the throttles, autopilot out, full spoiler, roll over into the descent, autopilot engaged again, and select max speed on the speed lock. The other pilot, when he was on oxygen, would do the checklist and liaise with air traffic and cabin crew. The aim was to get down to 10,000ft in under four minutes, requiring a rate of descent of more than 6,000ft per minute. Although we were often close, I never made it in less than four minutes. I remember well the first time I did this descent after I had started wearing half-moon specs, for near vision correction (particularly needed in the dim light of the cockpit). As I pushed my headset off to grab the mask, I managed to also knock my specs off and they dropped on to the cockpit floor. By the time I had established myself on oxygen, and recovered them from the floor, we were well into the descent. I was careful that it never happened again, and in fact on the last simulator before I retired I was pleased that I was the first on oxygen, and flew the descent.

In those days, most aircraft cruised in the high thirties flight levels, just a few, such as Learjets going up above 40,000ft. The 1-11 was running out of steam at cruise level, and, if we were heavy, 200/300 feet per minute rate of climb for the last bit wasn't unusual. We heard an interesting exchange on the radio one day, which made us envious. A Learjet was at FL370 badgering air traffic for a higher level. There was conflicting traffic, but eventually the controller said,

"Learjet 123, if you can expedite your climb, I can offer you FL410".

The Learjet assured him that he could expedite, and the controller replied,

"OK, in that case, Learjet 123, you are now cleared to climb to FL410, would you please expedite your climb, and report level."

The Lear replied, "Learjet 123, roger, cleared to climb to FL410, and in fact we are now levelling at FL410".

He must have been sitting at max speed, and zoom climbed to the new level. We were impressed.

There are many situations in airline operation which are not covered completely by 'the book'. I always understood that BA would back a captain's decision that was sensible in the prevailing conditions, even if it was not quite 'standard'. A couple of incidents for me showed that it wasn't so cut and dried.

I was operating a Frankfurt service from Manchester one morning. It was a period of congestion over Europe when slot times for take-off were very important. Sometimes we could be delayed a hour or more by the earliest slot we could obtain. On this occasion, we had a 'schedule' slot. This slot time meant we had to be airborne five minutes after our scheduled time of departure. About fifteen minutes before our STD, with passengers and baggage apparently on board, everything looking good, the dispatcher came into the cockpit looking worried. He told me that we had three passengers checked in, with bags, who hadn't boarded. If they couldn't be found, it would mean a baggage check, that is, all the baggage unloaded on to the tarmac, and the passengers asked to get off and identify their own bags. This usually took at least thirty minutes. I immediately called air traffic to request a delay on the slot. They told me that if we missed this one it would be at least two hours before the next one was available.

The minutes ticked by, and then the dispatcher came dashing out to tell us the he had found the passengers. They were still airborne, inbound on our delayed Tristar flight from New York, checked in for Frankfurt, with their bags, but the computer hadn't made it clear on the loadsheet. We were clear to go, with about five minutes to the slot. Doors shut, starting as we pushed back, warning the cabin crew that we were in a hurry, and of course, to add to our difficulty, using 06 runway, which was a long taxi. We taxied as fast as we could, but as we arrived near the holding point with a couple of minutes to go we realised there were about four aircraft ahead of us, and no chance of getting past them on to the runway. The controller offered us an alternative when he said we could make an immediate departure from the first intersection, Golf, which was about 200 metres from the start of the runway. This would mean we would just meet our slot time, and the alternative was at least a two hour delay.

The problem for me was that, although in the past our Flight Manual Volume 3, runway calculation details, had allowed us to depart from any of the first three intersections on 06, it had recently been amended to require that we always used the full length of 06 for take-off. This change was purely to improve our noise footprint over Stockport on the climb out, with no safety considerations involved. There was a decent headwind anyway and I didn't think Stockport would mind this one transgression. I made an instant 'captain's decision', and told the controller that we would accept his offer. We entered the runway, turned to port and departed. I thought later that if I had turned to starboard to line up, the long way round, I could have claimed we had back tracked. However, as we climbed away, I relaxed and thought we had done well to beat all the obstacles that had conspired to delay us.

That, I thought, was the end of it, until about a week later our flight manager called me into his office. I wondered why, but soon found out. He told me he had been sitting in the 5th floor office one day, from where he had an excellent view of the whole airfield, with 'somebody from London', when they had noticed a BA S1-11 take off from intersection golf on runway 06, when 'the book' said we had to use the full length. He was obviously talking about me, so I then explained what had happened on the day, and as I knew the full length requirement was purely a noise limitation, I had made the decision to ignore it. He, being quite definitely a 'book' man, told me my decision was wrong. I was astonished, and asked him if he thought I should have declined the offer of an intersection departure, and returned to the terminal for at least a two hour delay. He said that was exactly what I should have done. I couldn't believe it, told him I thought that was ridiculous, and said that we obviously thought and operated in different worlds. I said I thought I had made a sensible commercial decision which meant ninety-odd passengers arrived at Frankfurt on time, without compromising safety in any way. Once again, we parted without agreement. Rules for wise men and fools, I decided.

Another flight which required a decision, not so instant, was when we had to divert one night from Manchester to Leeds. It was foggy at Manchester requiring a Cat 2 or 3 approach, but the runway lights failed so we had to go to Leeds. As we approached Leeds, we were given the latest weather. The visibility was just above limits but forecast to drop below, and Leeds was Cat 1 only. More significantly the runway state was icy, with a braking action of medium, and poor in parts, and the controller advised that the runway ice was getting worse. When we checked our Volume 3 we found a restriction on the landing weight if the braking action was medium or less. Our landing weight would be a few hundred kilos above this weight. We had just enough fuel to divert to Prestwick immediately, but if we held to burn off fuel to make our landing weight legal, we would then be committed, and if the Leeds visibility went below our Cat 1 limit we would have nowhere to go. I decided that I would land now, technically above the icy runway limit. I briefed the first officer about careful use of reverse thrust to avoid asymmetric effects. We landed, carefully and successfully. A captain's decision which may have been difficult to justify if we had slid off the runway.

Around this time we were being exhorted by the company to carry just 'sword' fuel. SWORD was the computer program which produced our plan for each flight, and calculated the fuel required as the legal minimum, fuel for the flight, fuel to diversion, and 45 minutes holding, plus a small contingency. We were told that every extra kilo of fuel carried above this minimum cost money. This was obviously true, but I had already experienced occasions when unforecast weather had changed the situation dramatically. Sword fuel for Manchester London was about four and a half tons, but I never went with less than six tons, and seven if there was any doubt about weather or delays. Occasionally, if it was the first officer's leg, when technically he made all the decisions, he would ask for the sword minimum. I would say that he could have that fuel if he wanted, but I would have a bit extra, just for me. I knew that when the crunch came, whoever's leg it was, only one person would carry the can. There were a couple of cases of junior captains being intimidated by these policies, caught out with sword fuel, and landing with uncomfortably little. A flight manager was caught out in fog on a flight from Berlin, diverted twice, and finally had to do a Cat 3 landing below limits. Being a flight manager, that was OK, but I wondered if that leniency would have been shown to a line pilot. Rumour had it that the company kept a list of those captains who carried more fuel than 'necessary', and I was glad to hear I was in a leading position on it.

One occasion when I was more than glad I had 'my' fuel on board was an autumn evening Paris and return from Manchester. Season of mists and mellow fruitfulness, but the forecast for Charles de Gaulle was good, a nice clear evening, with just a prob40 (40% probability) of low visibility at about three o'clock the following morning. Sword (computer) fuel was between 5 and 6 tons, enough for comfortable diversion to any of the other Paris airports. However I decided on 7.6 tons (good for an extra hour), which almost filled the wing tanks. A more comfortable amount for me. As we approached Charles de Gaulle airport (CDG), with the ATIS advising reasonable visibility of several kilometres, we were radar positioned in sequence as usual for the north runway, 27R. There wasn't a cloud in the sky, and we could see the twinkling lights of the city spreading to the south. Radar turned us to join the ILS localiser at about eight miles, and as we turned we could see the runway and approach lighting clearly. We called established to radar and he told us to call the tower. I did this and advised that we were established. His reply made us sit up.

"Roger, Speedbird 5182, you are number one and cleared for the ILS 27R. The RVR is 50 metres".

I immediately asked him to confirm the RVR.

"RVR is fife zero metres", he replied, with Gallic indifference.

We were Cat 3 capable, and had prepared for a possible auto approach and landing, but 50 metres was below our Cat 3a limits (even below Cat3b limits), and meant we couldn't descend below 1,000ft on the approach. We continued down the ILS with the runway lights still in view, although we knew that with a low fog things would be different as we reached the last few hundred feet. Just before 1,000ft I checked the RVR again, still the same, 50 metres, so I advised the tower we were going around. He put us back to the approach controller, who cleared us for a standard go around climb to the holding beacon to the northwest at 3,500ft. Thinking quick diversion to Orly, I asked my co-pilot to call the company frequency at CDG and get the latest Orly weather. I listened as he did, and the company advised us that both Orly and Le Bourget were also 50 metres or less.

Back with approach we heard the aircraft following us calling on go around, and the controller asked us to climb in the hold to 5,000ft. I made an immediate decision to divert to Brussels, which was wide open, and requested a clearance from Paris. Their response was 'Standby'. Each aircraft on approach was now going around, as nobody had approach limits of 50 metres, and the situation was slowly becoming more chaotic by the minute. Aircraft were being pointed at various holding beacons in the Paris area, we were requested to climb to 7,000ft and then asked to descend again to 5,000. After about fifteen or twenty minutes in the hold, watching aeroplanes all over the sky, trying whenever I could get a word in to request diversion to Brussels, the overworked controller came back to us with a clearance to Brussels, but at FL50. At that height we would be gobbling fuel, and I requested higher. Once again, 'Standby'. It would take us about 25 to 30 minutes to Brussels, and we didn't have fuel to go there at FL50 and have much in reserve, so I eased the throttles back to make it go a bit further. However after about five minutes en route Paris cleared us to FL120, and put us over to Brussels. After five minutes at FL160 we finally landed with some relief. We would have been under much more pressure if we had departed with just Sword fuel.

During the eighties I considered a move to long-haul, and looked at the 747 rosters to see what sort of flying I might be doing on that fleet. We had moved to a rostering system called bidline, which originated in the states. This was seniority based, and we would receive one month's roster of all the work, about two months in advance, to select, in order of seniority, a line of work to our choice. During each roster month, any uncovered work was shown in the 'overtime' book, and pilots could also bid for this (seniority order) and be paid extra for doing it. At the time I was about number four in seniority at Manchester, so usually could rely on at least second or third choice, if not first. On the larger 747 fleet I would also have been quite senior, and so would have had a reasonable choice. However I wasn't keen on the long-haul lifestyle, the longer sectors meant an average of six or seven landings a month, whereas on the 1-11 we averaged 40 to 50. Our sector length averaged about one hour, and we did two, three or four sectors each day, which I found much more pleasant. I also did not particularly care for being based at Heathrow, and having to commute, so I didn't bid for the 747. There were rumours for a while of a Tristar base at Manchester, part of the British Airtours charter and inclusive tour operation, which was based at Gatwick. I thought that might have been interesting, but it never happened.

Some days were four sector days, such as a Geneva plus Amsterdam, Paris and Jersey, or Frankfurt and Brussels, and the company would obviously have preferred to utilise us this way all the time. Available pilots and the schedules didn't always fit however, so some days were just two sectors, such as Amsterdam or Paris. My choice (when bidline allowed) was an early Amsterdam or Brussels, and I would be home by midday. We normally worked up to FTL (Flight Time Limitations), particularly when doing extra days via the bid system. The longer days were often close to the daily limit (between 11 and 12 hours depending on sectors and start time). The FTL allowed 'captain's discretion' to be exercised to extend the duty day slightly if delays had been encountered. This only happened very occasionally, and the crew controllers would usually change the plan to avoid it, by swapping crews. There was never any commercial pressure in BA to operate beyond the limits. I read now, in Chirp for example, of companies where the captain is asked (told?) to exercise his discretion before the day starts so the schedule can be completed. That's not the way it's supposed to work. The only regular nightstop we had after Berlin finished was Paris. There was also an occasional Stockholm. Paris was a very pleasant break, either an early finish at Paris followed by an early start next day, or late finish with a late start next day. Occasionally it was a late finish, a day off in Paris, then an early start. The day off was a paid day on bidline, earning, as I remember six credit hours. I believe after I left, days abroad not working like this were counted as days off towards the minimum.

In the annual base and fleet bid for 83/84, Concorde appeared for the first time. There had been no movement on that fleet since its introduction, but now some retirements had created vacancies. Two of us at Manchester, Willie Wilson and myself, had the seniority to bid for it, and after some hard thinking I decided to try. I didn't really fancy the very limited routes and flying involved but nevertheless thought it was an opportunity that couldn't be missed. Willie and I put our bids in. There was a 'freeze' period on type after any bid, to justify training costs, three years for narrow body, and five years wide body. A few weeks after the annual bid closed I had a 'phone call one evening from the flight manager of the fleet at Heathrow. He said he was very sorry to say that it had only just been agreed with BALPA that the freeze period on Concorde would be seven and a half years. If I went on Concorde, at the end of my training I would only have seven years and four months left before retirement, and so my bid had been declined. I would have volunteered to work for an extra two months, but that wasn't an option. So near, yet so far, but I'm not sure if it wasn't a convenient way of weeding out those who may not have been the company's first choice. Willie didn't get it either. I settled down again happily on the 1-11 with no regrets.

With my seniority, I liked bidline. We had to work to 'cap', an agreed number of credit hours each month, and could then bid to work on days off, for extra pay. I could usually pick and get a line (28 days work roster) which gave me trips that I enjoyed. One strange part of the initial bidline agreement was the 'ringed' trip. The management pilots didn't work to bidline, so when the lines were drawn up, they would pick days on which they would fly. As this trip was already on a line pilot's month of work, it was circled, or 'ringed'. This meant the line pilot would get the pay credit for the day, but didn't have to fly. The agreement also meant that, if he really wanted to, he could operate as supernumerary and claim the expenses which he would otherwise lose. I don't remember anybody taking advantage of this. One month I had a line which included a ringed six day German tour. I thought I might pick up some extra work on a few of those days. In the event, the management pilot decided not to do the German tour, which meant it dropped into the overtime book, and of course I was the only pilot who had six days free to do the trip. So I was paid overtime to operate the tour which had been mine in the first place. I didn't complain. The ringed trip arrangement didn't last long, and was soon negotiated out of the bidline agreement.

Initially at Manchester we had airport and home standbys to cover eventualities, but they disappeared with bidline and the drafting system. Being paid extra to fly on a day off made a difference. Driving 46 miles to work down the motorway meant that occasionally I could have a problem. We had to report one hour before take-off, which was a minimum to do all that was required. On one occasion I was held up by an accident on the motorway and arrived breathless about fifteen minutes before take-off. The crew controller was more relaxed about it than I expected, and said,

"No problem, the first officer has done everything, and is waiting for you in the aircraft!"

Good first officers are worth their weight in gold!

Another time, luckily when we had airport standbys, a stretch of motorway was closed suddenly after an accident, and the resultant gridlock for miles around meant I was two hours late for a midday Geneva. I couldn't even get out of the car to use a phone box (before mobile phones). Several pilots and cabin crew had been similarly delayed, but the flights had all been covered successfully. The crew controller told me to go home, and wondered why I'd bothered to come, being so late. However these events were unusual.

In my early days as a Viscount first officer, I was on an 0800 departure from Speke. I didn't hear my alarm and woke at about 0725. My journey to Speke normally took thirty minutes, but I dressed in three and hurtled through the Mersey Tunnel, arriving at the aircraft five minutes before departure. The captain, Jimmy Jones, was in his seat grinning. I decided that it would never happen again, and thereafter I always had three alarm clocks, one of which was electric, on the far side of the bedroom, and it would ring until I got out of bed to switch it off. The system worked.

After a few years we lost the Berlin operation when the 737 fleet took over, however the S1-11 fleet was then scheduled to provide the back-up element of the Shuttle services between Heathrow and Manchester, Glasgow, Edinburgh, and Belfast. The frontline services were operated by the Boeing 757 fleet, the 1-11s providing the extra service if this was oversubscribed. I quite enjoyed the shuttle routine, we did six days on, which could mean sitting around all day at Manchester or elsewhere, or flying to any of the bases to operate. It also involved quite a lot of positioning as passenger. With the bidline roster system we were paid by the flying we did (flying hours, duty hours, or time away from base) and shuttle, because of its unusual nature, attracted an extra pay premium which made it even more attractive and enjoyable for me.

The variable nature of shuttle flying can be shown by a couple of example days. On earlys at Manchester, if we weren't used on the first few morning departures, shuttle control at Heathrow would often ask us to position an empty aircraft somewhere to do another flight. One morning they called us to say that if we weren't required to back up the 1130 departure, would we position the aircraft to London. We prepared the aircraft, and, having checked that the 1130 B757 was well under a full load, decided to go ahead of it. Just before we closed our doors, one of the flight managers from London came on board to say that he was positioning down, and as we were going before the 757, he may as well fly with us. No problem, and we set off for Heathrow. As we turned finals 10 miles out on 28R at Heathrow, the tower controller asked us to call shuttle control on the company frequency. We did, and the shuttle man asked us where we were. I told him on finals, and he replied

"Oh, I didn't think you'd be so close, but we need the aircraft in Belfast. Do you think you could you possibly go there now?"

We had departed Manchester with my usual six tons, more than sword, and looking at the gauges we had just over four tons remaining. I did a quick mental calculation, and told shuttle control that we would. Now about four miles out on finals, I called the tower,

"Tower, Shuttle 2G, you probably won't believe this, but we would like to divert to Belfast".

"I'd believe anything from Shuttle," he replied, "you're cleared to turn direct to Lichfield and climb to FL140."

We climbed further to FL280 and made it comfortably to Belfast on our four tons. We then did the back-up service to the next front-line and arrived in Heathrow about two hours later. The poor flight manager who expected to be in London quickly was well delayed. But he should have known better than to hitch a ride on a shuttle back up.

I was on late back-up one day, when Shuttle control asked us to position an empty aircraft from Manchester to Edinburgh, for a possible 4 o'clock back-up. It was a lovely summer afternoon, so we flew direct from Pole Hill to Edinburgh, with the help of military radar. We waited for the call to back-up, but the 757 departed with just a few empty seats. We weren't required. After deliberating for a short while, shuttle control in London decided that we should take the aircraft back to Manchester. As we flew the empty aircraft across Yorkshire again I said to my co-pilot,

"This is better than a flying club, and we get paid for it!"

That was life on shuttle back-up.

European flying was generally uneventful. I had favourite and unfavoured airfields, of course, and on bidline I could attempt to choose to which I flew. I think Amsterdam was number one. Slick air traffic, using up to three or even four runways at once, and, importantly, a distinct friendliness to the British. We would ask to keep up our speed on the descent and almost always be allowed. Then if the wind allowed we would ask to use the nearest runway, 19 (as it was, now 18C), and usually that request would be accepted. The 250kt speed limit below 10,000ft had now been introduced, but we would often ask if 'we could keep our speed' and knew who would allow it, leaving us to maintain maximum speed, and slow down when we wished, just like the old days. Amsterdam was almost always co-operative and Manchester could mostly be relied on. It was a waste of time even asking in Germany. Knowing us, they would often remind us of the speed limit as we approached 10,000ft in descent. We would then annoy them by reducing only slowly, prompting frequent requests to say our speed. We would just tell them we were reducing. Lufthansa, of course, stuck rigidly to the rules, and if we were just behind them westbound across the North Sea, we knew we'd be delayed in the descent. In that case, when we called Manchester, we'd ask to keep our speed and, if they were, as usual, co-operative, they would put us on a radar heading and we would slide gently past Lufthansa and land before them. It just balanced what they did to us in Frankfurt.

My least favourite of the European destinations was definitely Frankfurt. With two parallel runways, about 500 metres apart, and the terminal buildings on the north side, we could be sure of landing on the south runway, particularly if a Lufthansa aircraft was within ten miles. This meant a longer taxi and a wait to cross the north runway while aircraft (usually Lufthansa) landed. There was definitely a positive discrimination against British aircraft. On one occasion we had landed on the south runway, and stopped waiting for clearance to cross the north. A Lufthansa 737 was taxying for take-off on the north, but nowhere near the holding point, and another Lufthansa 737 was pushing back from the victor stands, just opposite where we were. The controller advised that we could expect to be cleared to cross the runway when the Lufthansa had departed. My co-pilot, Francis, was on the radio and replied, with just a hint of sarcasm,

"Roger, we'll be clear to cross after Lufthansa departs. That is the Lufthansa that is pushing back on the victor stands."

The controller, obviously missing the point, (Teutonic sense of humour) replied,

"Oh, No, I mean the one that is about to take off."

Which it did more than a minute later. We could have been parked well before that. Unlike Heathrow, the two runways at Frankfurt, were used for mixed landings and take-offs, which could be interesting at times. For landing they were supposed to maintain a two mile horizontal separation from aircraft on the other runway, but it didn't always work. Landing to the east one day, we had joined on a long final for the north runway, when a 747 was vectored on to the south runway. It ended up on final for that runway, but alongside us. The controller asked if we were happy to continue, and I agreed, but I felt I had to explain to the passengers why we appeared to be in formation with another aircraft alongside. On another similar occasion, we were established on the north runway and a Balkan TU134 was vectored on to the south, luckily two miles ahead of us, as the rules required. As the TU134 turned to intercept the south localiser, he overshot, and we watched as he went through the south centre line and then through our centre line, just ahead of us, before he eventually regained and settled on the south localiser. Not my favourite airport.

Madrid was another place where we didn't often win. One of our first officers was fluent in Spanish, and as his aircraft approached Madrid one day, he heard the controller (speaking in Spanish) tell an Iberia aircraft, which was behind them, that he would send the BA aircraft on a long downwind leg to allow Iberia to land first. The controller was breaking the rules by speaking in Spanish, but our first officer made it clear that he understood exactly what was happening when he replied to all subsequent calls in perfect Spanish.

Copenhagen was a pleasant operation. We flew there straight across the North Sea from Ottringham to Esbjerg, about 400 miles. In the middle we were a bit short on VHF reception and often lost contact with London before the border. Usually somebody a bit nearer London would relay for us, which helped. One morning we were cruising across quietly, too quietly in fact. We'd finished our breakfast, had a quick scan of the morning papers, when I realised we were getting quite close to Esbjerg, but were still on the London frequency. We smartly changed to the Copenhagen channel and called them. They weren't too bothered, their North Sea VHF reception was often as bad as London.

An interesting VHF anomaly occurred one morning descending into Manchester. We had called approach and received our final descent clearance, when another voice called us, loud and clear, with our callsign, and asked where we were. Intrigued, I told him we were approaching Manchester. He then replied, with his callsign, which I didn't recognise, to say that he was the tower controller at an airfield in Norway, and he had been receiving aircraft like us all morning. I explained to the equally intrigued Manchester approach controller what was going on, and to whom I was talking. An unusual and extreme example of duct propagation.

On our way home from Frankfurt one morning, we were in the cruise, approaching Brussels at FL310, when we saw something ahead, at our level. As we approached we could see it was a large radiosonde weather balloon, obviously stuck at our level for some reason. We altered track slightly to avoid it and asked Brussels if they knew about it. He replied that he didn't, but was only using secondary radar. When he switched primary radar on, he obviously saw it clearly, and we listened to him for the next ten minutes (even after we had changed frequency) frantically rerouting aircraft around the rogue balloon. We never found out if they shot it down.

Descending into Manchester one day, through layers of cloud, we spotted a hot air balloon just a few miles to port at about 8,000ft. We told the controller about it, and he said he knew of a balloon meet in Derbyshire, but they weren't supposed to be climbing that high. That was the problem with secondary radar, they couldn't see anything which didn't have a transponder.

One of the first officers, Hugh, introduced me to a novel navigational technique. We were plodding between beacons across Europe when the controller asked if we had INS (Inertial Navigation System), so that he could clear us direct to a distant beacon. Hugh replied,

"Negative INS, but we do have IGD."

The controller, obviously not wanting to show his ignorance, cleared us to proceed direct to the far beacon.

I was flying at the time and I looked across at Hugh with raised eyebrows for an explanation, and he told me,

"IGD, works every time. In the General Direction, a bit left of that VOR, right of that one, should do the trick."

An evening flight to Dusseldorf, over the North Sea, and the cabin crew number one appeared in the cockpit to advise that one of the passenger windows had shattered on to a passenger's lap. All was well at our end, but I decided to descend and depressurise. We did this (gently) and continued to Dusseldorf. The cabin windows had two pressure panels, plus a protective scratch panel on the inside. It was the inner pressure panel which had failed and the outer panel had maintained the pressure seal. I was concerned that the passenger alongside the window might have been upset by the lumps of clear plastic arriving in his lap, but in fact all he wanted was a piece of the window to show his friends. I was delighted to oblige, and he went away happy. The Dusseldorf engineers couldn't fix the window, so we had to fly back home unpressurised.

One very enjoyable operation was the Father Christmas flying, which started a few years before I finished. During December, we did a series of these, which for us was four flights in an afternoon. We flew to the Isle of Man and back, about thirty to forty minutes airborne, which, for the children on board, was to the North Pole and back. The flights were well organised, the aircraft were dressed externally with a red nose, a mouth, and antlers, all of which we had to help the engineers remove after the passengers had boarded, and replace on arrival, before they disembarked. We could see some of the parents looking at these decorations and wondering how we had managed to fly with them on. The ground staff, all volunteers, dressed up in animal costumes to keep the children happy while they were waiting to fly.

On board, 'Father Christmas' came in the cockpit with us for take-off. The cabin crew, some dressed as clowns, after their standard passenger brief, put a tape on which told the kids about the flight and our magical warp engine assisted take-off, and we, for our part, had to ensure that when we opened the throttles we were synchronised with the 'warp' engines winding up on the tape. If possible we would try to cruise just above a cloud layer, which, to the children, looked just like snow at the North Pole. At a suitable point in the flight, the cabin lights dimmed, and with suitable flashing lights and music on the tape, Father Christmas, now in full dress, would 'appear' in the cabin (from the galley) to the delight of the youngsters, and dispense his presents. I did several of these trips, and in 1989 managed to take my wife and three granddaughters, all aged about 5 or 6, the perfect age, on the last trip of the day. I did the same two years later with three grandsons, similar ages, and they all really enjoyed themselves, certainly a flight to remember.

I remember one trip, which was quite a humbling experience. We were doing an afternoon Amsterdam, and on the way back, the company called us with a request. The Jersey flight which should have departed about one o'clock, had been delayed by the weather in Jersey. The captain (the flight manager at Manchester) had delayed for so long that the crew were running out of hours. The crew controller asked us if we would mind operating the Jersey flight. It would mean being 'drafted', which was extra pay, so we didn't have to consider for long. The Jersey aircraft was almost ready for us when we landed, but one further problem was that about thirty of the full load of passengers were in wheelchairs. This meant using a modified lorry with a hydraulic platform to load them on to the aircraft, and then they were carried into their seats. This meant a further delay, of course. These passengers were a group, with their carers, and they were all quite severely disabled. They had travelled by coach from North Yorkshire, on the way the coach had a puncture, and they were delayed on the motorway.

We finally landed in the wind and rain at Jersey at nine o'clock that evening, about seven hours late on their schedule. After the able bodied passengers had disembarked, we then had the lorry routine again for those in wheelchairs. As this happened via the forward door, I stood by the flight deck door as they left to say goodbye, and ready to apologise for their considerable delay. Apologies were not required. Without exception, they were all happy, smiling, and at pains to thank me for an enjoyable flight which had rounded off their exciting day. They told me that, even though they had arrived late for their scheduled departure, British Airways had looked after them well, provided an excellent meal while they were waiting, and entertained them until the aircraft had departed. I was impressed by their attitude. If some of our business passengers on Shuttle had been delayed to that degree I am sure the response would have been slightly different.

The 1-11s were hush kitted in '84, to meet the stage 2 noise limitations, but they were unlikely to be able to meet the next stage, 3, so their days were effectively numbered. The noise and their rather voracious appetite for fuel, compared with later types, conspired against them. The similar vintage Tridents were retired before the 1-11s, accelerated by a wing spar fatigue problem, and replaced by the Boeing 757. It was amusing when positioning on a cockpit jump seat in a Shuttle 757, the first glass cockpit in BA, to watch the usually ex Trident crew coping with modern technology. As a 757 captain said to me one day,

"You can tell it's an ex Trident crew, when you hear the captain ask the first officer, 'What's it doing now?'"

I heard that the early 757s had an auto shut down facility when the system recognised an engine fault, such as low oil pressure. This was quickly modified when an aircraft had an engine shut down in this way, but shortly after the system diagnosed a fault on the remaining engine and decided to stop that one as well.

The 1-11 was recognised by BA as a good first aircraft for training new pilots, no flight computers and plenty of short sectors, so as sponsored cadets began to come through again in the late 80s, after a period when the only new entrants were 'direct entry' pilots from other airlines, we had a number of the new lads, and lasses, join us at Manchester. Selected from thousands of applicants, they were very impressive. During my last five years, I flew frequently with them.

They made me feel my age and that I was slowing down, but, of course, what they did lack was experience. It was interesting, talking to them about flying and the job, to find that several had applied for it simply because 'it was a good career', not because they were particularly enthusiastic about aircraft. Sign of the times, I suppose.

Several new pilots had been trained by BA some years before, but, due to the depression, there were no jobs for them when they qualified, so they were released until things improved. The only jobs available at that time were flying helicopters to the North Sea rigs. When the economy picked up again, BA welcomed them back. One or two of them struggled a bit at first changing from landing a helicopter at 5kts to a 1-11 at 120kts, but they soon settled in to the operation.

One of the two engine shutdowns I had on the S1-11 was with one of the new entrants. It was about three months before I retired. We were on our way back from Amsterdam, crossing the east coast at Ottringham, just starting descent, when we had an engine overheat warning. This was a shutdown item, and, as I was flying the aircraft, I indicated to the co-pilot to go ahead. I was surprised when he started pulling the aircraft manuals out of the bag alongside his seat.

I said, "What are you doing, don't you know the overheat drill?"

Looking a bit sheepish, he replied, "Yes".

'Well then, just do the drill', I said.

He did the engine overheat drill memory items, shut the engine down, told air traffic, and we were number one for approach. Although technically we were supposed to land at the 'nearest airfield', I didn't fancy Leeds, and we continued our descent and landed at Manchester. It was a false warning, which was quite unusual. For me, that was the end of it, but a few days later, I walked into our crewroom (quietly on the carpet) and my co-pilot was standing with his back to me talking to a couple of his contemporaries. He was excitedly describing the incident, telling them,

"I was panicking, looking for the books, and Cedric told me calmly, 'Just do the drill.'"

At that point, he turned around, saw me, and blushed to his roots with embarrassment, but I said to his mates,

"Don't worry, he was an ace, and he's got his first engine shutdown in his logbook, more than you have!"

The other engine failure was on a day when we had been delayed waiting for several aircraft to position back from Leeds. They had diverted the previous night and heavy overnight snow had meant de-icing them took some time. Eventually our aircraft arrived and we departed late for Belfast. It was dark as we rolled on take-off, the co-pilot flying, and as I eased the throttles back to climb power, one engine started banging and the aircraft rocked from side to side. From my previous experience at Speke I recognised a compressor stall, and watching the gauges could see number two engine indications flicking in unison with the bangs. We agreed on the engine and I did the shut-down items, then resumed control as required and did a circuit and landed. I thought it could have been some ice on the airframe at Leeds which had dislodged and gone into the engine, damaging a blade or two. Interestingly, the next day, one of our captains told me he had lined up behind us as we rolled and noticed a shower of sparks coming from that engine as we opened up. I suggested he might have told me and I could have stopped on the runway.

The Spey engines, though thirsty and noisy, were generally reliable. One minor quirk however was starting. First start of the day, particularly on a cold damp morning, required careful monitoring. The engines were rather prone to 'hanging' on start, unlike the easy Viscount routine of 'turning, burning, oiling and flowing' every time. The HP (high pressure) fuel cock had three positions, Closed, Start and Open. The routine was to initiate the start sequence, and as the HP rpm reached 1500 move the HP lever to Start. Then the TGT (turbine gas temperature) was watched and at about 500°C (or HP rpm of 5000), the lever was moved to Open. The Start position of the lever had a higher fuel flow than the Open. If the engine didn't accelerate properly, the increase in TGT would beat the rpm increase, and if the TGT reached the limit, the start would have to be cancelled. Sometimes the rpm increase would be slow and the TGT would also slowly increase, then one option would be to put the lever back to start and the extra fuel would (or might) restore the start progress.

One particularly cold and damp morning, when the aircraft had been parked outside all night, we managed to get both engines lit, and started our push-back. The engines still hadn't stabilised, and I was keeping an eye on them, when I realised that both engine rpms were slowly reducing, and the TGTs were steadily increasing. There was no option but to stop both engines, in the middle of the push, and tell the engineer that we would have to start them both from scratch. In this case, the engines, now having been warmed, started normally. But as I said, once running, the Speys were usually trouble free.

By the time retirement crept up on me, I had been flying the 1-11 for twenty two years, eight on the 1-11 400, and fourteen on the S1-11. I suppose I should have been just about getting used to it. In fact, a couple of years before I retired, I cut my hand badly and was off for two and a half months. When I returned I had to do a scheduled flight with a check captain supervising and I was interested to see how I would feel, after my longest spell off flying since I started. When I sat in the seat, it was as if I had been flying the day before, and I slipped back into the routine without a problem. It is nice to have that sort of affinity with an aircraft.

When we prepared to depart before a flight, we had a standard routine of briefing for take-off, and whoever was flying would ask the other pilot an emergency drill. It was good, and kept our minds concentrated on the procedures and possibilities. If we had time to spare, I liked to continue the brief, discussing the options and what ifs. I remember one time, we were doing this, developing the various outcomes of things going wrong, and at one point my co-pilot said to me,

"What if it..."

I don't remember the detail of his supposition, but I remember my response. Without thinking, I replied, "It wouldn't dare!", referring to the aeroplane, of course. Even though it was meant as a joke, I thought later that it did show my relationship with the 1-11.

Relaxed is good, of course, but it can become a little too much so. We were starting one day at Belfast, Aldergrove, and had set up for a departure from the main westerly runway. As we prepared to taxi, my first officer, one of the best at Manchester, suggested we could save a few minutes by using the shorter 17 runway, less taxying and a heading nearer our track for home. I agreed happily and we twiddled the flight directors for the new departure. A couple of minutes later we accelerated down the short runway. As we progressed it became apparent that we were going to use quite a lot of the runway. However, we lifted off comfortably in the distance available, but then looked sheepishly at each other as we realised that we had used the lower power setting of reduced thrust for the long runway, whereas we should have used normal take off power on the shorter one. Not too much of a problem, as we could have increased power at any time, as we would have done for an engine fail. But it shows that even at the top of the learning curve, there are traps for the unwary.

I think the airline operation has developed into probably the safest form of flying nowadays. Standard operating procedures mean that two pilots who have never met before can fly the aircraft safely and efficiently. Although not strictly necessary, it helps if the pilots do know each other and enjoy flying together. A relaxed atmosphere on the flight deck is better than the slight tension which exists when the pilots haven't met, or, worse still, have a poor or abrasive relationship. Short haul pilots tend to fly together frequently, whereas in long haul (as it was) this is less likely.

I was looking forward to retirement (normal at age 55 at the time), as the hassle part of the job was beginning to overwhelm the pleasant parts. I had just bought my retirement present to me, a new boat, a Fisher 37 wheelhouse cruiser, and was looking forward to some relaxed sailing, without the pressure of getting back at the end of leave. Security at airfields was increasing, and although it was obviously necessary, the way it was conducted left a lot to be desired, and some aspects were starting to annoy me, although I know it became much worse later, after I had finished. I remember one day going out to operate a Belfast service. We had a crew security check-point on the ground floor of the tower building, before we could go airside. The Belfast aircraft always had to be searched by two security officers before departure, and as we went through our screening, keys in the hat to stop it bleeping, routine, I noticed two security people by-pass this and walk straight out onto the tarmac. I guessed they were going to search our aircraft but asked our man what they were doing. He confirmed their destination. I then asked why they didn't go through screening as we did.

"Oh', he said, 'We know them".

I told him that wasn't the way it was meant to operate. I was flying the aircraft and had to be screened, so they certainly should have been. I put in a voyage report, but heard no more about it. Management weren't bothered. I know, from reading the 'Log' and 'Chirp', that it became much worse after I retired. I doubt that I could have coped with it.

I was happiest when I sat in my seat on the flight deck and started flying. Trouble was the number of hoops we had to jump through to get to that point, and that number was steadily increasing. Driving to work and finding a parking spot was the first, although the captains had a card to use the multi-storey car park at Manchester. The entrance to the park was on the third level and cars were then directed up, and you could end up at level thirteen or fourteen. We soon discovered that it was better to follow the exit signs down from the third level and usually find a spot nearer the ground. Only occasionally did I have to go out and start again. The next hoop when reporting was delays, slot times could be quite a problem. After that was sorted, it was just a matter of negotiating security to get to the aircraft. I'm afraid I never understood the logic (and still don't) of making crews go through such rigorous procedures.

It was time for me to go. I retired in January 92, at 55, the BA normal retirement age at the time, thirty one years after my interview with Geoff Perrott, twenty eight years in command, twenty two of them on the 1-11. Not bad for somebody who never planned an airline career, and how lucky for me that the airline was Cambrian and then British Airways. The timing was immaculate as, a month or two after I retired, the company began disposing of the 1-11 fleet.

7. RETIREMENT

In 1992, I settled happily into retirement. I had commissioned my new boat, *Kingfisher of Hoyle*, a Fisher 37, a year before, sailing it in February 91 from the builder's yard at Itchenor in Chichester Harbour, non-stop (72 hours) to Liverpool, which proved to me and my crew the benefit of a wheelhouse. I had, in 1989, discovered GPS, and had equipped the new boat with one of the first commercial receivers, made by Shipmate. The GPS system was still being set up, and wasn't operational, but even though there were only about nine satellites in the constellation, rather than the twenty one required for full coverage, we found that the receiver performance was extremely impressive. The Shipmate even predicted the times when it would be unable to obtain a fix, for maybe half an hour or so, three or four times a day, due to insufficient satellite coverage. The GPS system had been configured with a degradation element for civilian use, called selective availability (SA).

When I sailed my boat home, the first Gulf war was underway and this (SA) had been switched off, because the Americans were using yacht receivers in their tanks in the desert, these being the only sets available. The degraded accuracy of position was about 100 metres, but without degradation it was nearer 10 metres. We were impressed. It was December 1993 before the last of the block 2A satellites was launched and the GPS system was declared fully operational. To combat selective availability, a service called Differential GPS was introduced. Stations around the UK coast calculated the SA error and transmitted on MF the correction required. Ships or yachts equipped with a differential GPS set could receive this and the resultant fix would then be very accurate. Later Bill Clinton told the Department of Defence to switch off the selective availability to improve the system for civilian users, and the differential system wasn't required any more.

For the next few years I did lots of cruising in the new boat, as I had promised myself. We cruised the Irish Sea, Scotland, Eire, Channel Isles and English Channel, Bay of Biscay and northern

France. My wife, never an enthusiastic sailor, now refused to sail with me more than a few miles from Liverpool marina, where the boat was based, and so for several years I would spend a couple of weeks cruising with a crew down the Irish Sea, up the English Channel, round the corner past the Goodwin Sands, then up the Thames to St. Katherine's Dock, a very pleasant marina in the old docks next to Tower Bridge right in the heart of London. I would then go home to bring my wife down to join me for a few weeks, living on board and doing the tourist routine. At the time a berth in the marina would cost about £11 a night for a month's stay, not bad for night stopping in Central London. Then with a fresh crew, having taken my wife home, I would cruise back the same route.

On one trip up the Channel towards the Thames we stopped in Gosport for a couple of days. Peter Gates was crewing with me and we decided to have a ferry trip across to the Isle of Wight. There was a hovercraft service from Southsea to Ryde, and a catamaran from Portsmouth to Cowes. To try both, we started with the catamaran to Cowes, then caught a bus to Ryde for the hovercraft. On the first leg over to Southsea, the steward noticed I was wearing my 1-11 lapel badge, started chatting and said the skipper would be happy to have us on the bridge. So for the trip back to Ryde we sat upstairs on the bridge, and had a brief introduction to hovercraft operations. There was a fresh wind blowing from ahead and the skipper explained that better progress was made by tacking either side of the direct course, rather like a yacht. He was keen to chat to us, explaining that several colleagues were involved in commercial pilot training, as the hovercraft days were numbered, and he was thinking about doing the same. Back to Cowes on the bus for the last sector on the catamaran, and we decided to ask the crew if we could visit the bridge. They said 'no problem', and we were entertained by the skipper who told us of his experiences bringing the ship from Australia, where it was built a couple of years earlier. It was an enjoyable afternoon.

Many pilots enjoy sailing, it has similar attractions and difficulties to flying, the operational problems to be overcome are comparable, although the time scale is quite different. In a small boat, you can often put the kettle on and have a cup of tea while the options are considered. A description of a trip in my second boat, 'Greylag of Hoyle', may illustrate what I mean.

In 1982 I had been on our annual cruise in 'Greylag', my ketch rigged Westerly 33, from Caernarfon in North Wales, with a crew of friends. Tony, Ted, Jack and I had a two day sail to the Scillies for a pleasant night stop. Then across the Channel to Jersey, and to collect another friend, Arthur. On this leg, I actually took some sextant sights of the sun. I'd done astronavigation for the Board of Trade Yachtmaster exams, Coastal and Ocean, which I had completed a few years previously. Professing to be short of time, I delayed working up these sights at the time. In fact it was several months before I did them, in the comfort of home, but they were reasonably accurate. I decided I just needed a little more speed. Approaching Jersey early in the morning, Jack and I were on watch and heard on the radio that the Argentinians had surrendered in the Falklands. Jack told me that I would always remember where I was when I heard that news.

From Jersey, across to Lezardrieux then St Malo, gale bound there for a day, then back to Jersey, via Iles Chausey, to drop Arthur off and put Tony on a plane for home. After another wind bound day, Ted, Jack and I sailed for Guernsey, then across to Dartmouth, where Ted departed and Doug joined Jack and me for the trip home.

We were stuck in Dartmouth for a couple of days while another summer gale went by, and having sampled all the local delights, including the Dart Valley Railway, we were eager to be on our way. I hoped to make Caernarfon in one hop, as I was getting short of time. The forecast was westerly force 5 to 7 and I decided we would try getting as far west down Channel as we could. We set off from Dartmouth early on a bright, still June morning, but as we rounded Start Point, we met the promised westerly, about force 5 to 6. We motor sailed hard to windward all day, intending to make Falmouth at least. However the afternoon forecast suggested that the wind would ease before backing and increasing again, as the next depression followed a brief ridge. So we carried on, past Falmouth, and as we rounded Land's End in the dark that night, the wind had almost gone.

We motored into the new day on course for the Smalls Lighthouse off the south west corner of Wales, about 100 miles ahead. With dawn, the forecast southerly arrived, and with a fair wind we began to sail well at last. The morning forecast predicted an occluded front arriving that evening, wind increasing to southerly force 6 to 7, with rain and poor visibility. There would be a clearance behind the front with wind of south west force 4. At 1035 that morning there was a gale warning for Sole and Fastnet, just to the west.

During the day we sailed well, gradually reducing sail as the wind increased, until by late afternoon we were down to just No 2 jib and were still making 6 plus knots (that's fast), with occasional surfing bursts down the steadily increasing seas. We saw hardly any ships, although an RAF Nimrod visited us several times at low level about midday, probably using us for target practice. Dolphins joined us as usual from time to time, but disappeared as the cloud increased from the west.

After the previous day's early start, I'd had just about three or four hours sleep, and should have grabbed some more. As we approached St. George's Channel in the late afternoon I was getting tired, but I knew we had to avoid the Smalls Lighthouse with its various rocks and islands to the east (a pleasant passage on a nice day, but not in these conditions). It was also important not to stray too far to the west and get involved with Tuskar Rock on the Irish side. I wanted to pass between the Smalls light and the northbound lane of the Smalls TSS (Traffic Separation Scheme for ships off major headlands) and certainly avoid the southbound lane to the west. No problem if you know where you are in the first place! The front was now approaching, visibility was down to one or two miles, in drizzle and rain, and the promised southerly force 6 to 7 had arrived.

Position fixing in those pre Decca (or GPS) days, for my yacht, was a handheld Lokata RDF, hand bearing compass, and a sextant. The Lokata was the only option in the conditions. Now, about 70-80 miles from our last visual fix, I was trying to get bearings from Tuskar Rock and Strumble Head M/F beacons, which were well situated for a fix prior to the Smalls. The problem was in trying to use the Lokata RDF. The noise from wind and sea made the open cockpit impossible, and down below, where I could hear the beacons, the movement of the boat made the integral compass of the RDF leap about like a mad thing.

Finally, I found that the only compromise was to go to the fore cabin, the quietest place, tune Tuskar, find the null, and estimate the relative bearing. At that point, I shouted 'now' to the cockpit, so that the helmsman could give me the boat's heading at that instant (the heading of the boat was varying quite a lot). I could convert this to a compass/magnetic bearing and then repeat the procedure for

Strumble Head. The accuracy of this method left a lot to be desired, and although the resulting fix coincided roughly with our DR position, I knew that it could easily be ten miles or more in error.

Ten miles too far to the east at the Smalls would be unpleasant or much worse in these conditions. I considered going in to Milford Haven, but if the visibility dropped much more that entrance would be difficult to find, and it was a lee shore, so we continued on course. At one point early that evening, I stood in the cockpit peering ahead over the spray hood into the rain and tumbling waves, and experienced the classic illusion. I saw cliffs ahead! I went below for another attempt at RDF bearings, and convinced myself that we were at least twenty miles from any solid land. Next time I looked the cliffs had gone.

As we progressed north during the day, the VHF had picked up Milford Haven Coastguard, among other transmissions, and they had broadcast a general traffic information bulletin, warning of a large tanker of 100,000 tons due to enter the Haven that evening. I heard this broadcast several times, but thought no more of it. We were well clear of Milford Haven and I had enough to worry about trying to ensure that we cleared the Smalls with comfort.

At about 2130 it was getting dark (late June). The wind was now a good force 7 (28-33 knots) from the south, with rain and low stratus, and I knew we were getting near the Smalls. I was below again, still trying to get decent bearings, feeling tired and going through the 'What am I doing here?' and 'There must be a better way than this' routine, when there was a shout from the cockpit. I popped my head out and Doug pointed to port. There, on a reciprocal heading, was a very large tanker, about half a mile off.

"Well at least we missed him," we congratulated ourselves, and I went below again to navigate and worry. The voice on the VHF was loud, so I turned the volume down.

"White yacht on my port beam, this is Canadian tanker, 'Beaver State' " the voice came again.

I slowly realised who was calling whom. It was Milford's 100,000 ton tanker trying to contact us on the calling channel 16. I replied and we went to channel 6 (for ship to ship communication) and started chatting. He enquired where we were bound, told me that we looked pretty uncomfortable from where he was, and asked if he could do anything for us. I said (or lied) that we were relatively happy, homeward bound for Caernarfon, and at least had a fair wind. I added that a steak would have been appreciated, but didn't fancy going alongside for it. He said they had a couple of hours to kill awaiting the tide to enter the Haven, and, having spotted us on radar, decided to come and have a look at us. After a few more minutes chatting, we wished each other well and said goodbye. Opening the hatch to tell the crew the tale, I saw that the tanker had turned to port while we had been talking, and was crossing our wake, disappearing slowly into the mist.

I pulled the hatch shut again and thought,

'Diversion over, back to the serious business of trying to establish our position'.

Only then did the blindingly obvious hit me. I called the tanker on VHF hoping he would answer. He did, and, trying to sound as casual as I possibly could, I asked if he would confirm our position by giving me a bearing and distance on the Smalls.

"Sure thing, stand by," came the reply.

I imagined I could hear his slippers padding on the carpeted and steady bridge as he went over to the radar.

"040 degrees, eleven miles," he told me.

I thanked him and said goodbye again, feeling a warm glow of relief. Now I knew for sure, we were more or less where we wanted to be, approaching the edge of the northbound lane of the Smalls TSS. The kettle went on, and we relaxed over the best cup of tea that day. Just before midnight the front went through, the wind dropped to southwest force 4, visibility improved and the Smalls light shone clearly about four miles off to starboard. Next day we had a more comfortable sail across Cardigan Bay, past Bardsey Island and home to Caernarfon that evening.

The following year I fitted one of the first small radars for yachts, and the year after I had one of the new small boat Decca receivers. My next boat, Fisher 37 'Kingfisher of Hoyle', eventually had two fixed GPS sets, plus two handhelds, an excellent 36 mile Furuno radar, and a laptop with a navigation programme using Admiralty charts which, connected to any of the GPS sets, continuously tracked the boat's position, and also, with an AIS (automatic identification system) attachment, showed the position on the computer chart of ships in the vicinity, a similar system to transponders in aircraft. I have had people on board who ask if I think all these electronics spoil the fun of sailing. I would try to limit my reply to a simple,

"Not for me, they don't".

One interesting and fairly frequent occurrence when sailing some distance offshore, was birds (the feathered variety) landing on board. They were obviously tired and, seeing the boat, decided that anything would do for a temporary respite. Pigeons were frequent and they were often insistent on going below to the warm cabin. Not wanting to clear up the inevitable mess, I would make it clear to them that they were deck cargo, and no more. On one occasion sailing from Fishguard in South Wales to Wicklow in Eire we set a big cruising chute as a it was a nice day, and the light wind favoured it. This was a big coloured sail, like a spinnaker, and at the top, where it left the mast, billowing forward, it was initially horizontal. Soon after setting course, three little birds, like finches, settled on top happily, and sat there for the rest of the day. When we were a few miles from the Irish coast, they flew away, heading for land. I wasn't too sure, but it did seem to be planned. When I read about birds normally resident in North America which turn up in Essex or somewhere, having 'flown 3,000 miles across the Atlantic', I think it is much more likely they have been blown offshore a few miles, and landed on an eastbound containership for a rest. A few days later, suitably refreshed, they wait for the first indication of land only to find that they've arrived in the UK without a passport. On one occasion, about 20 miles off Dartmouth, sailing from Guernsey, a bat landed on deck. It stayed for an hour or two, posed for photos, then flew off, heading south towards France.

After retiring, I certainly didn't want to lose touch with flying, my ATPL was valid for another eight years and I could use it as a PPL to fly light aircraft. Dave Williams, long-time friend and colleague, who started as a first officer with Cambrian when I was flying the Viscount in the 60s, had always been active in the light aircraft world. Dave had been CFI of the De Havilland factory flying club at Broughton (Hawarden airfield) near Chester, in his spare time. He now had a couple of aircraft at Speke and was running a flying school operation called Deltair. A few months before I retired, Dave's son Anthony, also an instructor, had checked me out on the Cessna 172 at Tilstock, a disused wartime airfield near Whitchurch. I then hired this aircraft several times to take the family flying. I had first flown this Cessna in 1981, when Dave hangared it at Speke for a while. Apart from this, the only other single engine flying I had done since the club days was a trip with Dug Davidson (ex-Cambrian) in his Jodel 114 which he kept at Ash House Farm, a strip near Winsford, and the Aero Commander 112 at Staverton.

A year or so after I retired, Dave rang me to tell me he had just bought a Piper Super Cub, G-ARVO. I'd never flown one, so I agreed to try it. Anthony did a check flight with me. I was slightly surprised when we did about seven circuits and landings in it; for me it was just like an Auster and I enjoyed it. I flew it a couple of times later with my daughter's husband Rob, who is quite keen on flying. A few weeks later Dave rang me and asked if I would like to be the Cub check pilot. Apparently his instructors, all tricycle undercarriage experts, never having flown tail wheels, were not at all happy with this ancient little beast and its inclination to ground loop at the first opportunity. Dave told me that only PPL holders with more than 100 hours would be allowed to fly it, so there was no problem with me checking them on his behalf. I agreed, at least it meant somebody else would pay for my flying and, over the next year or so, I checked out quite a few pilots on the Cub, which was good fun and very interesting, watching the reaction of tricycle trained pilots coping on the ground with this directionally unstable little aeroplane. As one said to me, he felt like the tail was trying to overtake him all the time he was taxiing. We managed it all without a single ground loop.

Flying with people in the Cub took me back to my flying club days. Some of the private pilots were very good, but a few, as was the case previously, shouldn't have been allowed near an aeroplane. I checked out a couple of airline pilots on the Cub and there was a marked difference, which made it a pleasure to fly with them. They only needed telling something once, whereas with some of the private pilots I would say things several times but it still didn't appear to be going in. I thought it showed the subtle difference between the attitude of a professional and an amateur.

I gradually became part of Dave's establishment, unpaid of course, and did other flying, such as trial flights. Dave now had a fleet of Cessna 152s, a 172, Piper Tomahawks and a Cherokee, as well as the Cub. He had also bought three Bulldogs (G-BHXA, G-BHXB and G-BHZS) from Botswana, and his engineers were in the process of overhauling them for a Certificate of Airworthiness (C of A) for commercial operation, the first in the UK. Once the Bulldog was on the line, I also began to check people out on this delightful little aeroplane, and to do introduction to aerobatics for those who were interested. It was good to do aerobatics again and the Bulldog was an excellent aircraft in which to do them. The flight manual had three pages on spinning and recovery. The RAF had lost a couple from spinning accidents. It wouldn't recover from a spin by just centralising the controls, as many aircraft will. The correct drill was essential, identify direction, by turn needle if necessary, full opposite rudder, then steady forward movement of the stick (no aileron) until the spin stopped. We never had any trouble. I usually preferred to have full tanks flying the little aircraft and the Bulldog did have a lower max weight for aerobatics. We were probably a little overweight at times, and sometimes the Bulldog, if a little slow at the top of a loop, would do a gentle flick back to a normal level attitude. The pilots pushed the aircraft on occasions, such as stopping the roll half way round then pulling back on the stick to recover. With full throttle on, I'd have to chop the power to ease out of the resulting dive before reaching VNE. But mostly it was an enjoyable exercise.

During this time I was contacted by the owner of an Acrosport. George Brothwood, whom I knew as an air traffic controller at Manchester, had overhauled this pretty little single seat open cockpit biplane, very similar to a Pitts, and required an aerobatic assessment for its PFA (LAA) Permit to Fly renewal. George had done one, but they required an independent view. I agreed, of course, met George at Speke and he briefed me on the aircraft. I flew it for an hour and a half over North Wales and really enjoyed it, doing rolls, loops, stall turns and spins. The only difficulty, being open cockpit, was that it was necessary to throttle back to hear the R/T. The cockpit was small, but comfortable enough once in, although I couldn't stretch my legs full length and thought afterwards it would have been interesting if I had had a touch of cramp. However, I survived, and filled in the form for George. I didn't hear anymore, so I assumed the PFA were happy.

When I started flying the Cub, Dave suggested I find some grass strips which we could use, for which the Cub was ideally suited. I discovered several, of which Ashcroft Farm in Cheshire, and Llandegla, Greenlands and Rhedyn Coch (Emlyn's Field) in North Wales were favourites. I used them to take people to try grass strip flying and found it to be great fun, certainly for me. One of the aircraft based at Greenlands was a Nord 854, a little shoulder wing French aircraft, which belonged to John Tavener, whom I had taught to fly in club days. John had a temporary problem with his medical and asked me if I would check out a couple of pilots on it so they could fly with him. I drove over one day and did a few circuits in the Nord with Emlyn Jones, the farmer who owned the two fields, and John Mellors, with whom I had flown the Bulldog at Dave's school, and this kept John Tavener flying until he sorted his medical.

When the Bulldog came on line, I decided it would be interesting to take it into Greenlands. I flew over one day with Gordon Bancroft, a pilot I flew with at Dave's, to try it. Emlyn had briefed me on operating into Greenlands, which was usually occupied by sheep. Provided you flew over at low level before landing, the sheep, well trained, would all run to one corner of the field and stay there until you had finished and flown away. The Bulldog needed about 500 yards according to the book, but one runway at Greenlands (the field had three runways which were regularly mown), which was about 300 yards, had a very sharp upslope for the first 100 yards which, provided you landed right at the start, was a great help in slowing the aircraft. This runway was south westerly, and the longest runway, which was north westerly, about 400 yards with a nice downslope on the second half, was ideal for take-off, with the prevailing westerlies. On the first day I tried landing on the short uphill runway with the Bulldog it had been raining, so when we landed the grass was quite wet. I touched down fairly early on the upslope, but as we reached the level bit, about half way along the runway, I realised the brakes were pretty useless. As we were still moving quite fast, and it didn't seem likely we would stop before the hedge, I decided to swing the aircraft sideways to increase the drag. The Bulldog slid the last fifty yards at 90° to the runway direction, but the extra drag worked and we stopped about twenty yards short of the hedge. I decided to try a couple of landings on my own, and found that provided I came over the low fence at the threshold, power on, at minimum speed, stall warning bleating, and touched down in the first twenty yards or so, there was no problem and the Bulldog was almost stopped when the level part of the runway was reached. Thereafter I flew the Bulldog into Greenlands quite often, choosing the weather carefully, making sure the wind favoured landing on this runway, and allowed taking off on the longer northwesterly one.

About this time, I was in Shropshire with my wife, and realised we were quite close to the Long Mynd, the Midland Gliding Club base. I decided to call in for a look. After wandering around weighing up the operation, I enquired about a trial flight. One of the club staff (not an instructor) said he would take me for a trip. We climbed into a sleek sailplane, a K21 I think, at the launch point for an aero tow. The pilot explained to me what was going to happen, we were hooked up to the Piper Pawnee and away we went. The take-off was gentle by comparison with the winch launches I had observed, and when we reached about 2,000ft, having dropped the tow, he handed over to me. I flew along the ridge for about fifteen minutes, managing to find a bit of lift, and maintaining my height without too much trouble. I was surprised by my impression of the sailplane. I expected fairly crisp controls, but it was more like a Tiger Moth, and plenty of rudder was need in turns to maintain balance. It was just like a light aeroplane, without power.

We flew back to the field and the pilot resumed control for the landing (which disappointed me). He explained that he made his approach with reference to various landmarks around the circuit, ensuring that he was at a particular height at each point. I didn't say so, but I didn't agree with this technique, as I would have preferred to treat it like a forced landing, watching the touchdown point and adjusting the glide as required, keeping some height in hand, and using the spoilers (or side slipping) to lose height on short finals. I was in the front seat of the tandem cockpit, and as we crossed the threshold I realised we were heading rather close to the marker for the start of the landing run. This was three white painted tyres with a flag on a pole stuck vertically in them. As we approached this I realised that the pilot hadn't seen it from the rear cockpit, and we missed it by a couple of feet, just clipping the flag pole with our wing as we passed. An interesting exercise but it didn't impress me enough to consider taking up gliding.

Another interesting diversion with the Bulldog was when Dave was approached by the officer in charge at the Warships Preservation Trust museum in Birkenhead. Situated in the East Float of Birkenhead Docks, this comprised HMS Onyx, a submarine which was involved in the Falklands conflict, landing SAS troops onshore. There was also a frigate, HMS Plymouth, the surrender of South Georgia took place in her wardroom, and she saw action in the conflict, as well as the 'Planet' which served many years as the Bar Lightship at the Mersey entrance. These three were afloat, next to the tall derelict grain warehouses, and onshore was a German U-boat, U534, recovered from the seabed after 48 years. The Trust was organising an exhibition day, and one of the events was to be the hijacking of the frigate by terrorists, an assault by airborne troops and its recovery. They wanted an aircraft to take part and thought of Dave. The Bulldogs were ex Botswana Air Defence Force and were still camouflaged, which made them even more suitable. Dave asked me to get involved of course, so I went to see the officer and weigh up the options. The officer wanted me to make low runs past the ships, dropping the troops, (that bit relied heavily on imagination). On the day, with my son-in-law Rob as co-pilot, my wife, two daughters and several grandchildren on board the frigate, having been given a free pass, we set off from Speke, explained to air traffic what we were up to, and then had an enjoyable half hour, beating up the ships, down to about 50 feet over the water. The Float (East and West) is quite a large expanse so for the low stuff it was easy to stay over the water.

It was a great success, the troops rescued the hostages (girls from the Café), flushed out the terrorists, finally 'shooting' them and making sure they ended up in the water. They probably enjoyed it as much as we did. This was in July, and in August we had another request and did it all again. However I had recently read somewhere that to do this sort of flying required a display authorisation from the CAA, so when the next request came I decided to graciously decline. Still it was fun while it lasted.

For a bit of publicity, Dave arranged for me to fly the Bulldog with Ray Atkinson, our long-time friend and colleague from Cambrian days. Ray wrote an article about the flight in BALPA's 'Log' magazine. This possibly created some extra work for the Bulldog.

Dave had retired from BA a couple of years after me, but returned for a short spell as a first officer on the Boeing 767, when the company was briefly short of crews. Then Dave got a temporary job as 767 captain with Air Seychelles, on a two month rolling contract while they were training their own crews. He told me he was enjoying it, while it lasted, flying between Heathrow, Paris and the Seychelles.

One Thursday evening Dave rang me to say he was just going back to work, and asked if I would organise another trip with Ray, to try to drum up a bit more work for the Bulldogs. I agreed and said I would get in touch with Ray. Two days later, on Saturday, Reg, Dave's manager at the flying school, rang me with sad news. Dave had been snorkelling on a coral reef in the Seychelles with a friend from BA who was staying with him. They had become separated, and when his friend eventually located Dave, it was too late. Dave had drowned, after apparently being incapacitated in some way. It was a great shock for his family and friends. The flying school couldn't go on without him and was wound up. The Cub had gone away on a long term charter to a club in Kent, and a few years later Fenella, Dave's widow, rang to ask me to collect it when the agreement expired. A friend of Dave and Fenella flew me down to Rochester in his Piper Arrow, and I collected the Cub from Farthing Corner, a little grass field in Kent, and delivered it to Hawarden, Chester.

That, of course, was the end of my free flying at the school, and I looked around at the options available. Flying light aircraft at Liverpool wasn't enjoyable, with air traffic delays etc. I eventually discovered a flying club at Sleap in Shropshire. A former wartime airfield with three runways, no formal air traffic, delightful rural setting, the only restriction being its proximity to RAF Shawbury, three miles away. It seemed ideal, and after a look around, I joined the club and asked if I could be checked out on their aircraft. The young lady in the office who sorted my membership explained some of the club rules to me, including the fact that I would need a check flight on each of their types, and then fly each type every two months to maintain recency. After this she found an instructor to fly with me. He was a pilot with one of the airlines at Manchester and, after checking my logbook and ATPL, we went out to a Piper Cherokee Archer, did a pre-flight, then taxied out to fly. Three circuits, with a practice engine fail on take-off and a practice forced landing, and he was happy. I asked when we returned about being checked on all the aircraft, as I had flown all of them at Dave's, Cherokee, Cessna 152 and 172 for quite a few hours. He said they had to be careful with the PPL pilots, but I shouldn't worry too much about it. In fact, I didn't see him again.

I flew the Cherokee a couple of times, then one day rang up to book the 172. Nobody mentioned a checkout, so I didn't, and subsequently always flew it as it was a nice aircraft, less than twelve months old, in as new condition, unusual for a club aircraft.. It had a GPS, and I copied the handbook to learn how it worked. It was a fifty mile drive to Sleap, but I tried to fly every two months, midweek flying was cheaper than weekend, at about £85 an hour, which suited me.

About this time I saw an advert in 'Flight'. It was from Emerald Airways, who operated a fleet of Avro 748s from their base at Liverpool. The work was mainly freight, including a Royal Mail contract, with some passenger schedules and charter work. They wanted captains, full and part time, at several bases, including Liverpool. Although I was now 62 years old, I still had a current ATPL, and I thought part time, two, three or even four days a week, based at Liverpool, sounded interesting. I applied by post, not expecting much, due to my age, but I received a reply inviting me for interview, with logbooks.

I duly turned up at Speke (now John Lennon Airport)), with fourteen logbooks, but only took the last two in with me, and met the chief pilot and ops manager. I was informed that the airline operated the largest fleet of 748s in the world and after looking at my logbooks, they explained what the job entailed. They told me they required pilots based at Coventry, Newcastle and Liverpool. I pointed out, as I had in my letter, that I was only interested in part time at Liverpool. The (youngish) chief pilot explained to me that they had a lot of low experience new co-pilots. He then asked me if I thought I would be happy working to Standard Operating Procedures, for their benefit. I assured him that was exactly the way I had always operated in Cambrian and British Airways. He also explained that I would be 'bonded' to cover my training costs, but because of my experience he didn't think that would be more than £2,000 and twelve months. After a few more questions, they said I would be notified by post, and bid me goodbye.

A week or so later, I received a letter from the chief pilot, advising me that 'my application was unsuccessful', but wishing me every success in my future career (at 62!). Maybe I had been a little too positive in saying what I wanted, rather than listening to their requirements. I had a friend, Francis, with a boat in Liverpool Marina, where I kept mine, and I had told him about my interview. He was also ex BA, but VC10 long-haul. When I told him of my rejection, he smiled, and told me that a friend of his had worked for Emerald briefly, but left after a short time, not being happy with their operation. He told me he hadn't mentioned it before, but was certain that I would have felt the same if I had got the job. I had read of a couple of previous incidents to Emerald aircraft which didn't impress me. The company ceased operations in 2006 when their AOC (Air Operators Certificate) was suspended.

Soon after I started flying at Sleap the CFI rang me at home one evening after I had flown to tell me I hadn't filled in the tech. log correctly. I apologised. Shortly after I had another call after flying to say that I had flown when I was out of recency. I assured the CFI that it was just two months since I last flew.

"No," he said, "It is two months and one day".

I asked if he was serious, but he was. A few months later, I drove to Sleap with my son and his friend, having booked the 172. It was a crisp clear winter's day, with a northerly wind. I had checked the Shawbury forecast and actual that morning before leaving home and there wasn't a problem with the weather, wind forecast 15 up to 20 knots, easing during the day. When we arrived at the field, no aeroplanes were out. The routine at the club was that the first pilot to fly would go to the hangar, open up, get the aircraft out and taxy it to the club to refuel, if necessary, and book out. He would put it back in the hangar when he'd finished, or, if it was flying later, leave it for the last pilot to put away. I went into the office and the girl told me that there was no flying, as the wind was up to 35 knots, above the 25 knot limit for club flying. Astonished, I asked where she got that wind from, as I was certain the wind was far less than that. I estimated it about 15 knots, as forecast. She told me that the tower was manned, by an Air Britain member, and he was reading the wind from the anemometer. I said I'd go up to the tower to see for myself.

We introduced ourselves in the tower and asked about the wind. We were told that it was now up to 40 knots. I said that I could estimate wind speed quite well, (being a small boat sailor helped) and I was absolutely sure that the wind outside was nowhere near that strength. The tower wasn't usually manned during the week, just occasionally at weekends and in purely an advisory capacity. I said that as the wind was forecast to reduce during the afternoon, we'd get the aircraft out and then call for the latest reading. I noticed that the anemometer was mounted on a corner of the tower building, whereas it should have been sited on clear ground, on a mast at a height of 10m (33ft).

An hour or so later, having opened the hangar, moved several aircraft to get the 172 out, I started up and taxied for the northerly runway. Alongside the taxiway was a hedge, and I pointed out to my passengers that the leaves and branches were hardly moving. Lining up on the runway, I called the tower, requesting the wind speed. I was astonished by the reply.

"35 knots, gusting 45 to 50 knots".

The aircraft was sitting quietly on the runway, not moving at all in the wind, which it certainly would have been if the wind was as reported, and the ASI (minimum indicated 40kts) wasn't indicating any airspeed. I told the man in the tower that I considered his instrument was grossly in error, and, using my discretion and estimation of the actual wind, which I reckoned was no more than 15 knots, I intended to fly.

We flew for about an hour or so, returning half way through for the passengers to change seats, so each of them could have a go at flying the aircraft. We put the aircraft away, and when we went to the office to pay, the girl told me she would have to report me to the CFI for flying above limits.

"No problem," I replied, "I'll explain what happened to him."

Sure enough, that evening the CFI rang me and asked why I had flown when the wind was well above club limits. I told him the story, and that I thought the anemometer needed calibrating.

"No," he replied. "The anemometer is correct; in fact, I calibrated it myself".

I pointed out that the actuals at Shawbury during the afternoon when we were flying gave the wind as 10 to 12 knots, with no gusts. He retorted that the conditions at Sleap and Shawbury (just three miles apart) frequently differed considerably. I said that I could not believe that in the prevailing conditions that afternoon a meteorological situation existed to create a difference of 38 knots between airfields separated by three miles, and anyway, quite simply, in my estimation, the anemometer was obviously wrong. I was getting nowhere and gave up.

My initial enjoyment of flying at Sleap was steadily being eroded, and a couple of incidents were the final nails in the coffin. I had booked the 172 to fly with a couple of friends, but when we arrived the aircraft was u/s, and all that was available was a 152, a two seater, so this meant flying twice to take them both. As I was doing the pre-flight, I couldn't find the fuel shut off valve. This could have been anywhere, but was usually under the pilot's seat. There was only carpet where it should have been. I thought I would check with the young instructor on duty. He came out with me to the aircraft, insisting that it should be there. When we investigated more thoroughly we discovered that the carpet had moved and become fixed in a position which covered the fuel valve, under the pilot's seat, and even the cut out in the carpet for the valve had disappeared. With some difficulty we repositioned the carpet, so the valve was accessible. I thought it strange that nobody else had noticed the obscurity of the shut off valve. That, I thought, was that, but the instructor then asked me,

"How long is it since you flew this aircraft?"

I hadn't flown a 152 at Sleap, the last time would have been at Dave's, two or three years before. I knew that wouldn't go down too well, so professed to not being sure.

"Is it more than two months?" he insisted.

I agreed that it probably was.

"In that case, you'll need a check flight", he said.

"Oh, OK, let's go and do a few circuits," I replied, thinking that this was becoming a bit laborious.

"Gosh, No", was the reply, "We'll have to do a full hour's check , handling, stalls and circuits."

For a Cessna 152! I told him it wasn't worth the effort, and we didn't bother flying.

Another occasion was when I was getting close to licence rating renewal, and needed about two hours to revalidate. I booked the 172, and on the day, it was foggy in the morning, but it had cleared as we neared the field at about 1230, to leave a clear sky with a fairly thick haze. I saw the 172 landing as we drove in, and was relieved that flying hadn't been cancelled. As I prepared to book out, I couldn't see the aircraft and asked where it was.

"Oh, the CFI has taken it back to the hangar to put it away, he thinks it's too hazy for flying".

I dashed down to the hangar, just in time to stop them putting the aircraft away. I explained that I needed to fly, was happy with the conditions, and would do the flying in the circuit, if necessary. The CFI reluctantly agreed, and advised me to be careful.

"When you are flying downwind in the circuit, into the sun, it's quite difficult to see where you are going", he told me.

Keeping a straight face, I assured him that if I had difficulty, I would use the compass. The aircraft had a full panel. I put my wife in the passenger seat, taxied out, and took off. We did a couple of circuits and then I thought I'd climb higher to see how high the haze went. At 3000 feet we were CAVOK on top in bright sunshine. I transmitted blind (no tower operator) that we were clearing the circuit to the west. Forward visibility into the haze was poor, but the ground below the aircraft was in good view, and the GPS (plus ADF and VOR) was working well, and I told my wife that we'd fill the time in with a trip over Wales, which we did. Just as we left the circuit, another instructor on the ground called me to ask what the conditions were like. I told him it was CAVOK on top, and he said he'd give it a try.

On another beautiful day when the wind was up to about 20 knots, I had to wait for the duty instructor, who was flying, to authorise me to fly. He'd decided that nobody would fly that day without his specific authorisation. When he landed, he briefed me that it was quite turbulent on the approach below 500 feet, asked if I was sure I'd be able to cope with the conditions, and advised me to be careful. I promised him I would be, and had an enjoyable flight.

After a couple more similar incidents, I decided I didn't seem to fit in at Sleap, although the restaurant was very good, and I started looking for something different. I had enjoyed the video of Jack Brown's seaplane training school in Florida, and decided to investigate. I soon found that Marilynn McDonald, of Caledonian Seaplanes, operated a Super Cub on floats at Loch Earn, Perthshire, in the Highlands of Scotland. I contacted her, and received full details of the course, for the seaplane rating on my PPL. It comprised a minimum of five hours flying instruction, a flight test, a written seamanship exam., and short oral technical exam. In the brief, Marilynn offered a copy of 'How to Fly Floats' by J. J. Frey, which I bought and it was a very useful introduction to what was to come.

Caledonian Seaplanes was based at the Drummond Hotel at St. Fillans on the banks of Loch Earn, just where the loch becomes a river. Marilynn, a charming Scottish lady, had been instructing for more than twenty years, the last six on seaplanes. The Cub, with a 135hp Lycoming, and floats, wasn't amphibious. Marilynn suggested three days would be sufficient for the course, so I booked into the hotel for six nights in early May 2004, having had experience of Scottish summers sailing in my boat.

My wife and I drove up to St. Fillans the day before the course was due to start. As I entered reception at the hotel, a lady was standing by the counter. I guessed it was Marilynn by her wellies. Introductions over, she suggested as it was a fine evening we start flying immediately.

I was introduced to the aircraft, a smart yellow Cub, moored alongside a fixed wooden pontoon, bows on to the gravel shore immediately opposite the hotel. The pontoon was covered by an inch or two of water, as the loch level was high, due to recent rain. I was glad I had brought my sailing wellies – I wore them for all the flying.

Leaving the pontoon was the first interesting exercise. There was a light westerly wind, about 10 to 12 knots, and a gentle current flowing from the same direction into the river. We moved the aircraft by hand to the end of the pontoon, facing wind and current, and Marilynn held it there while I climbed into the front seat and prepared for start-up. I was glad of this arrangement, because climbing into the front seat was, for me, a fairly slow and difficult procedure, whereas she, I soon discovered, could leap in or out of the back seat like a bunny rabbit. As soon as I was ready, I pushed the starter and, as the engine fired, Marilynn leapt on to the float and into the back seat in one graceful movement.

The Cub began to move, of course, as soon as the engine was running. I carefully manoeuvred between the moored boats and the shore until we were in clear water. It was steered on the water by a retractable rudder at the after end of the starboard float. Most seaplanes have one on each float, but this Cub managed well with just one. The water rudder is linked to the rudder pedals, via a cable and spring connection, which allows for the water rudder to jam and not inhibit the flying controls. The rudder is retracted by lifting the cable from the cockpit floor and attaching it to a hook.

At rest, the floats are in displacement mode, ie. supporting the aircraft weight by their own displacement, and they sit quite low in the water. Taxying short distances is done with about 1,000rpm, and steering is easy in light winds. The aircraft, left to its own devices will weathercock into the wind and if the wind is strong another technique for turning must be employed.

Marilynn said that wind conditions on the open loch were near the limit for flying. I would have classed it as a nice day for sailing, with about 15 knots of wind on the open loch and just a light chop on the water. We did the power check by opening up to 1700rpm in a clear area and checking mags etc. The take-off explained all. Having briefed me, Marilynn let me get on with it. The standard floatplane pre take-off check is CARS. Marilynn had modified this to FCARS; Flaps set half: Carb Heat off: Area clear for take-off: Rudder (water) Up: Stick hard back. I quickly did my own TMPFGH which I use for all light aircraft, and then followed up with FCARS for Marilynn.

So, all done, stick hard back, and full throttle. The next bit was quite alarming at first and it was several take-offs before I got used to it. The aircraft noses up in two stages, first about 10° nose up, and then another 10°, and forward visibility is lost. It feels like it is trying to climb out of the water, which of course it is. After a pause of about five seconds, the stick is eased towards neutral and the aircraft is planing on top of the water, and you can see ahead again. Now my 'light chop' felt as if we were accelerating across concrete logs. I eased the aircraft into the air as soon as I could, and it became a normal Piper Cub. Landing was straightforward, holding off using a bit of power to ensure a gentle touchdown, and as the after end of the floats touched the water, power off and stick back. It felt like landing on a soft cushion and it was all over in about 100 yards.

Taking off again, we flew over a gap between the mountains to Loch Tay, just to the north, and found conditions here quite different. It was more placid, so a few more take-offs and landings and estimation of water conditions from the air (an essential part of the training), noting the glassy water in the wind shadow on the windward side of the loch, and estimating the wind direction by the wind lines parallel to the wind and the wavelets moving perpendicular to it.

In light winds, unless you are careful, it is easy to get the wind 180° wrong. When the wind is stronger it is easier to judge. The mountains surrounding the lochs create quite a variety of wind effects on the surface, from calms to mini squalls. The scenery is outstanding. Back to Loch Earn, checking Ts & Ps before we left the water to cross the mountain.

Contrary to my initial view that engine failure over land would be a major problem, apparently a floatplane is the safer option. The large surface area of the floats means that you can safely force land on surfaces that would be a problem for a landplane. Ploughed fields, gorse or boggy ground can be accepted by floats with little or no damage, and less chance of nosing over. Grass is almost as good as water. Marilynn told me that she had dismantled the Cub and transported it by road for its first winter maintenance at a nearby airfield, but subsequently she flew the Cub in, landing on the grass, carefully, and for take-off, she had a small four wheeled dolly made. The Cub sat on this for take-off from a runway, leaving it behind as it lifted off. Impressive.

At the end of my first flight, we landed at St. Fillans and berthed the Cub on its pontoon, cutting one magneto as we approached the berth, to slow the engine, and cutting the engine when I judged we would arrive gently alongside. No brakes, but this was more like a boat, and I felt happy doing it. Marilynn was quickly out, holding the Cub against the pontoon. I slowly levered myself out, onto the float and then the pontoon, and held the Cub while she began to moor it. Thinking to help, I stepped back on the float to reach a rope from the cockpit and, stepping back, missed the pontoon and dropped into the water, luckily holding onto the strut – so I was only soaked to the top of my legs. Marilynn and my wife onshore were convulsed with laughter. I realised that any hoped for respect for my years of sailing experience and almost 16,000 hours in the air had just disappeared in a splash.

Marilynn suggested an early start for the following day, mentioning six o'clock, but I managed to ease that back to 8 o'clock and we were airborne soon after. It was a quieter day, so we flew across to Loch Tay and found that the water there was like glass. This introduced an important technique, namely glassy water landings and take-offs. I had read of this phenomenon, but was not prepared for its significance.

Although conditions appear benign, the glassy water landing is potentially the most dangerous part of floatplane operation. In fact, as Marilynn explained, below about 100 feet you have no depth perception, and height estimation in the normal way is impossible. The routine is to pick something such as a small promontory on the shore and use this as your 'last visual reference'. Establish a normal powered approach, but using only half flap, and aim to cross the reference point at about 200 feet. At or before the point, raise the nose just above the horizon and, when the speed reaches 40 to 45 mph, feed in enough power to stabilise the rate of descent at 150 fpm. Then just hold that and wait. Waiting was the bit I had difficulty with, it seemed to take forever to reach the water.

I surreptitiously squinted sideways at about 50 feet, with Marilynn exhorting me to look ahead, to watch the nose and not anticipate touchdown, and realised I definitely could not judge my height in the usual way. Marilynn explained that as the aircraft entered ground (or water) effect there would be a slight nose down tendency, which should be countered with a touch back on the stick. Initially I found this hard to appreciate. As the aircraft touched the water, I closed the throttle, brought the stick back and that was it. An alternative option to this routine is to drop something, such as a cushion, on the water to create ripples, and then land before they subside.

Glassy take-off technique starts as normal, stick back, full power, on to the step, but then, as the aircraft tends to 'stick' to the water more, being in it all the time instead of skipping on wavelets, the drag is reduced by lifting one float out of the water. So stick over and slightly back until one float is clear, then hold that until flying speed and away. Great fun!

Next came step taxying, in which you get the aircraft on to the step then ease the power back to about 2,000rpm and you are planing along the water just below flying speed at 30 to 35mph, and you can turn the aircraft gently, a strange experience as it feels as if you are skidding sideways. This can be part of the technique for a restricted area take-off when, in light wind conditions, you can start downwind and turn into wind for take-off, or in calm conditions make a circular take-off. It is also the best and quickest way to taxi for a long distance. One glassy take-off I did flapless by mistake, instead of the usual half flap. This simply extended the whole process. However, runway length is not usually a problem, Loch Tay and Loch Earn are about 11nm and 5nm respectively.

Plough taxying was the next item to learn. This is employed to turn the aircraft in stronger winds. As it weathercocks around its centre of buoyancy, which at rest is about a third of the float's length from its bow, the technique is to move this aft to about two thirds, thus putting more fuselage area forward of the centre of buoyancy and the aircraft will in fact tend to weathercock downwind. To achieve this, the throttle is opened, stick hard back, until the high nose up attitude is achieved. Then power is reduced enough to hold the attitude and as the centre of buoyancy has moved aft the aircraft can easily be turned downwind. The water rudder is left down and as the downwind heading is achieved the power is eased and heading maintained, taking care not to go off that heading or the aircraft will weathercock into wind again. Complicated? Plough taxy is only used when essential as forward visibility is poor, engine cooling suffers and water pick up by the propeller causes leading-edge erosion.

Then came sailing and beaching. Sailing is manoeuvring the aircraft without power. The engine is switched off, the aircraft weathercocks into wind and begins to drift slowly back, tracking along the fore and aft line of the floats, and making 1 to 2 knots in even a light wind. Putting full flap down increases the speed noticeably. The direction of drift can be modified within about 25°-30° each side of the downwind track by putting the stick in the direction you wish the tail to go and the rudder the opposite way (air rudder, the water rudder is up). Thus it is possible to have a degree of control of where the aircraft will end up.

Beaching is a matter of choosing a place to go ashore, checking from the air first is a good idea, and Marilynn had several spots which she knew were OK. The beach is approached with caution, checking for underwater obstructions then nosing gently onto the beach, cutting the engine at the appropriate point. If the wind is stronger and onshore the aircraft can be nosed into wind and allowed to drift gently on stern first, water rudder up, but wave conditions may preclude this. We practised beaching then flew back to Loch Earn.

Back at Loch Earn I tried to improve the glassy landing technique by cutting the approach and managed to thump it onto the water. I briefly touched the throttle for a go-round, but Marilynn dissuaded me. I decided I would stick to her prescribed routine. We then did a landing near a buoy, taxying to the buoy and stopping near enough to put a rope on it.

Marilynn was now briefing me for the test, encouraging me to slow down and not rush, but also to forget about normal circuits and simply fly close to the chosen patch of water watching it in case conditions changed. A tight circuit at about 300 feet was recommended, 500 feet was 'high'. No windsock and no advice from the ground. There was a lot to remember for the test and although she seemed reasonably confident, I wasn't sure. Over a coffee in the hotel, she said to my wife,

"He doesn't listen, does he?"

My wife, of course, agreed, but I can stand criticism, it's good for the character.

We had been flying for four days, mostly Lochs Earn and Tay, but one day we had done a few landings on Loch Lomond for a change, and beached outside a hotel for coffee. The test was booked for the fifth day at 1200, and I managed an extra 55minutes in the morning to practise. I had now done 6 hours 50 minutes, and considered the 5 hours for the course an absolute minimum. Marilynn went off in the Cub with another student and I hung around waiting for the examiner to arrive. A seaplane flew over and landed and I realised it wasn't the Cub, but an Aviat Husky, a Cub lookalike. I helped the solo pilot to moor to another pontoon and then discovered he was the examiner, Neil Gregory.

After form filling and other formalities, the Cub was back and Neil suggested I did the pre-flight. As Marilynn had usually prepared the aircraft, I was a bit slow and missed the fact that Neil had sneakily dislodged one of the float bilge pump covers. However, once that was sorted he told me I was to treat him as just a passenger and I would have to do the departure on my own. Marilynn had mentioned to me that this had happened previously, but I still wasn't expecting it. It required a plan. I lashed a rope to the end of the pontoon, moved the Cub to its usual position for departure and tied the rope with a slipknot onto the wing strut where I could release it from my seat. We both then climbed aboard and I prepared for departure. When I was ready, I started the engine (luckily first time), slipped the rope, and we were away.

As I applied rudder, I realised I hadn't lowered the water rudder and quickly rectified that. We taxied away with a few more questions on the way, found a clear patch for the 1700rpm run-up and mag check, then took off and flew, as instructed, to the western end of the Loch. I climbed to 1500 feet and was asked to demonstrate a stall and recovery, then an incipient stall in a turn with power on, and a 360° steep turn in each direction.

Next, having designated a small area at the head of the loch to which I should limit my operations, we had an 'engine fire'. Diving the Cub towards the water, having done the vital actions, I managed to misread the very light wind and got the direction 180° wrong! It was the opposite direction to the other end of the loch, where we had departed. Tricky from 1500 feet, but from 200 feet it was obvious. My excuse was that the wind was so light and as we were on fire it didn't really matter. At 100 feet we did a go around.

We then flew to Loch Lubnaig, a loch I hadn't used so far, and again, an area at one end was designated as 'my loch'. At this point I decided I'd made enough mistakes and was trying too hard, so I was just going to relax and enjoy the rest of the flight (back to the old philosophy). It worked and I did. There was enough wind, about 12 to 14 knots, to do normal and rough water take-offs and landings in different parts of the loch. Rough water landing is fairly straightforward, minimum speed with power, holding off and choosing the moment to ease power and land. Rough water take-off is normal on to the plane, but without flap, then at about 35mph apply full flap. This kicks the Cub off the water and into the air. You then hold it in ground effect just above the water, carefully ease the flap in and climb away.

Neil then asked if I had done a damaged float landing, and I said I hadn't. This would be used when you hit an obstruction on take-off and suspect that one float is badly damaged. The idea is to land on the good float, put some power on and keep the aircraft planing on one float, steer towards a suitable beach, cutting the power at a point when you will run onto the shore, or at least shallow water, before the float sinks. Neil demonstrated one for me, then I did the same, without the last bit, of course.

A few more circuits, taking off and landing crosswind, engine failure after take-off, and a restricted area take-off, which means getting on the plane crosswind then turning and getting airborne into wind. This is the only occasion when it may be necessary to leave the water rudder down for take-off, to maintain directional control on the crosswind part. Neil was urging me all the time to forget normal flying, and enjoy the close in, low level circuits, putting the wing almost in the trees on the steep sides of the loch. Finally we flew back to Loch Earn where there was glassy water for that exercise.

I did a reasonable glassy water landing as previously instructed, but Neil said it wasn't necessary to make such a long descent onto the water. He then demonstrated his method in which he crossed the last visual reference at about 90 feet, set up at 40 to 45mph and 150fpm descent. I agreed that I preferred this method, which reduced the long wait for touchdown, but he then rather spoiled the effect by hitting the water just as hard as I had done on my lousy landing in training. I completely agreed when he said,

"You can't win 'em all!"

Once ashore, he shook my hand and told me I had passed the flight test. Next came the technical oral, which I'm afraid I'd forgotten about and hadn't given much thought. I guessed my way through some questions like,

"What is the wing spar made of?"

I guessed wood, but it was aluminium. I didn't know the designation number of the engine, I thought 135hp Lycoming was near enough. I certainly hadn't done enough swotting on the technical side of the aircraft. However for a yachtie, the seamanship written exam was a doddle, tides, buoyage, etc., and I managed 100%. That was it, and I was a qualified Single Engine Piston (Sea) rated pilot.

The course was harder than I expected, but great fun and a unique flying experience. No radio, no ATC, low level circuits, magnificent scenery, slope soaring along the mountains. We saw red deer frequently, and Marilynn showed me a couple of osprey's nests, from a safe distance. The only catch was that none of the seaplane schools in the UK would allow you to rent an aircraft, unaccompanied. I think insurance may be the difficulty. Understandable, as the riskiest part of the operation for the aircraft is the time on the water, manoeuvring and mooring. I understand Jack Brown in Florida operates on the same basis. Nevertheless, I went back several times and flew, accompanied, for recency and renewal, with Marilynn, and also with Neil, when he had his school set up. He operated the 180hp Husky amphibian from his water sports centre, at the western end of Loch Earn. I flew it for a couple of hours with Neil, using several more lochs, including doing nine touch and goes without turning on Loch Tummel. Most of the lochs in Scotland are available for use by seaplanes, unlike England, and quite a few are officially designated on the CAA charts as water aerodromes. I finally landed the Husky on a runway at Perth, when we'd finished our flying, quite a strange feeling putting the floats with four wheels onto the ground.

Between flying at Sleap and the floatplanes I'd flown another little aircraft, a Thorpe T18. Willie Wilson, a friend and colleague from Manchester, had spent about eight years building from plans a Rand KR2, a wooden two seat low wing aircraft with a VW based engine. He kept it in Deltair's hangar , and I often saw him when I was there. Willie was in touch with many aircraft owners at Speke. In 2001 he rang me to tell me he had just completed the five hours test flying on the Thorpe for its permit. The owner, who wasn't very experienced, having completed his PPL on his ARV with Dave at Deltair, had asked Willie to fly with him while he got used to the aircraft. Willie wasn't keen, never having instructed, and told me the aircraft wasn't the easiest to fly. He'd suggested to the owner that I might be interested. The aircraft had come from the USA and the owner had overhauled and rebuilt it over a couple of years. I went to Speke and met the owner and the aircraft. It was a very nice little aeroplane, and I did a few circuits to try it. First problem was that there was no apparent effect when carb heat was selected. When we investigated we found that warm air was on all the time. That was soon sorted. The aircraft was a pleasure in the air, 120 knots on its 130hp Lycoming, with excellent handling. I stalled it later and found a very positive stall with a pronounced wing drop. Not a problem, but it obviously needed care. The main problem was its ground handling, being very short coupled the rudder was extremely sensitive, and on the ground I felt it was a ground loop looking for a place to happen.

For the first hour or so the owner had difficulty just taxying. I started flying with him, doing quite a few circuits, including an hour or so at a quiet Mona, in Anglesey, where I almost did my first ever ground loop. The owner lost it on landing and the aircraft began a rapid swing to the edge of the runway. It would certainly have developed into a ground loop, but I applied full rudder and a touch of power which stopped the swing, and then, rather than trying to regain runway heading and risking a ground loop the other way, I allowed it to run onto the grass, luckily missing the runway lights. After more than six hours flying I made the difficult decision that the aircraft was simply too much for the owner, and he needed more experience, particularly with tail wheels, before he'd be able to cope with it. He wasn't too pleased when I put it to him, but I genuinely considered that it was the only option. I heard later he tried with a local instructor who came to the same conclusion.

Just after I retired the Sl-11s were all disposed of by British Airways. A company based in Bournemouth, Hurn, bought most of them. They advertised in 'Flight' for pilots to fly the aircraft. I considered applying, although I didn't fancy driving all the way to Hurn to work. While I was thinking about it, I spoke to Willie Wilson at Speke, and he'd obviously considered it like me. Willie had flown the Sl-11s for some time, and finished his time at BA on the 747-400. When I mentioned the advert to Willie, he told me he had already been in touch with the company. He said they had told him, in no uncertain terms, that they were not interested in employing ex-BA pilots. We were not too sure of the reason for this attitude, you would think that pilots who were experienced on type would be a natural choice. We decided that they only wanted pilots who could easily be moulded into their operating routines, much as, I've heard, some of the low cost operators prefer. In other words, pilots who would not resist pressure to operate as the company decided they should.

When I was flying from Speke with Dave's school, I had noticed a small grass airfield at Ince Blundell, north of Liverpool. Gordon, who flew with me, and lived in Maghull nearby, investigated and found it was a microlight flying school and club. However, we learned that, at that time, although you could learn to fly with the club, when you were qualified the regulations didn't allow you to rent an aircraft. So, having learned to fly, you had to buy your own aircraft to continue. A few years later Gordon enquired again and found that the rules had changed and it was now possible to rent. The school operated flex-wing and three axis microlights. The three axis, conventional aircraft was a high wing, Ikarus C42. I visited the field and met John North, the CFI, and Richard Thornborough, the other instructor. I joined the club, was checked out on the Ikarus, and started flying from Ince. I had discovered the world of microlights.

I quickly settled into flying at Ince. Three grass runways, all about 400 yards (or metres), no ATC, apart from an occasional advisory service if an instructor was around, just transmitting your position and intentions. Not all aircraft had, or used, radio, so it meant a sharp lookout at all times in the circuit, with a circuit height of 500 feet. It certainly beat flying at Liverpool. I began to fly the Ikarus regularly, taking family for trips, and it was a pleasure, back to basics flying from grass, a friendly relaxed atmosphere, altogether just what light aviation should be.

Talking to pilots and owners I soon realised that several aircraft were home built. Some years before I had seriously considered the Kitfox home build, but hadn't gone any further. I now joined the Popular Flying Association (PFA), later to become the Light Aircraft Association (LAA), investigated and found there were many options to choose from, building from plans, part built kits, and various types of construction, wood, composite (glass-fibre), aluminium, etc., etc. I browsed magazines, brochures and all the information I could get from the PFA. I definitely wanted a conventional three axis aircraft, rather than a weight shift, or flex wing, microlight, and eventually one aircraft stood out as offering all I needed. This was the Evektor Aerotechnik EV97 Eurostar, a very conventional all metal, low wing, two seat, tricycle undercarriage aircraft, produced by a proper aircraft manufacturing company in Czechoslovakia, which built other aircraft and also made components for Boeing and Airbus. It was powered by the ubiquitous Rotax 912UL, a horizontally opposed four cylinder geared engine which produces 80hp from just 1211cc at 5800rpm, the prop geared down by a 2.27:1 gearbox. I contacted the UK dealer, Cosmik Aviation, who offered the aircraft in kit form, or as a ready to fly option, and they sent me full details, prices etc.

I wanted to fly the aircraft before a final decision, so called Cosmik and made an appointment for a 'demonstration', as they called it. In August 2005 I drove down to their base at Deppers Bridge in Warwickshire. I met Chris Theakestone, the builder of Cosmik's ready to fly aircraft, BMAA inspector, microlight instructor, company pilot and demonstrator. Chris showed me around their small but well organised factory, and I inspected Eurostars, finished, part built, and in boxes.

We then went to Shotteswell, a few miles away, where the demonstrator aircraft was hangared. It was a breezy day, up to 24 knots, I don't think Chris was too keen on flying, but I managed to persuade him, and we climbed into the aircraft. Chris taxied out and took off on the longer, 600m, grass runway, the wind right across. The field is perched atop a small ridge which accentuated the wind effect. After take-off, Chris handed over to me and I flew around for fifteen minutes or so, doing turns and stalls. I immediately liked the aeroplane in the air, crisp, sensitive controls, a real fingertip aircraft. We flew back to the field, Chris took over and landed into wind on the short 300m runway. At this point as we began taxying towards the hangar, I realised that the 'demonstration' was over. I quickly pointed out to Chris that my interest would go no further without my flying the aircraft properly. After he was reassured that I thought I could cope with the conditions, I was allowed to do two circuits, including take-offs and landings, using the longer runway for take-off and the short one for landing, as before. Chris insisted on my maintaining 70mph on the approach, which I considered rather fast, and we floated for 100yds before touching down, but with the fresh wind it wasn't important.

I was now happily convinced that the aircraft was the one for me, and shortly afterwards placed an order. The kit was part built, the company had originally also offered a basic kit with sheets of aluminium and lots of rivets, but so few were sold that they stopped supplying it. The engine was the Rotax 912UL 80hp, the 912ULS 100hp had also been an option, which I might have gone for, but also since dropped. Another withdrawn option was a wing folding kit. Flying controls were rod for elevator and aileron, cable for rudder and elevator trim, which explained its sensitivity. The kit comprised the bare fuselage, structurally complete with canopy fitted, and six large boxes, three containing two wings and elevator and tailplane, one box on a substantial base with the engine inside, and the other two (one very large on a pallet) with all the various components, undercarriage, brakes, spats, control rods, cowlings, fairings, propeller, instruments, radio, and dozens of plastic bags, all marked, with nuts, bolts, fittings etc., etc.

Next problem was where to build. I wanted to be close to home, considered industrial premises (expensive), decided airfields were too far away, and then one day while having a shower I looked out of the window and realised my neighbour opposite had a huge two car garage which wasn't really utilised, as he lived on his own and usually left his car out. I approached him and explained what I needed, measured his garage and found it perfect for my requirements. I offered to rent it from him for up to twelve months and let him use my single garage for his car. He was amenable to my plan, not even bothered about the rent, and we agreed on the deal.

I continued with my plans, now well into the paperwork side, a plethora of information and advice from the PFA, plus a maze of rules and regulations pertaining to microlights and home builds which were quite new to me. I needed a permit application and an inspector. I arranged Dick Davison as my inspector. I knew Dick and, conveniently, he lived just a mile or so from me. He'd owned a J3 Cub for many years, and now had a Super Cub. Ken Davies, another inspector who lived near Chester, agreed to be standby, if required. I finalised the order and arranged a pick up date.

At this point, I discovered that microlight flying hours didn't count for renewal of my PPL. When I mentioned this to Chris he told me that the Eurostar EV97 microlight could be registered as a light aircraft, an EV97A , rather than a microlight, and this would solve that problem. The only difference in the kit build would be the fitting of an additional electric fuel pump, cost £50, but an advantage would be that the EV97A had a max take-off weight of 480kg, rather than the max microlight weight of 450kg. There is also a maximum empty weight for microlights, to comply with meeting the requirement to able to carry one hour's fuel plus two 82kg people. It is a challenge for the builder of the Eurostar to stay under the weight, but with the extra 30kg the EV97A doesn't have this problem. Nigel Beale of Cosmik found that his factory built aircraft had difficulty meeting this maximum empty weight, but solved it by some excellent lateral thinking. The one hour's fuel requirement was calculated at max continuous rpm, 5500. Cosmik simply changed the placarded max continuous to 5200rpm, decreasing the one hour's fuel weight, which allowed an increase in the max empty weight figure.

For me it was all proceeding to plan, and then, four weeks before delivery, my neighbour dropped a bombshell. His brother was coming to live with him, with car, and he would have to pull out of our arrangement. Rapid change of plan. I looked again at my single garage, 16ft by 8ft wide and 10ft high. I bought some 8x4 chipboard and built a temporary extension with doors, giving me a length of 20ft which I reckoned would be just enough, aircraft overall length is 19.5ft, a bit less with the rudder off. In the event, it was the best outcome. Although it was a bit cramped at times, particularly after the engine was installed, the convenience of having the aircraft at home far outweighed any disadvantage. I could work, or stop, whenever I wanted, tools, parts and tea were always to hand. I even managed to go to the 'hangar' at one o'clock in the morning to check something I'd been thinking about in bed.

February 8th 2006, I set off early in a hired 7.5 ton truck, accompanied by a couple of friends, Andy and Gordon, for Deppers Bridge. A couple of hours loading fuselage and six boxes and we were on our way home. On arrival back at base, 45 minutes had it all unloaded, wing and tail boxes in Mike and Barbara's garage next door until required, the rest filling my garage/hangar, and I couldn't imagine how this was going to work out. One step at a time, I decided, the old adage must be right.

Over the next few days I gradually sorted through and emptied the boxes, stowing bits in the two spare bedrooms, rudder, propeller, fairings, undercarriage, spats, control rods, etc. I was left with fuselage and engine box in the hangar. The engine would stay in its box, supporting the fuselage (when it was on its undercarriage) until required. Cosmik had a plan for the order of construction, but with my limited space, I had to devise my own. There was a very thick build manual from Evektor as well as a smaller but useful one, plus a CD, with good advice, from Cosmik. The large manual occasionally presented some interesting translation challenges. When working on the nose leg bungees I was stumped by reference to an 'ambulatory bundle'. I eventually realised they were talking about a 'knot'. Apart from that sort of thing the instructions were good. All small parts, nuts, bolts, etc., were in plastic bags labelled with 'pos numbers'. These numbers related to the drawings and instructions in the manual, making it easy to follow. The only time this didn't work was for the flap lever assembly, when they didn't make sense. Cosmik told me that the pos numbers were wrong in this case, so I had to spread the bits on the floor and work out where each went.

As the basic airframe is substantially complete, the build is essentially fitting out. Undercarriage and brakes, flying controls, instrument panel and instruments, fuel system and tank, electrics, radio and, of course, engine, propeller, and cowlings. There was plenty for me to do, enough for satisfaction as each stage was completed, but not so much that the end was too far away. All the aluminium skin of the aircraft is anodised, which is even better for an aircraft which is to be kept outside.

First job was the undercarriage. I put the fuselage on trestles, with help, and started. The two GRP legs are each secured in the airframe by two 8mm bolts. The book says use a reamer to get an exact fit for the bolts. Reamers are expensive. A phone call to Chris, and I learned that a hole drilled with a 7.9mm drill would provide a push fit hole for the bolt. Chris was a great help in the early stages, But I gradually settled into making my own decisions, in consultation with Dick. My aircraft work as an apprentice from years ago also helped. Typical problem was the undercarriage again, when the legs had to be positioned exactly in their locating channel 8mm from the rear spar. I was scratching my head thinking about this when Andy called to see how I was getting on. He suggested sitting an 8mm allen key on top of the leg using the short part to position the leg 8mm from the spar. It worked a treat, good to have friends. The bolts went in from above and the washers and nuts had to be fitted in a blind space. I sorted this myself by Aralditing washer to nut, sitting them in a ring spanner and 'feeling' the spanner on to the bolt. It worked, again. That was how it progressed, one job, one day at a time, not looking too far ahead.

Undercarriage fitted, engine box holding the tail up, with the turtle deck removed, just having been held on by a few temporary rivets, I fitted the sticks, control rods for elevator and aileron, and trim cables, having first done rudder pedals and brakes. Some items didn't fit first time, like the mainwheels which wouldn't go on the axles. I had to 'ease' the axles with some Brasso and very fine wet or dry. When fitting the hydraulic brakes I needed a hypodermic syringe to fill the cylinders on the rudder pedals with fluid. I tried everywhere to buy one, at chemists etc., without success. I was finally directed to the 'harm prevention unit' of a local hospital where I was given several, free, and they didn't want to know what they were for, even though I tried to explain and offered to pay.

Tensioning the rudder cables called for some innovation. I used an old spring balance, having calibrated it to the required 25kg, using petrol cans and bathroom scales. My two sons, when available, were useful assistants. Brian helped with the tensioning, holding the tension on while I marked the cable and then made the eye. The system worked. The routine for most jobs was to read the manual, look at the bits, think about it, read the manual again, and if possible do a dry run with the bits. Some jobs could be assembled, and taken apart easily, but some were 'one shot' and you had to get it right first time.

The instrument panel was interesting, just a shaped but blank piece of aluminium. To cut the holes I bought a circle cutter, but wasn't happy with its operation, so resorted to the old fashioned method of making a circle of holes with a 3mm drill and then carefully filing the hole to size, laborious but accurate. I decided I wanted a full panel, even though permit aircraft are VFR and day flying only. I found two second hand 12 volt turn and slips for £70 each and was so pleased I bought them both. Permit aircraft parts are not required to be certificated, as for C of A aircraft. Electric artificial horizons (AH) and direction indicators (DI) were expensive (£900 to

£1000), and as vacuum versions were much cheaper (£300), I decided to fit a venturi to power them. I bought the biggest venturi, and fitted it on the port side of the fuselage, just aft of the engine cowlings . Fitting it was a modification, so I had to produce drawings for the PFA.

The PFA required the build process to be signed off by the inspector at various points, and Dick did this as required. He often called in when passing to see how I was progressing. When all the holes were done in the instrument panel, I did a dry run with all the instruments fitted, then considered its paint finish. The Austers I flew in the fifties had a nice black crackle paint finish. I researched this on the internet, and found tales of gloom. Expensive two pack paints requiring an oven for finishing and usually failure at the end. Then, in the Light Aero Spares (LAS) catalogue, I spotted an aerosol crackle paint for £4.99. When I ordered it I was told to follow the instructions to the letter, which was mainly to make sure the temperature was above 25°C, and ensure that the accurate timing of the three coats over four hours was strictly adhered to. On a warm sunny day in early April the temperature in our conservatory with doors and windows closed and a fan heater on was nearer 30°C. After the third coat at four hours it was done. Not much happened at first, it looked just like a flat paint finish. However over the next hour or so the crackling, or pickling as we used to call it, slowly started and spread all over the panel to give a very satisfactory effect. I was delighted. £4.99 was a bargain.

The build progressed steadily during the spring, most days I managed about four hours in the hangar, sometimes more, sometimes less, as the rest of life had to be fitted in. The estimate for time to build the kit was 500 hours, which was about right, but I'm not sure if that included thinking time, an important element. One day, with Brian and Andy helping, we pushed the fuselage out onto the drive to temporarily fit the tailplane and rudder. The 8ft span tailplane was too wide to be fitted in the hangar. I had done the rudder angle settings inside but on this day we fitted the tailplane, did elevator angles, elevator trim settings, and tailplane fairings. All done, the fuselage went back in the hangar, rudder back to its bedroom and tailplane in Mike and Barbara's garage. This job was my first use of Rivnuts, threaded rivets for screw attachment. I'd bought the Rivnut tool from Cosmik, but couldn't get it to work on experimental bits of aluminium. Exasperated, I bought another tool locally, which worked perfectly. I sent the original back to Cosmik, it was found to be faulty and they refunded me.

Back in the hangar the fuel tank was fitted (easier said than done), and the cockpit seats. Fuel flow rate was checked using the electric pump. I monopolised the kitchen table for about ten days while I fitted the instruments to the panel and as much wiring as I could do at this stage. Complete with instruments, switches, and fuses, the panel was finally installed in the aircraft.

I fitted a fire extinguisher on the cockpit floor, just forward of the main spar, where I could reach it easily. Although an extinguisher wasn't a legal requirement, I thought it made sense, and it was to prove so later. When I commissioned my boat, Kingfisher, I had specified BCF extinguishers to be fitted, instead of the standard, dreadful, dry powder ones. We had BCF on the 1-11s, and I had used them in training and been impressed by their efficiency. Some years later, they had been banned from yachts, because of their effect (only when used) on the 'hole' in the ozone layer. However they were still permitted in aircraft, as there was no reasonable alternative. I had removed four from my boat, and I fitted one of these in the aircraft.

I was now at the engine fitting point. The manual recommended fitting engine to the bearers then the whole unit to the airframe. Cosmik recommended fitting bearers to airframe then the engine. With my lack of space, this was the only option. I fitted the bearers, removing water pump and carbs from the engine as advised, and organised Brian and Andy to help. With engine suspended by rope on a piece of 4x4, they held it in position as I inserted the four mounting bolts. Three were easy, but of course the fourth wouldn't line up. I struggled for five minutes, trying to push the bearer into line for the last bolt, as they became increasingly impatient with my efforts, until I finally succeeded and they could relax.

I was then able to continue on my own, refitting carbs and water pump, fitting exhaust system and making all the connections to the engine, throttle and choke cables, and mechanically synchronise the carbs. All the electrical connections were next, mag switches, master, fuel pump, radio master, and gauge connections for oil pressure and temperature, cylinder head temp, and coolant. I filled the fuel tank one litre at a time to calibrate the fuel gauge, and prove the system. Next came the cowlings, which had to be carefully measured and drilled for the fasteners, which had to line up with their corresponding holes in the other cowling or bulkhead, and then I fitted scuttle between the cowlings and cockpit.

With the oil system all connected, and oil level in the tank checked, I motored the engine over, minus plugs and prop, to check oil pressure. Zero. This was covered in the manual and it suggested pressurising the system by a fairly complicated procedure involving air bottles. I simply attached the valve from an old car inner tube to the filler of the oil tank, pressurised it to a couple of pounds by a foot pump with a gauge, motored the engine over again, and the oil pressure came up on the gauge. The turtle deck was replaced on the fuselage using all the rivets this time. The rivets were the type in which the head of the pin is retained inside the rivet as it breaks off. So no hunting for rivet heads. However all the rivets (including all those done in the factory) have to be sealed with a blob of sealant, and as there were no volunteers for this boring job, I had to do it. I didn't count them, but there are a lot of rivets on a Eurostar.

After I had fitted the spats to the wheels, there was not much more to do to the fuselage. The radio aerial was fitted on the turtle deck just behind the canopy. There were two radio positions in the cockpit, and as there was more hangar room on the starboard side of the aircraft, I plugged a headset in that side for a first trial. It was dead. I checked the power to the interface, and continuity to the socket, as well as the aerial connections. No joy. When all else fails, read the instructions. The radio handbook advised me that the first trial of the radio must be made from the port, number 1, position. Thereafter either position would work. I did as instructed and the radio worked well. I could even hear aircraft going into Liverpool from inside the hangar. Finally the propeller went on, that was easy, but the spinner had to have cut-outs to allow it to be positioned over the prop. The paper template wasn't much help, so it was a slow process of carefully filing the fibreglass away until the correct shaped cut-outs were made.

I had sourced locally decals for the registration marks and fuselage decoration, and another local engraving company who did the various placards for the panel. With two tone blue registration and go-faster stripes finished, the fuselage was finally wheeled out onto the drive, and the wings and tailplane from next door's garage were brought into the hangar. Apart from the registration marks, and the dreaded rivet sealing, work on the wings was minimal. Ailerons and flaps were factory fitted, so after control rods to ailerons and pitot head on the port wing were done they were ready for trial fitting to the fuselage. This could only be done one wing at a time, due to space on the drive, so, in turn, each wing had flap and aileron connections finished, and wing root fairings finished with Rivnut fittings.

With the aircraft on the drive, it prompted comments from neighbours and passers-by such as,

"You'll have to take the phone wires down to take-off from Hilary Drive".

And the more obvious comments,

"It'll never fly like that, it should have two wings, one each side."

Dick, my inspector, thought it might be a good idea to give the engine its first run on the drive, but I'm afraid I didn't have the courage and deferred that to the airfield. That definitely would have produced a few more comments.

This was it, we were ready, and I organised the truck again. I made two 4x4 beams with padding so four men could lift the fuselage onto the hydraulic lift and into the lorry. It went well, we loaded wings and tail and lashed them all down. With two sons, Brian and Peter, we set off for Ince. The fuselage had moved slightly by the time we arrived, it would have been better to let most of the air out of the tyres to make it more stable, but it survived. It was fine and dry. Gordon met us there at 11 o'clock, and by 5 o'clock we had two wings and tailplane/elevator fitted, and most importantly, the engine had its first run. I didn't have a hangar (one reason for choosing an all metal aircraft), so we tied it down securely on its parking spot under the trees, with straps to anchor points screwed firmly into the ground. This is it G-CFTJ, welcome to the real world, no more heated hangars. The bespoke registration, an unnecessary expense, comprised my initials and my wife's.

After the first day at Ince, we fitted the rudder, then spent the next few weeks doing engine runs, taxying, fuel flow tests, adjusting and setting flying controls, compass swing, etc. Dick was involved doing his inspections. During the engine running I discovered that the alternator was only producing a trickle charge (no ammeter), and with engine running the voltmeter was down to 11.5volts. It was amazing, and very nice, when doing something to the aircraft with cowlings off, how people would appear from nowhere to watch and offer advice. When investigating the low charge rate, somebody told me he'd had a similar problem, and pointed out the two yellow wires from the alternator to the cut-out regulator box, which he said were the cause of his problem. When I fitted the box, I had thought that the spade type connectors on the box weren't very tight, so now I removed them all, including the two yellow ones, tightened them, and refitted them to make really firm connections. Starting the engine, the voltage came up to 14 plus immediately. Problem solved, but I thought that screwed connections would have been better than the spade type.

After Dick's final inspection, I received my PFA permit to test on Saturday 15th July, requiring five hours flying, including a two hour flight, and at least fifteen landings. I had already been approved by the PFA to do my own test flying. I didn't tell them that if I hadn't been approved, the aircraft would go back in the box. All that work for somebody else to fly it, no chance.

It was now the hot summer of 2006 (July was the hottest month on record), and temperatures locally were up to 35°C at times. So I was at the field early on Sunday 16th (just over five months since the boxes arrived) to prepare the aircraft and make the first flight in the relatively cool part of the day. As I worked in the sunshine on my aircraft, a flex wing microlight flew overhead at about 500ft and as I looked up the pilot waved to me. I waved back, and that was the moment I decided that I'd died and gone to heaven. An aeroplane, a grass strip, and sunshine, what more could a pilot want?

Peter arrived in time to video the first flight, for posterity (or the accident investigation!). No, completely confident, at 9 o'clock I taxied out. People often asked what it felt like making the first take-off in an aircraft I had just built, but it felt no different to flying any aircraft for the first time, and I had already flown a Eurostar. After engine and pre departure checks I lined up on runway 11, opened the throttle and at about 40mph eased the nose up and lifted off at 45mph. I climbed to 3000ft and did four stalls, one for each flap setting, 0°, 15°, 30° and 50°. TJ stalled at 43mph with flaps up, about 33mph with full flap, and there was adequate warning by nose nodding and wing wobbling before it happened. Controls were positive and light, and at cruise speed of 100mph it flew straight as a die. The fixed tab on the rudder only needed a slight adjustment. I landed after fifteen minutes and we did the recommended check of all attachments, finding them all OK. I flew three more times that day, doing nine landings in all. I was very pleased with my little aeroplane.

I continued the test flying over the next few weeks, and all went relatively well. Because of the hot conditions, I found that the oil temperature rose fairly quickly in the climb and was at 120°C by the time I reached 2500ft. The recommended range was 90° to 110°, normal operating limit 120°, and maximum allowable was 140°C. I throttled back to a low cruise rpm, and then it settled back to about 100°C. This wasn't acceptable. I had asked about the need for the optional oil cooler when I had ordered the aircraft and was assured it wouldn't be necessary for the frozen north. However when I called Cosmik and told them about my temperatures, they said,

"You need an oil cooler." I ordered the cooler kit.

Passengers weren't allowed during test flying, but some flying was required at max weight, and 'observers' were allowed to assist in recording flight details, so my two sons (when available) were happy to fulfil this role. The required two hour flight, restricted to 25nm from the field, was completed, flying over to the Clwyd Valley in North Wales, and refreshing acquaintance with the various strips, but not landing. We hadn't fitted the oil cooler at this stage, so the engine required gentle treatment, with low revs, and we didn't go above 2000ft. Shortly after this flight, the kit arrived and I fitted the oil cooler. Due to the nice weather, it wasn't a problem to fit at the field, but it would have been easier in my hangar. It made the difference, the oil temps dropped to a reasonable level, and I wasn't restricted in climbing.

The only other hitch during testing was suction, or lack of it, for the gyro AH and DI. Although the instruments both worked well when airborne, in fact the AH usually erected before take-off, the suction gauge indicated well below the required 5ins/hg. I decided to fit a second venturi into the system to power the gyros, and when I had done this the suction was in the green. Mounted on each side of the fuselage between the engine and cockpit, the venturis provided some suction on the ground from the slipstream but needed airspeed to bring suction up to normal operating level. The LAA were happy with an addendum to my original modification.

Test flying complete, I filled in all the forms and sent them off, with the fee, to the LAA. About four days later, August 10th 2006, I received my Permit to Fly for TJ. Six months and two days after the boxes had arrived at my hangar.

I quickly settled into flying my little aircraft, getting thoroughly used to it, and exploring its capabilities. I didn't change my initial view, in fact the more I flew it, the more satisfied I was with my choice. All I wanted now from my flying was to be able to fly when and where I wished. Just to fly locally for half an hour or so was often all I required. The pilots at the field often went off to a fly-in en masse (or maybe three or four) and also planned, and did, more ambitious trips to France, Germany or Ireland. They invited me to join them, but I wasn't keen on the water crossings. One point about flying my aeroplane which gave me frequent cause for thought was that it had only one engine. So far seven engines had let me down, luckily only one being in a single engined aircraft. Once I got used to my aircraft and had practised forced landings, I was happy that if the engine failed I could put it into an open space of about 200m at a low speed and would have an excellent chance of walking away uninjured. However I had no desire to stretch my luck by flying any distance over water. Seventy miles of English Channel to Cherbourg, or Irish Sea to the Isle of Man, was not an option for me. An unwritten agreement with my guardian angel meant that now I wouldn't push my luck unnecessarily.

In my earlier flying club days people only very occasionally wanted to fly to the Isle of Man, and if they did we suggested that they flew up the coast to St Bees Head, and climb to about 8,000ft for the thirty mile crossing, reducing the time at risk to a minimum. When I resumed flying light aircraft after retirement I was horrified that pilots thought nothing of flying the 75 miles from Wallasey to the Island at 1500ft. I was asked several times when flying the Bulldog if I would fly there with somebody. When I declined and explained, they would say to me,

"The engine doesn't know it's over water"

My standard response would be,

"Maybe not, but I do."

One interesting difference between the Eurostar, being essentially a microlight notwithstanding its registration as a light aircraft, and most of the other light aircraft I'd flown was inertia, or lack of it. This meant it was more affected by wind variations near the ground, and airspeed could change very quickly. The Pilot's Handbook gives an approach speed of 68mph, which is cautious but sensible. The standard 1.3VS (stall speed) for approach cannot be safely applied to aircraft as light as these. I used a short final speed of about 60mph, or even 50mph in calm or light wind conditions, but with more wind and turbulence, because of the speed variations, it was better to maintain a minimum of 60mph. Crosswinds weren't a problem, although it was difficult to keep the aircraft in line with the runway on the ground, as it would tend to blow sideways. On grass the aircraft could be kept tracking along the runway, and allowed to turn slightly into wind, tyres sliding on the, usually damp, surface. I tried landing one day on an out of wind runway, with about 20kts across, and this technique worked well, simply landing with drift on. All this was helped by its low speed controllability. Airborne, with responsive controls all the way down to the stall, a proper stall rather than a mush with poor elevator authority, the aircraft is a pleasure to operate. Stalling in turns is a non-event, even when doing steep climbing turns with just a little power on, which is fairly stupid flying, the aircraft simply shudders, then the nose drops, the wings level and it recovers without any help. Non aerobatic, but it stall turns beautifully (not an aerobatic manoeuvre), and recovers from an accidental spin positively. Intentional spins are not permitted. I had a copy of the comprehensive LAA spinning test, which hadn't shown any problems.

At the end of 2006, one of the club members, Peter Morgan, contacted me to say that he had bought a new ready to fly (RTF) Eurostar from Cosmik. He had arranged some dual on the type with a school at Oxford and was trying to arrange somebody, at considerable expense, to deliver the aircraft to Ince for him. I offered him an easier (and no cost) option, which was to go down with him to fly the aircraft back, and then I'd fly with him until he felt happy with it. He was delighted with this plan, and in January 2007 (on my 70th birthday) Pete's wife drove us to Deppers Bridge, and, taking off from Nigel Beale's 300m, slightly bent, strip, we flew his aircraft home. Over the next month or so I did a few hours with Pete, until he was thoroughly familiar with his new aircraft.

During early 2007, another club member, Mark Sanders, was doing his initial NPPL course with the school on the Ikarus. He'd just bought a second-hand Eurostar and had it delivered to the field. Mark thought he'd like to complete the rest of his course on his aircraft, but discussing this with John North we agreed that it would only complicate matters. So Mark finished his course on the Ikarus, and during this time I flew with him once or twice in his aircraft. Once Mark had his NPPL we then flew his Eurostar together, as I had done with Pete, until he was confident to fly it on his own.

When Mark's permit came up for renewal, after the inspection he had to do a test flight, which is the usual routine. The LAA wouldn't allow him to do it himself, because he had less than 100 hours flying. As I had been approved to do all my own initial test flying, he checked with the LAA, and I did the test flight with him. Soon after, Peter Morgan's Eurostar permit was renewed, and he also had to do a test flight. As Peter's aircraft was factory built, it was licenced by and under the control of the BMAA (British Microlight Aircraft Association). At Peter's request I wrote to the BMAA to ask if I could do his test flight, explaining that I had done the same for mine and Mark's aircraft. I filled in the form from the internet requesting permission to do the flight, listing my experience. I didn't get a reply, so I rang the BMAA.

The young lady I spoke to explained that to test fly a BMAA aircraft I would have to be qualified as a BMAA test pilot. I asked her how I could qualify, and she said I would have to do the test pilot course and exam. She suggested I contact the BMAA chief test pilot. I did this, by several emails, but as I didn't even get a reply I decided to give up, and told Peter that he would have to find an approved and qualified BMAA test pilot. Although I am a member of both the LAA and BMAA, I find that the LAA has a much more practical and pragmatic approach, which I find suits me. I'm glad that my aircraft is under the wing of the LAA. As previously mentioned. if I had been required to ask somebody else to test fly my aircraft having spent six months building it, it would simply have gone back in the box!

In my first year of operation, I flew down to Sleap to meet Willie Wilson with his Rand KR2, a friend of Willie's with another KR2, and George Brothwood, now with a Sipa 903, having sold his Acrosport. It was my first use of tarmac in TJ, which was interestingly different to grass, particularly on take-off, when the aircraft was almost airborne before I had fully opened the throttle. The interconnection between the rudder and nosewheel was much more noticeable than on grass, as any slightly coarser use of rudder showed up, whereas on grass, which I was used to, it wouldn't be noticed.

Even though my club membership was still current, I was charged a landing fee, which disappointed me. Even more disappointing, the restaurant was closed. I didn't bother renewing the following year.

I much preferred operating to private strips, and was surprised when investigating again just how many there were. Even better when there was no landing fee, and best of all when a cup of tea was on offer. Ken Davis, my stand-by inspector for the build, had a strip south of Chester, and I arranged with him to fly in. At his request I drove there first to examine it at ground level. Later that day I flew in to the 300yd grass strip, and let Ken try TJ. He was impressed that the Eurostar could happily fly from his strip with two up, as his current aircraft, a Gardan Minicab, was limited by the available length, and he only flew it solo. Ken had a hangar for the Minicab, and a caravan crewroom, with tea. Bliss!

Dick, my inspector friend, kept his Super Cub at Rhedyn Coch, Emlyn's Field, where he had a substantial hangar. Emlyn's field was not as smooth as Greenlands, and had cows as well as sheep. Dick's hangar was in the field adjoining, which was fairly short and had quite a downslope away from the hangar. It was just enough for Dick, on most occasions, to take off downhill, but not acceptable for landing. For landing, Dick had to chase the sheep and cows clear, land in Emlyn's, then open the gate to his field, and taxi up the hill to his hangar. Amazing what people will do to fly. I arranged one day to fly into Greenlands, Dick met me with his car and drove me to Emlyn's so I could acquaint myself with the field. He dropped me back at Greenlands and I then flew to Rhedyn Coch and did a couple of landings. The field is surrounded by tall trees which adds to the interest. A mile or so away, across the A55, is another strip, Bryngwyn Bach, which is home to a couple of aircraft, one of which is a Spitfire. Something else to look out for.

Dick also introduced me to Alan Chalkley, who recruited me into the North Wales Strut. Struts are the local element of the LAA, and very useful as a meeting point for like-minded individuals. Alan, who is also BA retired (he started on Stratocruisers), has owned a Piper J3 Cub for many years, and has a strip, Rhos Field, at the western end of the Lleyn Peninsular. Having spoken to Alan, and received his airfield brief, I flew to the strip with Bernie. Super little airfield, with one 400m grass runway and two much shorter ones, suitable for the Cub in strong winds. Alan took us to his bungalow, just half a mile from the field, for tea and cakes. Suitably refreshed, we went back to the airfield for Alan to fly TJ. He enjoyed it and was impressed enough to write a complimentary article about the aircraft in the LAA magazine. Bernie and I flew home via Pwllheli, to have a look at what was left of the old Broom Hall airfield.

Alan put me in touch with Bill Williams-Wynne who operated a strip at Talybont, just north of Tywyn on Cardigan bay. Bill had just bought a Eurostar kit, and, having contacted him for the necessary brief, I flew to the strip with Brian in April 2007 to meet him. Nice little field, 460m grass runway, from which Bill had moved the sheep to safety behind the runway fencing. Bill was obviously interested in my experiences building and flying my aircraft. We flew TJ together, and Bill did three landings which I think convinced him he'd made the right choice. Talybont is situated on Bill's farm, and he drove us back to his beautiful house (just slightly smaller than Buckingham Palace) for lunch, and to show us his other airfield, just a large grass area, with sheep of course, and his hangar with his Eurostar kit ready for action. I'd brought some useful bits and tools from my build which would help Bill, and he asked me about several points which he had already realised were not easily understood. In the hangar at Talybont was Bill's Vans RV6, which he was in the process of selling. He told me it wasn't really suitable for the short strip. However, I've since heard that Bill has bought the Vans again. Brian and I had a nice flight home, via Lake Bala and the mountain route, rather than the usual run along the coast.

Bill sometimes hosted a fly-in at his Talybont field. I flew down with Andy to one fly-in about a year after visiting for the first time. It was very hazy as we left Ince, but the visibility improved as we passed Anglesey. Dick had set off from Emlyn's about the same time, but didn't like the poor visibility and turned back to land at Ken's strip. There were three other Eurostars at Talybont, including Bill's, now completed. The weather was humid and unsettled and, after a barbeque lunch, we heard the rumble of thunder to the south in the early afternoon, so decided to make our way home, as did the others. The cu-nims were moving slowly up from the south and as we appeared to be beating them, we decided to call at Ken's strip on our way home. After a cup of tea with Ken and Dick another rumble suggested we should move. Taking off from Ken's, we called Liverpool for a quick zone transit. As we crossed the Wirral it was black over

Speke, with frequent flashes, and we listened to Easy Jet and Ryanair aircraft trying to dodge the worst bits on their way into the airport. When we arrived at Ince it was getting blacker by the minute and we saw a couple of lightning strikes fairly close to the field. We landed and just managed to tie the aircraft down and make it to the club caravan as the heavens opened.

In June 2008 I flew down to Truro in Cornwall to visit my sailing friend Arthur. I had promised to show him the aircraft and was hoping to take him flying, possibly across to the Scillies, where we had often sailed. I had flown with Arthur, and our wives, some years earlier in Dave's Cessna 172. We had flown from Speke to Caernarfon, looking at our sailing haunts. Arthur had really enjoyed the trip, and he had taken to flying like a natural. He had recently been diagnosed with a brain tumour, and even after an operation, the prognosis wasn't good. Andy and I flew down on a beautiful day, visibility 50 miles plus all the way, landing at Eaglescott for fuel as Truro didn't have any. When we arrived I was disappointed to hear that Arthur wasn't well enough to come to the airfield, but his wife Gwen picked us up in the car and we spent the afternoon with them. We flew home, via Eaglescott, and sadly, just a week or so later, Arthur died. I was disappointed that he didn't see, and fly in, my aeroplane. He would have enjoyed it.

After my ATPL expired I had been issued, and been flying with a PPL. In June 2006 I'd applied for, and been given an NPPL, but hadn't used it. I was given a SSEA (simple single engined aircraft) rating which allowed me to fly light aircraft, microlights and SLMGs. This new licence was originally intended as an alternative to the JAA PPL, being easier to obtain and keep valid, but with more restricted privileges. Day flying and VFR only, single engined aircraft max weight 2,000kgs, and no more than three passengers. Rather than a Class 2 medical, self-certification with a GP's countersignature was all that was required. A self-checking system of rolling recency was used at the time. In due course, however, it became more complicated.

A year later I decided to use my NPPL. The reason for this requires some explanation. When I failed my first RAF medical in 1953, aged sixteen, I was naturally slightly hesitant, three years later, about taking what was the same medical, for the CPL. The president of the medical board asked me, when telling me I had passed, if I was worried about passing. I confirmed that I was, but didn't tell him why, and he mentioned that my blood pressure was a little high, caused by my anxiety. Thereafter, I had my class 1 medicals as required, initially without any problem. However during the sixties I went to an AME (aviation medical examiner) for several renewals, and on one occasion he told me he couldn't pass me, due to an indication of sugar in my urine sample. I knew what that indicated, and asked,

"Does that mean I might have diabetes?"

He said it was possible and I would have to go to my GP to arrange hospital tests. I drove home thinking about my large mortgage and what this meant for the future. I went straight to see my GP and told him the tale. He said he would arrange for the hospital tests (glucose retention) as soon as he could. He then asked if I was worried about it, and I told him that I certainly was, as my job depended on the outcome. He said,

"Stop worrying, I can tell just by looking at you that you don't have diabetes."

That helped, but I was still worried. A day or two later I went to the local hospital for the test. After a couple of hours of glucose drinks every twenty minutes, plus blood and urine samples, I went home to await the results. My GP was very good and obtained the results quickly and called me to see him. He told me the tests were fine, and rather than any inclination to diabetes, I was right at the other end of the scale. I asked why my urine sample had shown the sugar trace, and he told me that it could happen to anybody, anytime, but unfortunately it had happened to me at my medical. He sent the results off to the CAA and I went back to work. I was relieved, but thought that the AME might have reassured me, as my GP had done.

Some years later, same AME, I had an ECG (electrocardiogram). These tests had been introduced after the BEA Trident crash at Heathrow. The doctor did the procedure himself and that, I thought, was that. At the time, based on age, I was required to have the ECG every three years. A few weeks later I received a letter from the CAA. This advised me that, 'due to an irregularity in your recent ECG, you are required to have another ECG at next renewal', in six months. Thinking heart problems at least, I phoned the AME to ask what it meant. He told me it wasn't a problem, and nothing to worry about. I put the phone down and continued worrying. I then decided to contact the medical department of British Airways. I told the doctor the story, and he said it was almost certainly a simple procedural error in the ECG. Slightly reassured, I still had to wait for my next medical to be sure.

This time I went to the CAA medical centre at Heathrow. When the doctor had apparently finished the ECG process, he then asked me to breathe in and hold my breath. He then ran the ECG machine again for a short time. He explained that with some people the position of the heart created a small negative wave, but when the breath holding routine was followed the trace became normal. Subsequently I noticed that when the ECG operator reached the end and looked at the trace, they (usually a nurse) then asked me to do the breathing in bit and were satisfied. On one occasion when the nurse didn't ask for it, I asked her why. She said it was a very minor irregularity, but nevertheless she then did the routine, and commented that the CAA were particularly pedantic about these small discrepancies. I explained my reason for not wanting to upset them.

As time went by, I was obviously beginning to be slightly apprehensive each time I went for a medical. I had a spell with an AME in Liverpool, who would frown when he took my blood pressure and suggest I cut down on my drinking. At the time, I hardly touched a drop. I guess he wondered why my blood pressure had gone up next time he saw me. I then discovered another AME on the Wirral, near home. I went with the now usual trepidation, and met a doctor with a very pleasant bedside manner and even found we had a mutual friend. After the first few items we came to the dreaded sphygmomanometer. I thought,

"Here we go, new doctor, how will he react?"

He pumped away, and I watched carefully for a reaction. None – good! He went back to his desk, wrote on the form, smiled, and continued talking about our friend. After a couple of minutes, he came back, as I thought, to retrieve his machine, but to my surprise he quickly took my blood pressure again. Of course, he caught me completely off guard. He then told me he had heard of the condition, but never actually observed it. My first reading had been 'very high', but the second was quite normal. He told me that I obviously pumped it up to order, and called it 'white coat syndrome'. At the time, I admired his expertise in fooling me and beating it. He was quite happy to pass me. I continued having medicals with him for some years, until he dropped off the AME list.

At this point I decided to buy a sphygmomanometer to check my BP for myself. Since 1986 I have kept a record of my readings, and always found them to be quite normal. I expected the syndrome would ease when I retired, but it didn't happen. The condition was well established, and whenever a strange doctor or nurse took a reading, such as at a hospital visit, it would go sky high. An attempt to be a blood donor failed when they managed a reading of 230/110. For the last few years when I was working and for several after retiring I went to an AME in Liverpool, Andrew Zsigmond, and established an easy relationship with him which certainly helped. After a few years of medicals with him, I mentioned the problem and told him about my records. He told me he had noticed my tension and simply made allowance for it. Not making an issue of it made the difference. I was now operating with a PPL and Class 2 medicals still having ECGs.

The crunch came when Andrew retired. Looking at the list of local AMEs, I found the one in West Kirby, who had originally diagnosed my problem, was available again. I arranged my annual renewal with him. He remembered me from my visits twenty years before. The blood pressure check was left to the end of the examination. It was very high and he reacted with horror, saying I must have treatment immediately, and he couldn't possibly clear me. I reminded him of his diagnosis years ago, and showed him a copy of my normal readings. To no avail. He said he must see those readings when he took my blood pressure. I told him the more he made an issue of it, the less likely was the possibility of that happening. I could see that he wasn't going to change his attitude, regardless of what he'd told me all those years ago, which I couldn't understand. I gave up.

At this point I realised that I already had an NPPL. All it needed to be valid was a signature from my GP, confirming my statement of fitness. No Class 2 medical and ECG. I went to see my doctor and explained the situation. She was much more sympathetic, took my blood pressure, and suggested some medication to lower my 'normal' pressure a little. She was quite happy to countersign my statement, and my NPPL was valid. The cost, about £30 for the GP signature, rather than almost £200 for a PPL Class 2 medical, was a bonus. Problem solved.

The Ince Blundell Flying Club was often invited to fly into local airshows. The Hoylake RNLI show was a regular venue, the aircraft landing on the beach in front of the lifeboat station. There was a flying display each year, with the Red Arrows, helicopters, parachutists, aerobatic teams, etc. In August 2007 we had a full turn out, 2008 it was windy and cold and I went with Brian, but nobody else bothered. 2009 was another reasonable day, and Dick joined us in his Cub, for his first beach landing.

In July 2008 the Wirral Show was held at New Brighton, and the club was invited. The tide times were favourable, leaving a smooth 800m stretch of hard sand just off the sea wall from mid-morning until late afternoon. On the Saturday, the wind was quite strong so just the three instructors and myself flew in, with the Ikarus, two flex-wings and TJ. On Sunday the weather was better and a full contingent of club aircraft enjoyed a day on the beach.

Another regular fly-out was to Southport. This is a flying show over the last weekend in September, well attended, and featuring an excellent display, with a wide variety of aircraft. For one reason or another, I didn't join the fly in until 2009. The local council, who organise the event, prepare an area of sand by the pier, scraping and rolling and marking three 500m runways on the sand. They also establish a mini control tower, with R/T, and a couple of controllers who oversee the aircraft flying in, as well as the actual display itself. We flew in from Ince on the Saturday, well briefed regarding arrival procedures before we took off. When I heard the controller's voice on the Southport frequency, I was immediately transported back to flying the S1-11 from Manchester. It was Tony Brown, one of the long standing air traffic controllers at Manchester, now retired. He has a particularly distinctive, calm and relaxed voice which was always a pleasure to hear when calling Manchester after the anonymous voices of the controllers when crossing Europe.

I was delighted to hear him again at Southport, and, after landing, made my way to the 'tower' to see him. He and his wife were running the control tower. I was pleased to learn that their son Peter, who had been a first officer with me at Manchester, was now a captain on the BA Boeing 777 fleet. We flew in on both days, even though the weather was cloudy and rather cool. Peter came with me the on first day, and Andy joined me on the second. The show (the biggest in the northwest) was impressive, with the Vulcan, BBMF flight, Red Arrows, and various aircraft, Typhoon, Catalina, Sea Hawk, Seafire, etc. It was good to land on the beach at Southport, more than fifty years since I last landed there. That was when Norman (Gerry)

Giroux operated his Fox Moths from the beach, taking people for pleasure flights. In busy periods, such as bank holidays, he would borrow an Autocrat from us, and I would fly it to the airstrip.

I didn't attend the 2010 show, due to reasons to be explained. The Sunday show was cancelled due to bad weather, which caused the organisers to reschedule the 2011 event for a weekend in July, to avoid the usually inclement equinoctial weather of September .

The reason I couldn't attend the 2010 show, regardless of the weather, was because my flying was restricted by the aircraft only having one wing. In June 2006, a German registered Eurostar had crashed in Switzerland. The investigation found that it had broken up in an area of the Swiss mountains known for turbulent conditions. However further investigation of the crashed aircraft eventually showed (after three years) that the metal used in the main wing spar caps didn't meet the required specification. Although it didn't meet the specified tensile strength for the material, tests showed that it was still above the required strength for the airworthiness standards, and it hadn't contributed to the accident. Another aircraft tested showed similar deficiencies. To cut a long story short, the CAA decided that all British Eurostars should have their wing spar caps tested. Until then, we could fly, but with restricted speeds.

The test, mainly by electrical conductivity, required a fairly high standard, in my view, to pass. It was a difficult time for Cosmik, the aircraft UK agent, but they rose to the occasion, organising testing for more than 150 aircraft in the UK. Any wings failing the test would have to be returned to the factory in Czechoslovakia for new spar caps to be fitted. The aircraft manufacturer, Evektor, was covering the cost of transport from UK and repair. When Chris came up to check the three aircraft at Ince, each had a wing that failed. One of my wings only just failed to meet the requirement, but a fail is a fail and it went off with the others. Chris took the three wings back on his trailer, and they were away for about two months, but it was good to have a reliable agent and manufacturer behind us, and the only cost to the owners was for Cosmik's travelling to test and transport the wings to their base. It could have been much worse.

Another notable incident occurred in October 2008, and could have had a disastrous outcome. I had changed my RPM gauge on a miserable wet day, and I ran the engine to prove that it was OK. As the aircraft was surrounded by pools of water, I couldn't open up to more than 3,000 rpm, so I decided I would go for a short flight to check the rpm over the full range with my optical tachometer. I stopped the engine, so that I could remove the tie downs, chocks and pitot cover. Back in the cockpit, the engine was still warm, and the Rotax 912 is notoriously reluctant to start when warm. I wound it over for four or five seconds with no response. I thought it may have cooled down so tried again with a bit of choke. That was probably a mistake. It didn't respond, so after a short wait, I tried again, without choke. This time the engine fired a couple of times, without starting, but as it did, I saw smoke coming from the engine starboard cooling intake at the front of the engine. I then saw a flicker of flame in the smoke! I switched off and grabbed the extinguisher from the floor beneath my legs. I jumped out of the aircraft, I'd like to think it was as quick as a flash, but that is a relative term for a septuagenarian. I dashed to the front of the aircraft and emptied most of the extinguisher into the intake. I finished off by emptying the remainder into the oil check flap on top of the engine cowl.

The smoke dissipated quickly, and I removed the top cowling to investigate. The fire had obviously been in the port carburettor intake and had destroyed the air filter. There was some minor damage to the throttle cables, melting their outer covers, some cable clips showed heat damage at their tips, and the top glass fibre cowling was a bit scorched inside, but that was all. The top of the engine and bulkhead were black with soot, which looked bad until it was cleaned off, quite easily. I had obviously caught it in time with the extinguisher. There was a fresh breeze from the port rear quarter of the aircraft which had blown the flames forward through the intake.

Nobody had seen what happened as the few club members about were in the club caravan. I went there for a cup of tea and showed them the air filter. I received sympathy and theories, of course. After my therapeutic cup of tea, we went to the aircraft for more investigation. One offered theory was a stuck inlet valve, allowing explosive gases back to the air intake. It seemed feasible. We turned the engine over and one compression seemed a little weak. I removed the rocker covers on the port side to check but the valves appeared to be operating normally.

I knew what had happened, but not how and why. I'd had enough for one day, and went home. I rang Dick, my inspector, to brief him. Next morning I rang Skydrive and spoke to Conrad Beale, who probably knows more about Rotax engines than most. He said he'd never heard of a stuck valve on a Rotax, and not to worry too much about lack of compression. It would probably be temporary, caused by the vagaries of the hydraulic tappets. He did say that a fuel soaked air filter after a prolonged start wasn't unusual. He was interested and asked me to keep him advised.

I went back to the aircraft to remove the carbs and cables, the port carb was sticky inside with deposit from the burnt filter. While I was doing this, I caught my finger several times on some strands of braided cable which was cable tied to the engine bearer next to the port carb.

At home I cleaned both carbs, and set them up for reinstallation. I was now convinced that the problem was simply an intake fire, but didn't know what had ignited it. The carbs have a drip tray beneath them to prevent any excess fuel, from such as a stuck float, going on to the exhaust under the carb. I found it hard to believe that fuel would have ignited on the exhaust, which wouldn't have been very hot anyway.

Next day I went back to investigate. Remembering my snagged finger, I removed all the ties holding the screened cable beneath the engine bearer, so that I could move it round to examine it. I was astonished, and horrified, to see that the braided cable had been chafing on the corner of the carb drip tray. It had chafed through the copper braiding, and was half way through one of the two wires, which were the connection from the AC generator to the regulator on the bulkhead.

I now knew how the fire had stared. Fuel soaked air filter, broken genny wire shorting to the braided screening just underneath, igniting the fuel vapour. I was relieved I had found the fault, could fix it, and prevent it happening again. Reassembled with clean carbs, mechanically and pneumatically synchronised, two new air filters, new throttle and choke cables to both carbs, genny cable repaired with a junction box, well protected from chafe, and I was serviceable again.

There are two other Eurostars at Ince, and while I was working on mine, Mark, the owner of one, came over to hear my tale of woe. After seeing my engine, he went to examine his aircraft, and shortly after called me over. He had found an almost identical chafe of the same wire, but on the starboard carburettor. The screening was chafed through, but the wires inside were still intact.

A few days later we checked the third aircraft and found a similar chafe, but not as bad as ours. The weak spot of the Rotax is chafe. There are so many hoses, wires and cables, and it is essential to keep on top of it with frequent inspections, coupled with sensible anti-chafe measures.

Apart from these minor dramas, my flying continued in a more pleasant routine. From the beginning at Ince, I had invited various pilots to fly TJ with me and allowed them to do it all, including take-off and landing. It was interesting to see how they coped, and it did show the benefits of flying from a small grass field, rather than an airport like Liverpool. Being quite used to landing on a short strip, they had a better awareness and control of the final approach than some of the private pilots I had flown with at Speke. When you have a mile of runway in front of you landing a light aircraft, you don't have to concentrate too hard.

I also let the instructors try the aircraft. At the time John was the only one who flew the Ikarus, and Richard flew the flex-wings. John enjoyed the Eurostar, although it is quite different to the Ikarus. Richard, who had been instructing on the flex-wings for several years, also enjoyed trying the Eurostar, but, as he told me, he had to think carefully before each control movement, as the basic controls operate in the opposite sense. But, after a few circuits, he was getting it sorted. I had exactly the same problem when I was eventually persuaded by Richard to try flying a flex-wing. However, soon after flying with me in TJ, Richard started instructing on the Ikarus. Carl, another pilot who was in the process of getting his instructor rating, also tried TJ, and when he qualified also began to instruct on the Ikarus.

One interesting point arose when flying with different pilots. One or two said that they found difficulty flying my aircraft with their left hand (left hand stick, right hand throttle) when they were used to using the right hand in their own aircraft. I had never really considered this before. I had flown my aircraft from both seats without difficulty. When I started flying I'd flown Austers first, left stick, right throttle, and then the Maggie and Tigers, right stick left throttle, and thought nothing of it. Later the Rapide, right stick, left throttles, and the Anson, left stick, right throttles. Airline flying was all left hand for the stick, apart from first officer time. Flying with either hand was something I'd always taken for granted and I was quite surprised that they even noticed or regarded it as a problem.

Flying with either hand, reminds me of another incident in keeping with my habit of giving myself a fright at regular intervals. I had been flying with my friend Andy, and after we'd finished, as he'd done most of the flying I decided to do one quick circuit on my own. I jumped in, fastened my straps, pulled the canopy shut, started up and taxied out. Quick run through pre take-off checks as I approached the runway and away. I climbed to 1500ft in the circuit and thought I'd fly for a short spell clear of the field. As I levelled at about 2000ft and increased speed to about 100mph there was a bang and the canopy opened, with a roar. It is hinged at its forward edge, and it lifted to about twelve to fifteen inches open. The only effect on the aircraft, apart from the noise, was to pitch it slightly nose down. I reached up for the handle with my right hand and pulled the canopy down. I wasn't able to pull it fully down, and it wouldn't go to a position where I could twist the handle to lock it. I turned back to the field, holding the canopy down with my right hand, and subsequently landed back at Ince just using my left hand for the stick, with occasional excursions to throttle, flaps or trim. When I closed the canopy before take-off, I had obviously not fully turned the handle over its spring detent, and it had vibrated back to the open position. Now I check it visually when I close it, and again in the pre take-off checks. Some people have to learn the hard way.

I fly the aircraft all year round, and in the winter this can mean an hour or so de-icing it before flying. If the sun is shining, pushing the aircraft out of its parking spot in the shelter of trees and leaving it for half an hour or so will do the job naturally. On a cloudy day, however, it requires a couple of cans of de-icer and physical removal of the ice. The ailerons, elevator and elevator trim surfaces use piano hinges, which I regularly lubricate. I discovered the hard way that these hinges, by their very nature, are a good water trap. I had taken off one very cold but bright winter day and climbed to about 6000ft.

As I cruised gently around I realised that the sideways movement of the stick was restricted. I had no more than about a quarter of an inch of aileron movement, before the stick resisted. I didn't force it, the rudder was OK (not piano hinges), and so I descended quickly and found by the time I'd reached 1000ft the ailerons were moving more normally. The water trapped in the hinges had frozen. Subsequently I found it only happened to the ailerons and elevator trimmer. The elevator never appeared to be affected, I was pleased to find, possibly because of the warm air from the engine. I tried various ways of ice proofing the hinges, but found that even the application of de-icer before flying had little effect. Probably, helped by the wind chill effect, even this de-icer would freeze. I just had to be aware of the problem and try to avoid it.

About this time, Roger Breckell, (one of the more experienced pilot-owners at the field), Richard and Carl bought a tail-wheel Thruster between them. After a short period of ownership, they did a swap with the owner of a MiniMax from Barton. They kept this aircraft for less than a year, but during this time Roger offered me the chance to try it.

The MiniMax is a single seat, low wing, tailwheel aircraft with a Rotax 447 two-stroke engine (first time I'd flown with a two stroke). Roger briefed me thoroughly as I sat in the cockpit. It has full span flaperons, but, interestingly, a notice in the cockpit requires that the flaps should not be used. Roger explained that the flaps were primarily to allow the aircraft to meet the maximum stall speed requirement for permit aircraft. The flaps have a negative, 'reflex', position which gives an improved cruise speed, and two landing settings.

I flew the MiniMax, carefully, and found it a pleasant little aircraft, which handled well. I stalled it, but didn't touch the flap lever. Back at the field, after a gentle fly-by, I made a soft, flapless, three point landing, in deference to the solid undercarriage. The only suspension is via the tyres, which means a fairly hard ride on a summer-dry grass runway.

The flaperons are large in relation to the size of the aircraft, and at the time I felt that at the full flap setting there may have been some limitation to fore and aft control by the relatively small elevator. Subsequently I searched the internet for information, and discovered that in America (it's an American design) the flaps are used, both positive and negative, but common advice is not to use them, and apparently the Pilot's Handbook warns that, if landing with full flap, plenty of power must be used to ensure full elevator control.

When I first received my NPPL, the revalidation was a simple system of rolling, self-checked, validity, and non-expiring ratings. However it was soon changed to the same routine as the PPL, requiring a biennial one hour of flight with an instructor, and revalidation of the ratings in the licence at the same time. My initial rating was SSEA, (Simple Single Engined Aircraft), which also allowed me to fly microlights and SLMGs, (Self Launching Motor Gliders). The changes required a separate rating for each group. At my first revalidation in 2009 I was given two ratings, SSEA and Microlight, but then there was a further requirement for at least one hour as pilot in command in each rating within the minimum twelve hours. This created an anomaly because as my Eurostar is a light aircraft, my flying in it didn't count for the microlight rating renewal. In 2011 I had to borrow Pete Morgan's identical (but microlight) Eurostar for an hour, which did count. All this to revalidate the NPPL, which was introduced to simplify licencing for light aircraft pilots.

In 2009, I did my 'hour with an instructor' with Richard in the school GT450 flex-wing. Richard had been pushing me for some time to try the weight shift aircraft. On the day, it was quite breezy, but during the afternoon the wind eased and we decided to fly. Taxying was the first problem. The 'rudder bar' (a misnomer, as there is no rudder) is connected directly to the nosewheel and steers like a bicycle, ie push right, go left, not like an aircraft rudder, push right, go right. Just to further complicate matters, on the left side of this rudder bar is a foot operated brake pedal, and on the right side is a throttle pedal. So taxying out, with reverse effect rudder, and left foot for stop and right foot for go. The Hammond organ would be easier. Once lined up on the runway, you are warned not to use the 'rudder' on take-off as enthusiastic use can cause the aircraft to roll over. The large and heavy wing, which pivots above our heads, is controlled by a substantial athwartships bar, which is held by both hands.

So, off we go, feet holding the rudder central, right foot pushing the throttle open, and at the appropriate speed pushing the bar forward (not back) to increase the angle of attack of the wing, and we are airborne. Don't ease the pressure with the right foot or the engine slows, and watch the speed. If the speed drops, ease the bar back, and don't use the rudder as a rudder, it doesn't work. This is really hard work, just like it was for Richard when he first flew my aircraft, and I think he's enjoying it. After more than fifty years of flying aircraft by moving controls one way, I am now having to move them in the opposite direction to fly.

Turning is next, and the bar has to be pushed to the left to go right. If you think about what you are doing to the wing each time you move the bar, it is easier, but it still requires a positive thought process each time, rather than the instinctive movement I am used to making. That is the problem, it is, for me at least, totally counter instinctive. We climb to 3,000ft and level off, and I fly around, desperately trying to relax and enjoy it. Richard shows me a stall and I try one, but it is more of a mush than a clean break. He shows me some steep turns and wing overs, but I don't even try them. We head back to the field after almost an hour, to find the southerly wind has increased again to 23kts on the ground. I'm glad that Richard decides to do the landing, but, as he needs to have both hands on the bar extensions, and so cannot use his hand throttle, he asks me to apply throttle via the foot pedal, as he requires. The landing in the gusty wind, about the limit for a flex-wing, is interesting to say the least. I cut the throttle on Richard's call, and he makes a smooth landing with the bar leaping about in front of me, and I can't even follow the movements.

The biennial hour can be done in parts, so in 2010 I flew a flex-wing with Richard on a quieter day for about 45 minutes. This time after take-off, we flew across to Formby Point and did a couple of touch and goes on the sand. This made it easier for my first attempts, using the vast expanse of sand, rather than being confined to the short grass runways at Ince. I was still having 'think before moving anything' problems, but it was beginning to feel a little easier. Then back to Ince, where lining up with the runway and getting the approach right pushed me to the limit again. The first attempt on runway 18 was high, and not having the finesse to cross the power lines on short final at the right height, we had to go around. I managed the next two landings more or less OK, after which I was worn out. One very odd effect is that as you round out and hold off for landing, by pushing the bar forward, the 'trike', which you are sitting in, doesn't change attitude (as would a conventional aircraft). It simply behaves as a pendulum. So, no holding the nose up as you land, and no flying by attitude, quite disturbing to somebody who uses attitude as a primary indicator.

As we taxied in Richard said I should be able to go solo after a bit more time, but I assured him that I had no desire to fly a flex-wing on my own. I'd decided that it would be quite dangerous. The more relaxed I became, the more likely it would be that I would react instinctively, and incorrectly. There have been several accidents attributed to exactly this scenario. Additionally, it was hard work, and I much preferred to enjoy flying my easy, finger-tip controlled Eurostar, which reacted instantly to my control inputs exactly as I expected. Something to do with getting older, I imagine. Nevertheless, an interesting experience, which I wouldn't have missed, and I may even summon up the courage to do it again one day. Later I completed my 'instructor hour' with Richard in the Ikarus, which was very relaxed.

There is lots of good natured ribbing between the two camps, the three axis versus fixed wing pilots. There are a few, such as the school instructors, who regularly fly both, but the flex-wing pilots are particularly vociferous in defending their choice of getting airborne. But on a cold winter day, I usually manage to stress the fact that I have just been flying, in shirt sleeves, in a dry, heated cockpit.

An interesting excursion in 2010 was when I was approached by Mike Lewis, long-time friend and publisher of 'Rapide' magazine. Mike is a member of the RAF Auxiliary 610 Squadron Association, whose HQ is at what was left of Hooton Park airfield, where the squadron was based in the fifties. Vauxhall had built a car factory on the airfield, but about 300yds of the runway and some of the tarmac area remained. A transport company used the old hangars for storage and their lorries entered via the old runway. Mike was keen to prove the viability of the mini airfield, and obtained permission from the owner of the land, and cleared the operation with ATC at Liverpool airport, a mile or so away on the opposite bank of the Mersey.

On the day, the weather was fair, and I landed on the short runway next to the factory. Half an hour stop for photos by the HQ and I departed for Ince. I was able to call Liverpool from the ground before take-off for clearance. I checked my logbooks, and found it was fifty four years and two days since the last time I'd landed at Hooton, when it was a working airfield.

During retirement I have kept in touch with several former colleagues, and those who were still working after I retired assure me that I left at the right time. One or two, like Dave Williams, tried working for other airlines but usually didn't stick it for too long. Working for BA was a hard act to follow. Bernie and I keep in touch, as we go back to the beginning of time, or primary school, which is the same thing. I regularly see Bernie, his wife Pat (who flew as cabin crew with me in Viscounts and 1-11s) and their daughter Anna, and he often flies with me in my aircraft. Bernie hasn't lost his flying touch, having trained on tailwheel aircraft, he can land TJ like a veteran.

As mentioned, I never expected to be an airline pilot, it just happened. All I ever wanted to do was fly, but once I settled in to the job, I realised that there were far worse ways of earning a living. Today, seeing young pilots, or would be pilots, struggling to get a decent airline job, I realise, once again, just how lucky I have been.

So, then, left base, turning finals.

8. ON FINALS

So that's it. Fifty seven years of flying, so far, and I hope to be flying for a few more years yet. Nothing exciting, I hope, just pottering around in my little aircraft, but it will keep me happy. I take a camera with me when I fly and usually take a few photos. It's amazing how varied the sky over Ince can be. Every time I fly, it's different. That is the pleasure of flying. I often remember the feeling I had, preparing my little aircraft for its first flight, and looking up and waving at the pilot of a flex-wing. I decided at that point I had died and gone to Heaven. Nothing has changed. A little aeroplane, a grass strip and a nice day... what more could a pilot want?

Many memories from airline flying over the years.

- Flying across the Alps on a clear winter's day. 37,000ft at night over France watching the cu-nims glow with lightning like huge lightbulbs.

- The satisfaction of a smooth autoland in limiting conditions, then taxying in (at Heathrow or Manchester) in thick fog, using the directional green centre line lighting which guided us individually to our parking stand.

- Climbing out of Charles de Gaulle airport after a Paris night stop early on a summer morning, then being served breakfast with delicious little garlic sausages and hot croissants (crumbs all over the cockpit).

- Getting airborne from Amsterdam on an autumn evening just as the sun had set, then climbing fast to bring it above the horizon again and watch it set for a second time in the cruise to Manchester.

- Crossing the North Sea watching the Northern Lights.

- Hand flying the 1-11 whenever we could, usually on descent, approach and landing.

- Cleared for a visual approach to Cork, from 40 miles out, then running along the southern Irish coast on clear sunny morning, at 350kts and 1,000ft.

- Descending into Glasgow on a crisp winter day, snow covered mountains spread across the horizon, and the distant Western Isles standing out in the crystal clear visibility.

These memories and many more will last. Airline flying and aviation changes with time, but, in my view, this was one of the best and most enjoyable periods.

~ End ~